FOR ORGANS, PIANOS & ELECTRONIC KEYBOARDS

E-Z PLAY TODAY

363

SONGS OF 1930s

ISBN 978-1-4950-6268-1

HAL•LEONARD®
CORPORATION

7777 W. BLUEMOUND RD. P.O. BOX 13819 MILWAUKEE, WI 53213

Visit Hal Leonard Online at
www.halleonard.com

All of Me

Registration 4
Rhythm: Fox Trot or Swing

Words and Music by Seymour Simons
and Gerald Marks

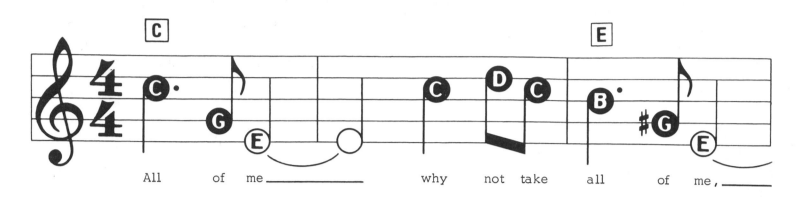

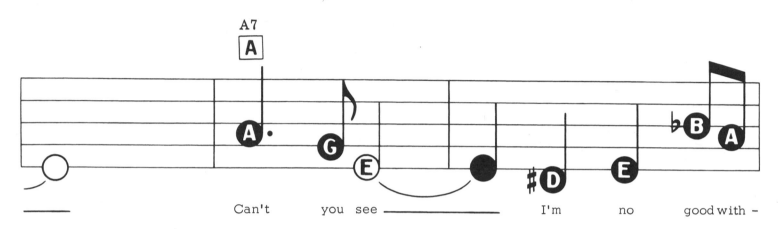

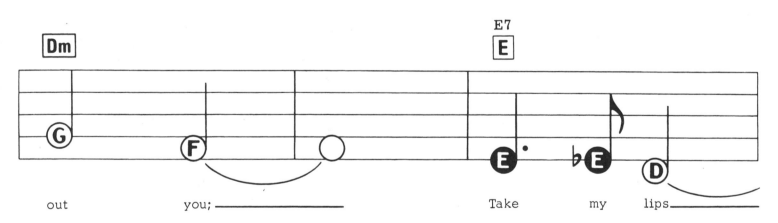

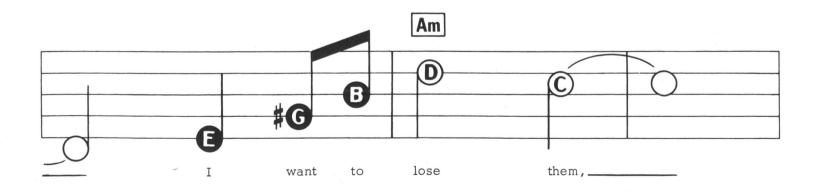

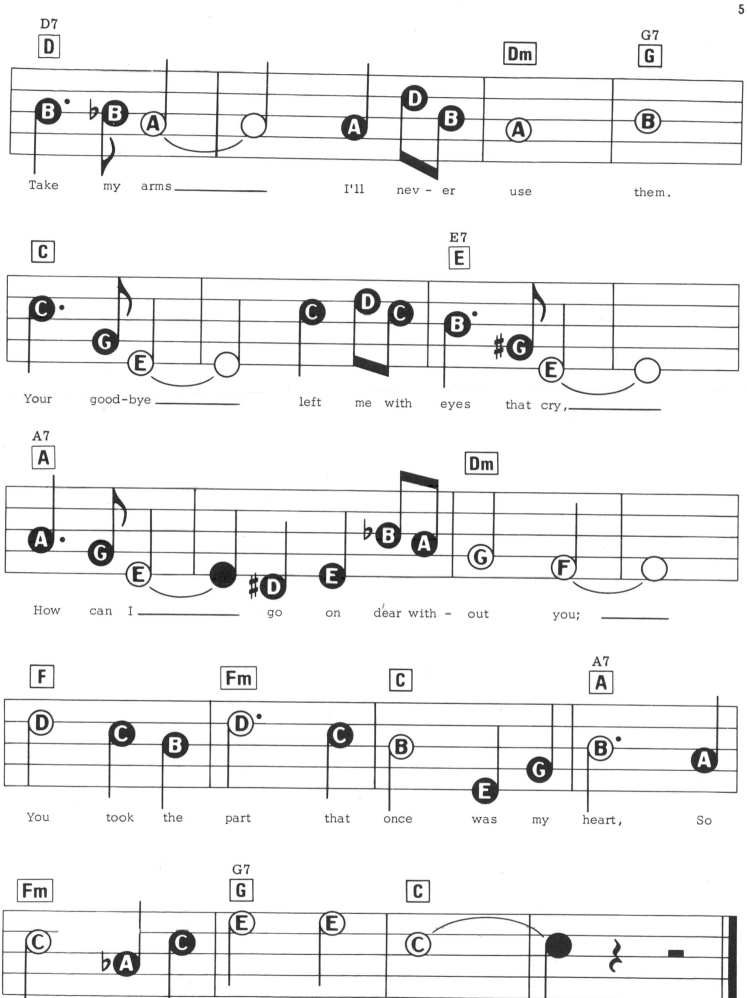

All the Things You Are

from VERY WARM FOR MAY

Registration 2
Rhythm: Ballad or Swing

Lyrics by Oscar Hammerstein II
Music by Jerome Kern

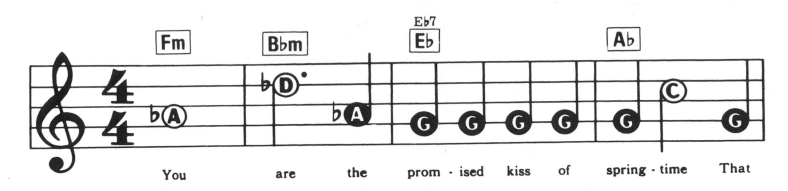

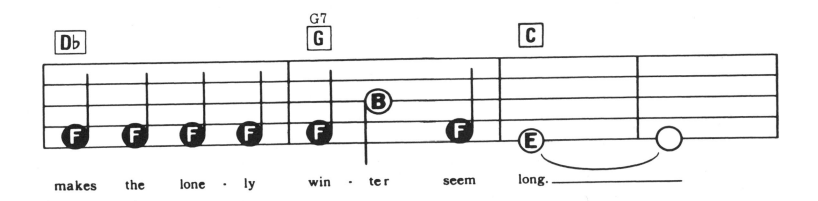

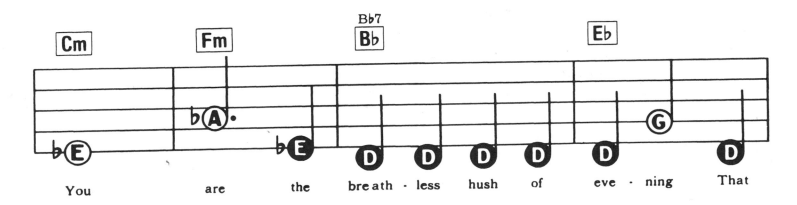

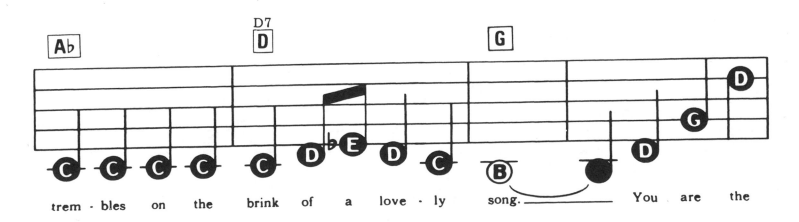

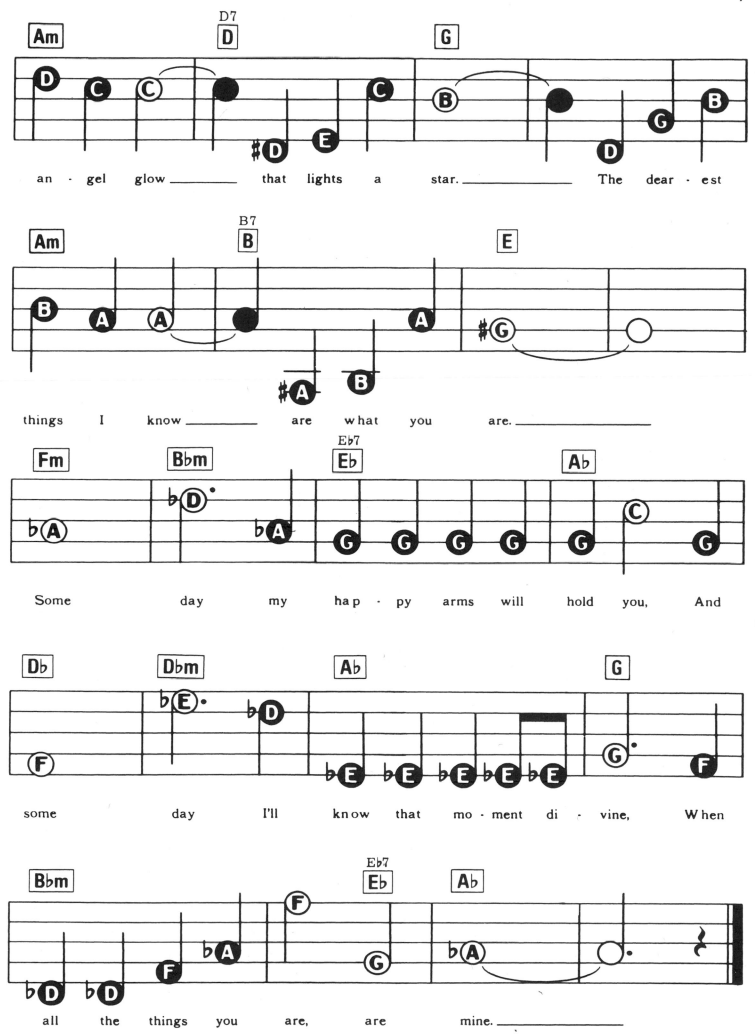

And the Angels Sing

Registration 1
Rhythm: Jazz or Swing

Lyrics by Johnny Mercer
Music by Ziggy Elman

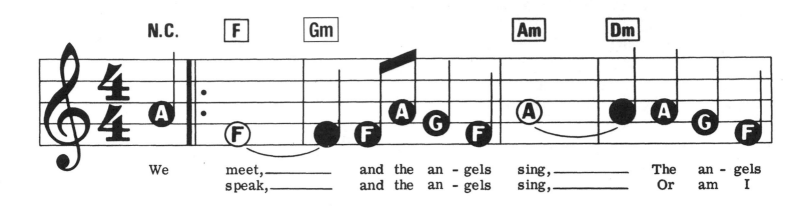

We meet,_____ and the an-gels sing,_____ The an-gels
speak,_____ and the an-gels sing,_____ Or am I

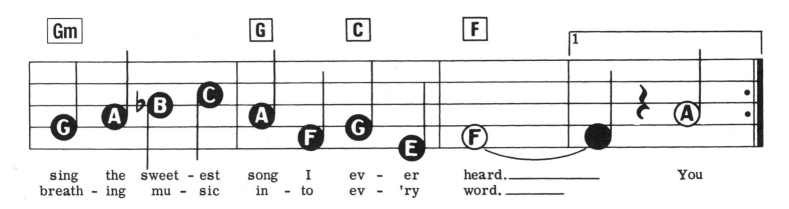

sing the sweet-est song I ev-er heard._____ You
breath-ing mu-sic in-to ev-'ry word._____

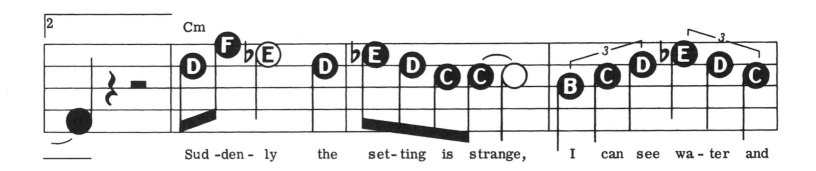

_____ Sud-den-ly the set-ting is strange, I can see wa-ter and

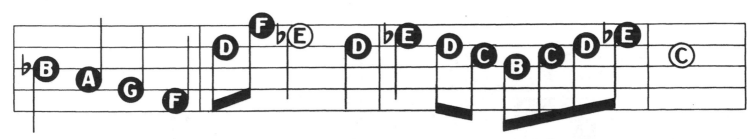

moon-light beam-ing, sil-ver waves that break on some un-dis-cov-ered shore;

F   Cm

Then sud-den-ly I see it all change,___ Long win-ter nights with the

Gm   G7 G   C7 C   F

can-dles gleam-ing, thru it all your face that I a - dore.___ You

F   Gm   Am   Dm

smile,___ and the an - gels sing___ And tho' it's
kiss,___ and the an - gels sing___ And leave their

Gm   1 G   C   F

just a gen-tle mur-mur at the start,___ We
mu - sic ring - ing

2   F

in my heart.___

April in Paris

Registration 2
Rhythm: Fox Trot or Swing

Words by E.Y. "Yip" Harburg
Music by Vernon Duke

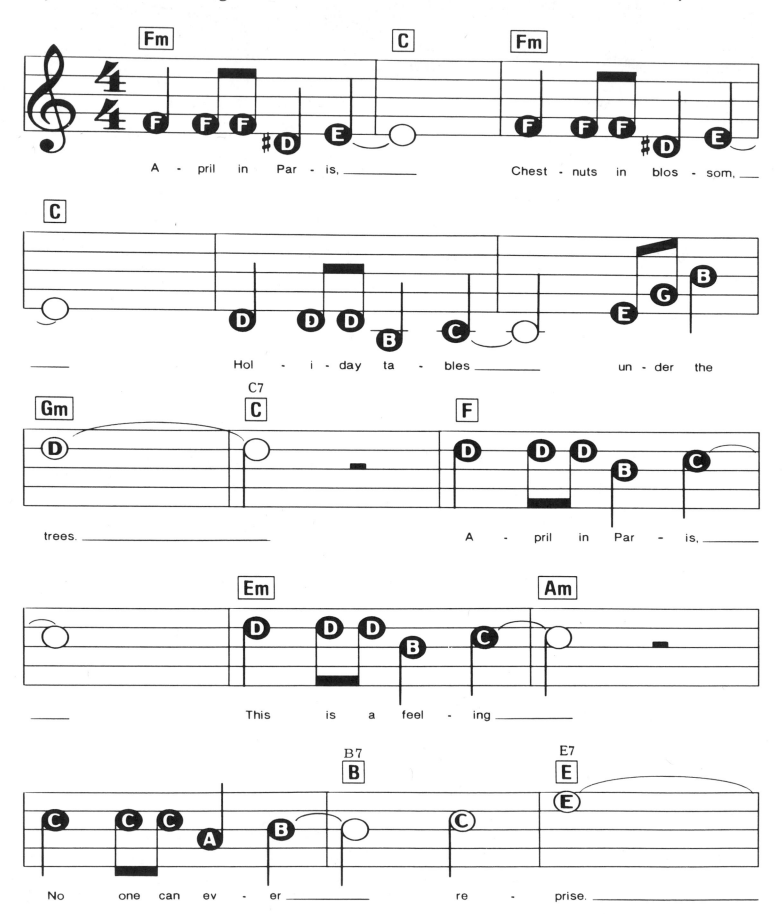

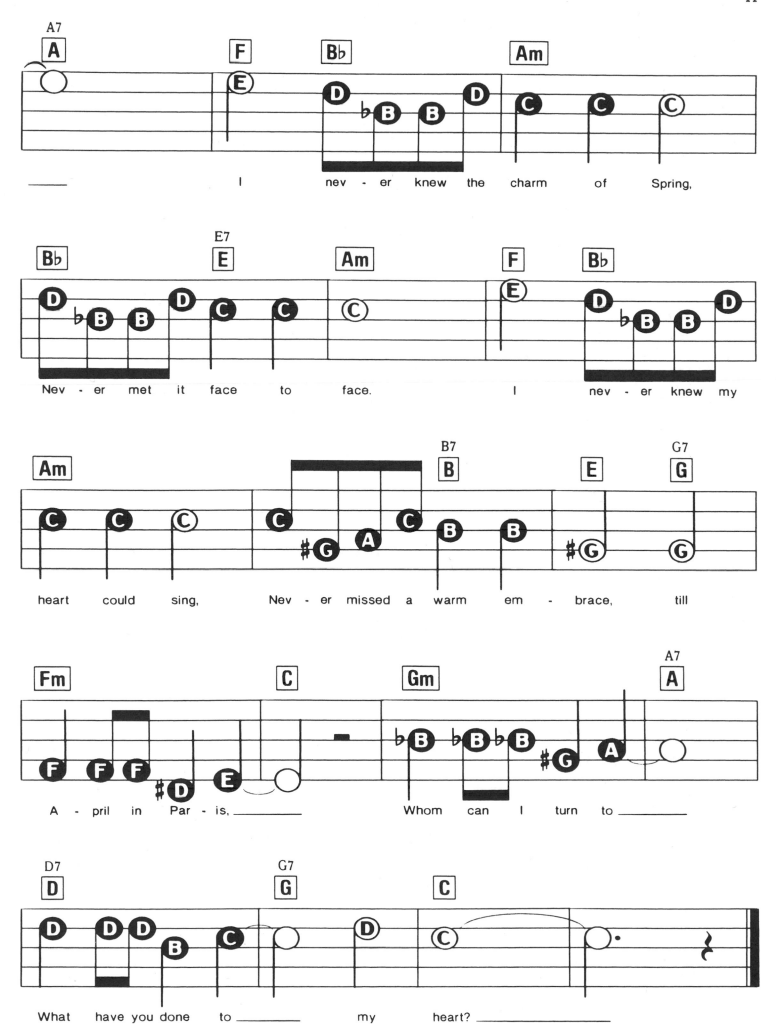

As Time Goes By
from CASABLANCA

Registration 8
Rhythm: Ballad

Words and Music by
Herman Hupfeld

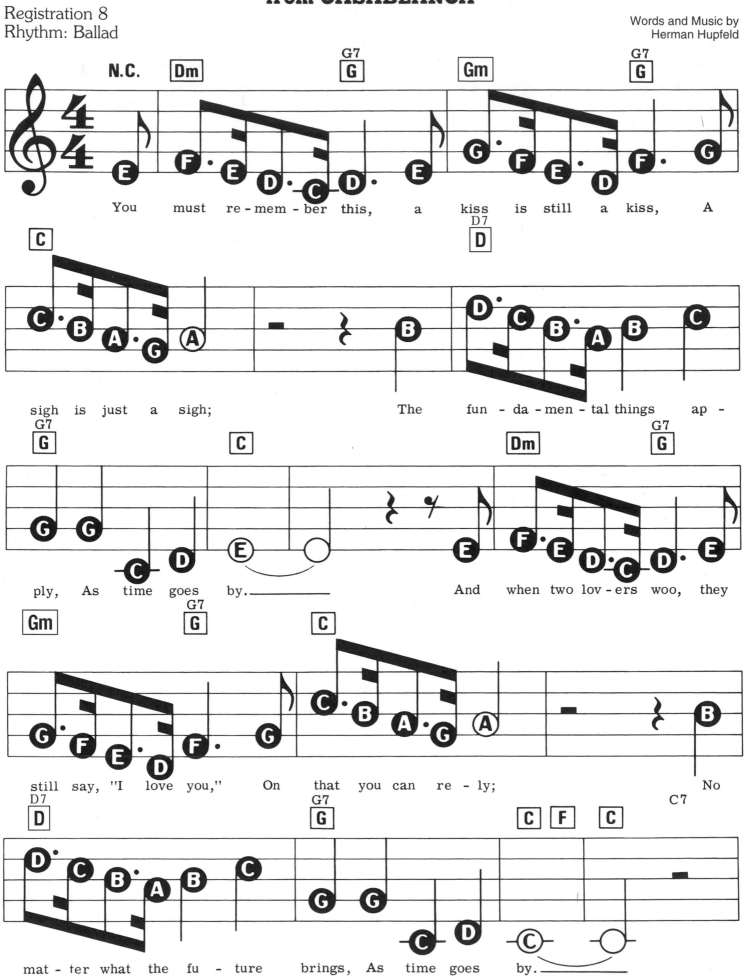

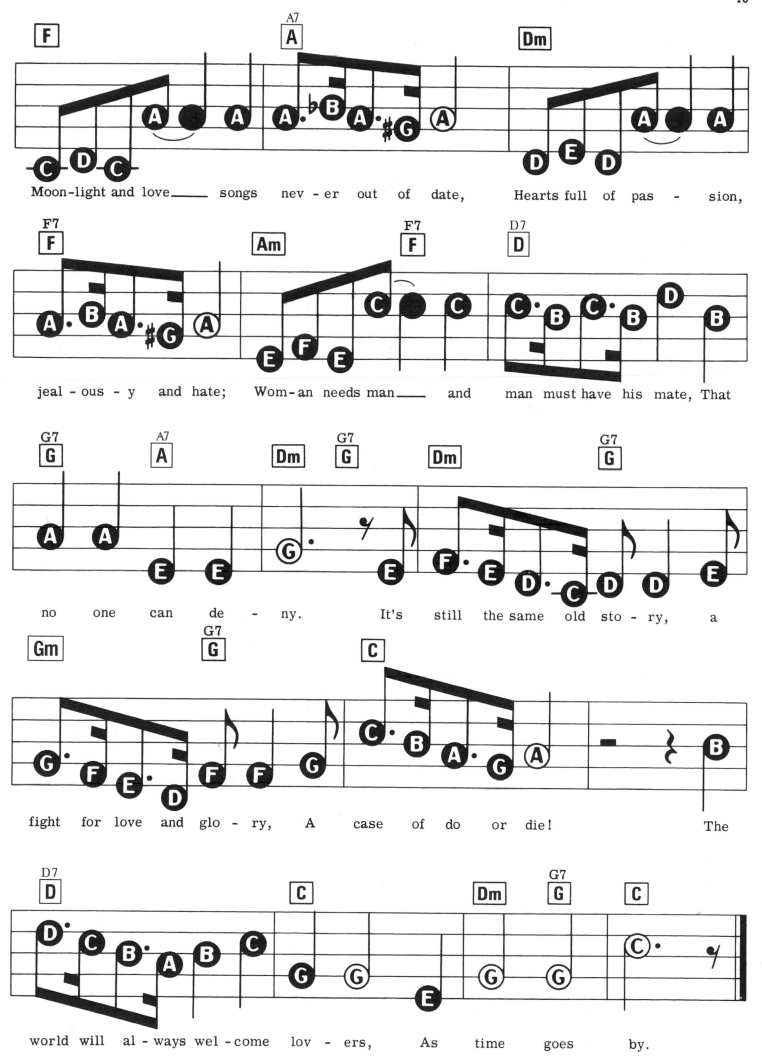

Autumn in New York

Registration 8
Rhythm: Swing or Jazz

Words and Music by
Vernon Duke

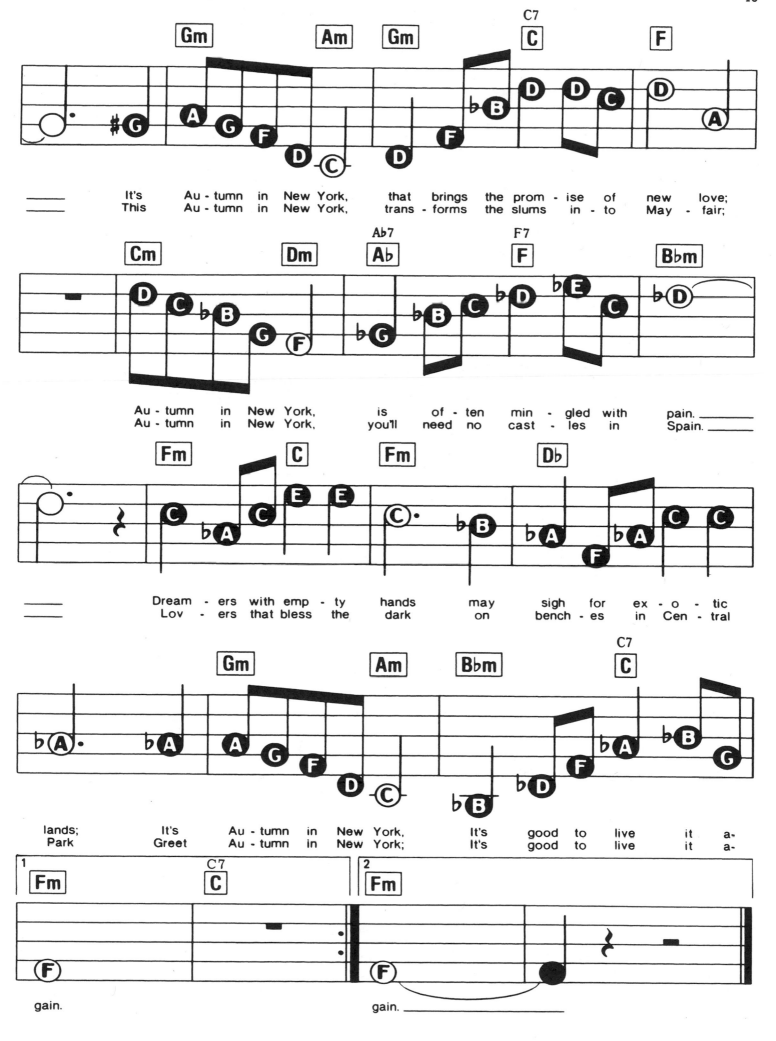

Begin the Beguine
from JUBILEE

Registration 2
Rhythm: Latin or Beguine

Words and Music by
Cole Porter

17

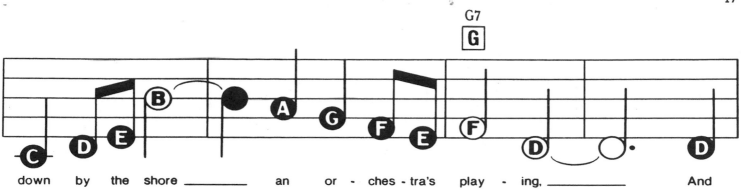

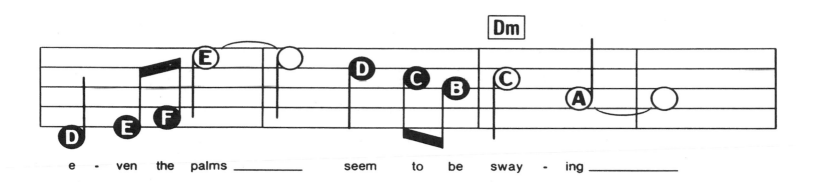

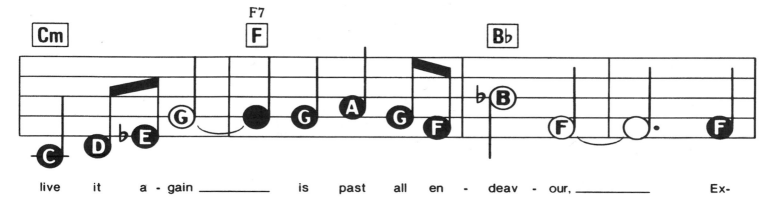

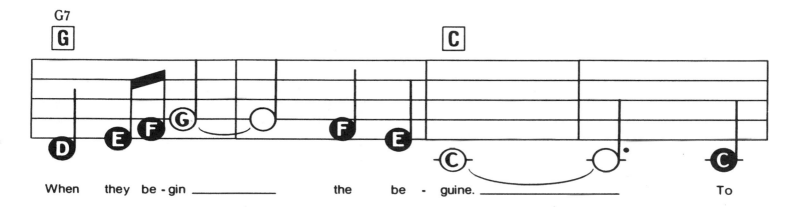

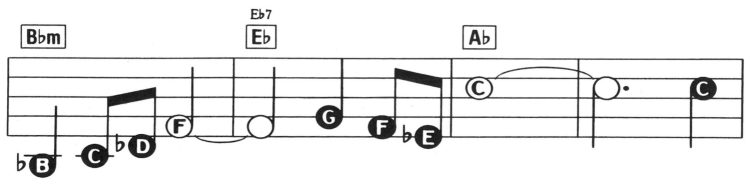

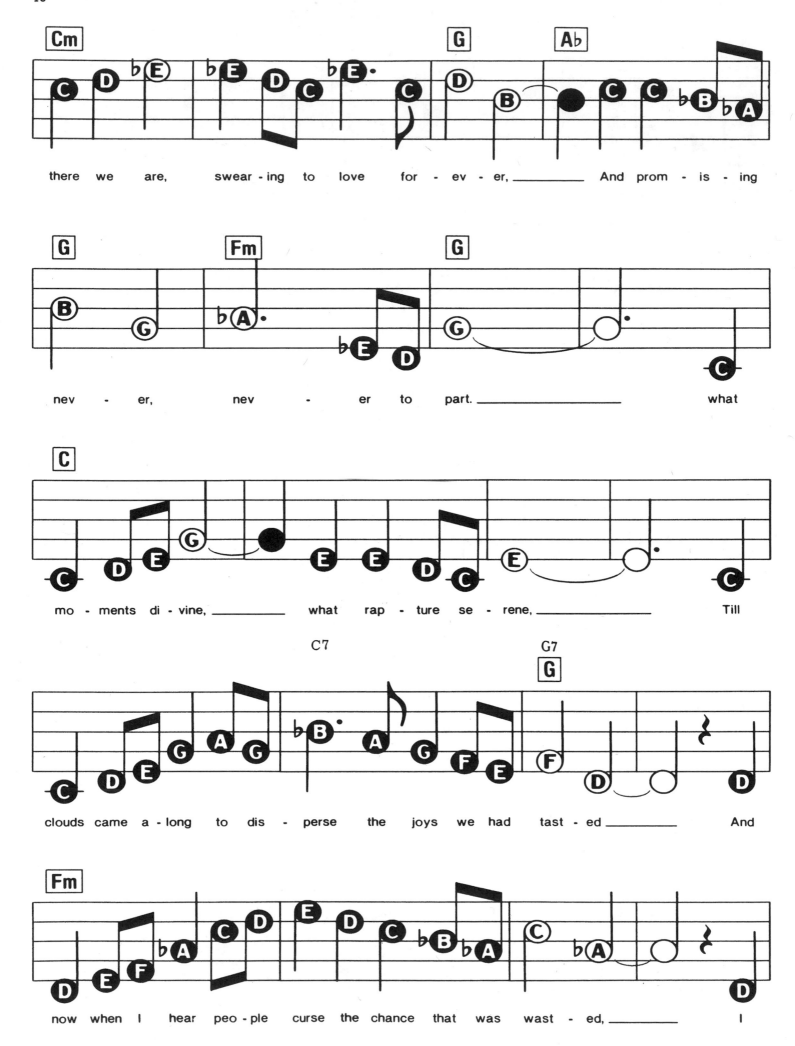

18

19

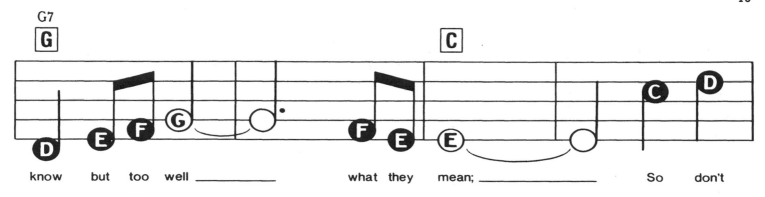

know but too well _____ what they mean; _____ So don't

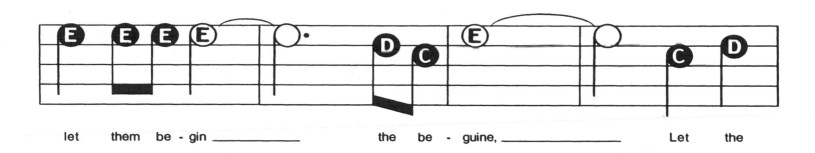

let them be - gin _____ the be - guine, _____ Let the

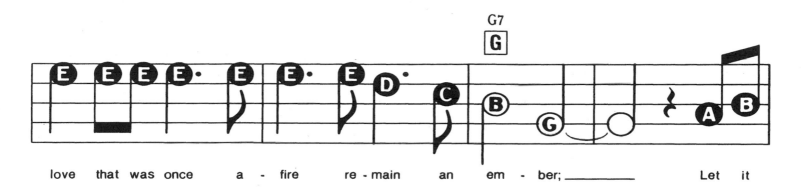

love that was once a - fire re - main an em - ber; _____ Let it

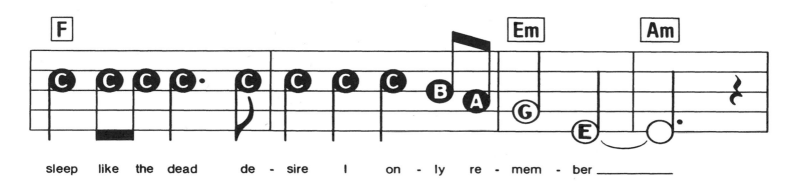

sleep like the dead de - sire I on - ly re - mem - ber _____

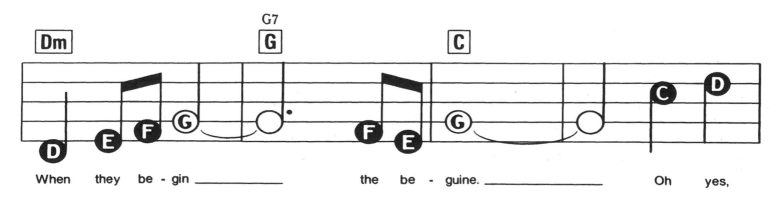

When they be - gin _____ the be - guine. _____ Oh yes,

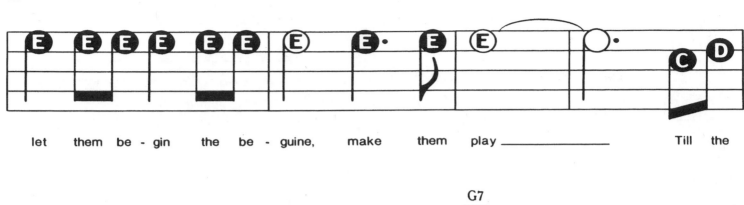

let them be - gin the be - guine, make them play _____ Till the

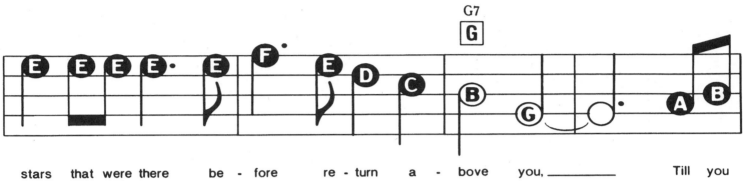

stars that were there be - fore re - turn a - bove you, _____ Till you

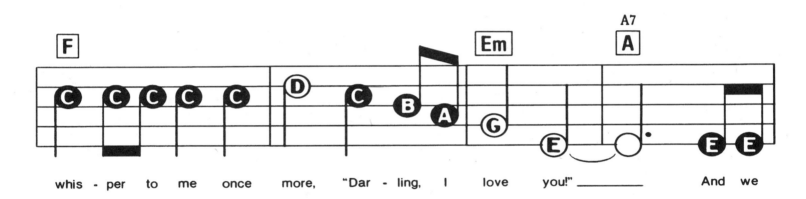

whis - per to me once more, "Dar - ling, I love you!" _____ And we

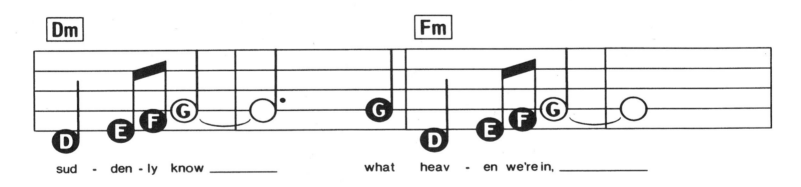

sud - den - ly know _____ what heav - en we're in, _____

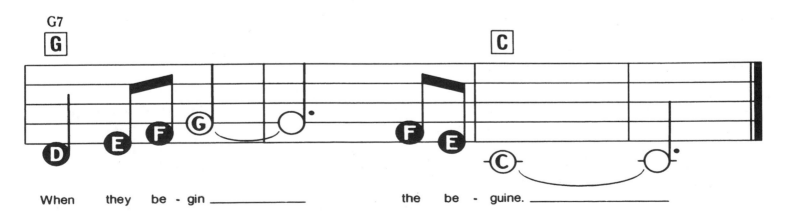

When they be - gin _____ the be - guine. _____

Cherokee
(Indian Love Song)

Registration 2
Rhythm: Swing

Words and Music by
Ray Noble

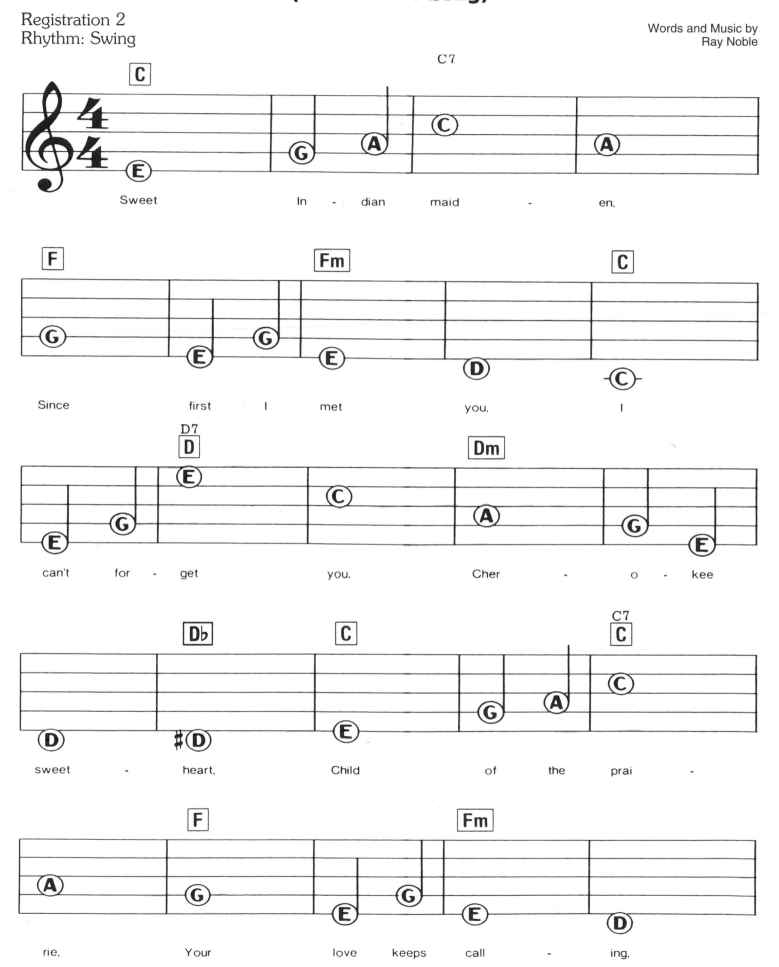

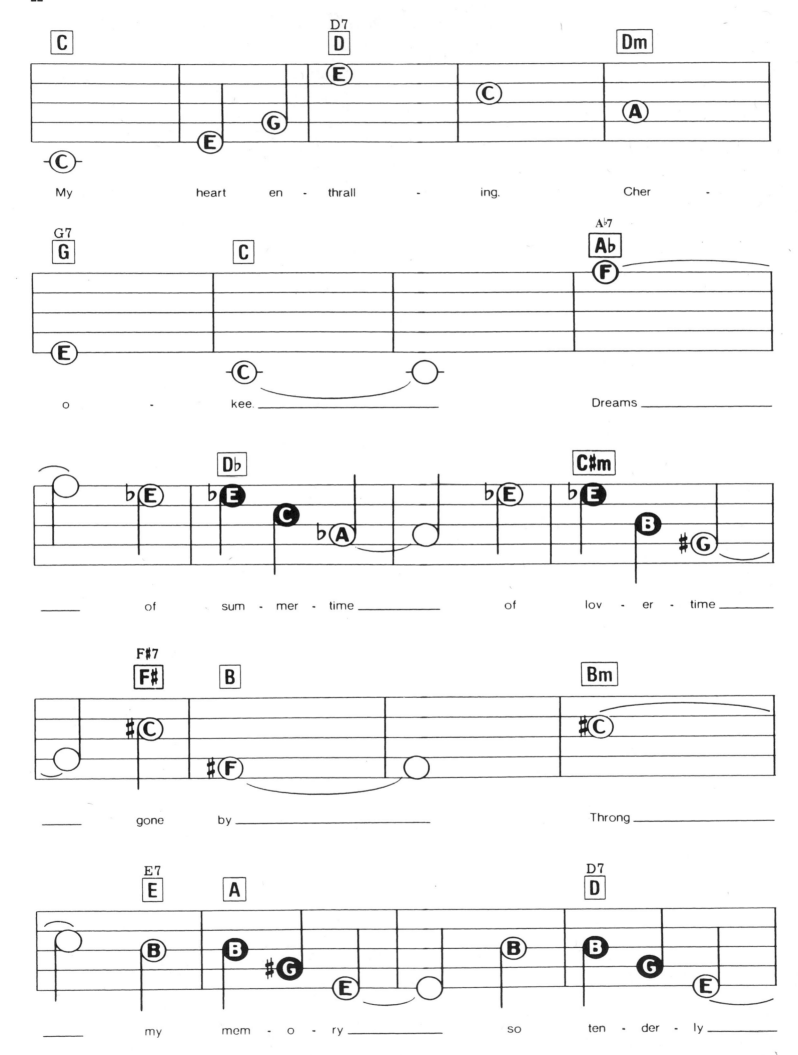

23

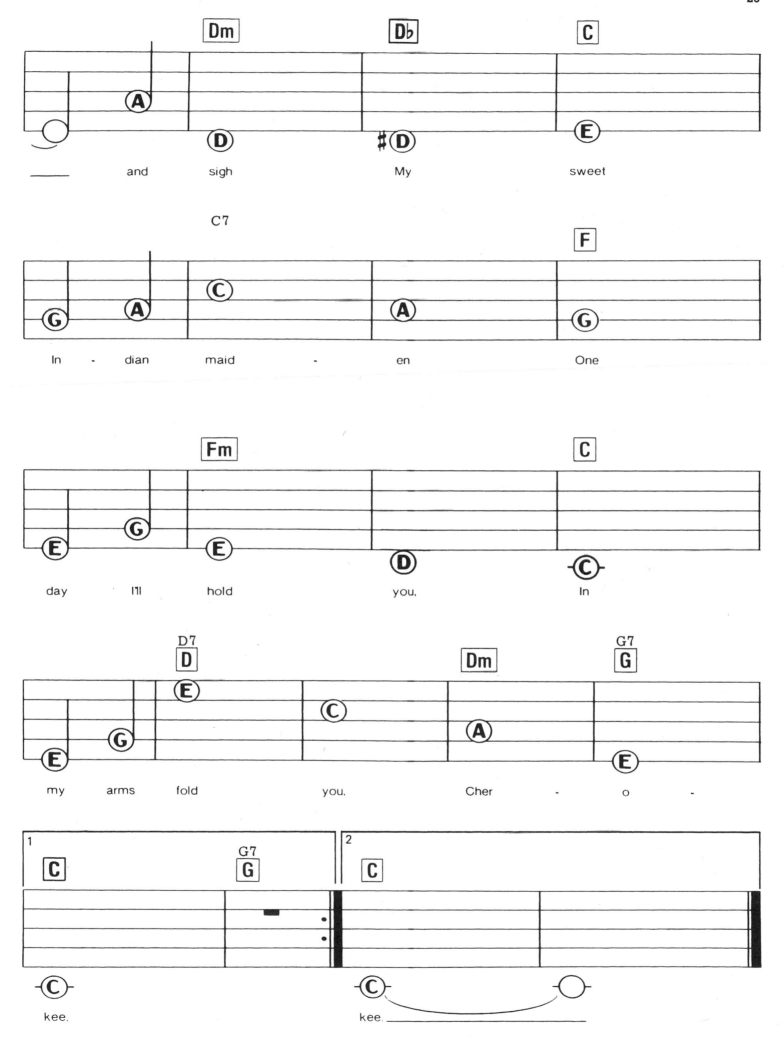

Blame It on My Youth

Registration 10
Rhythm: Pops or Fox Trot

Words by Edward Heyman
Music by Oscar Levant

You were my a - dored one, then

you be - came the bored one, and

I was like a toy that brought you joy one

day, a bro - ken toy that you pre - ferred to

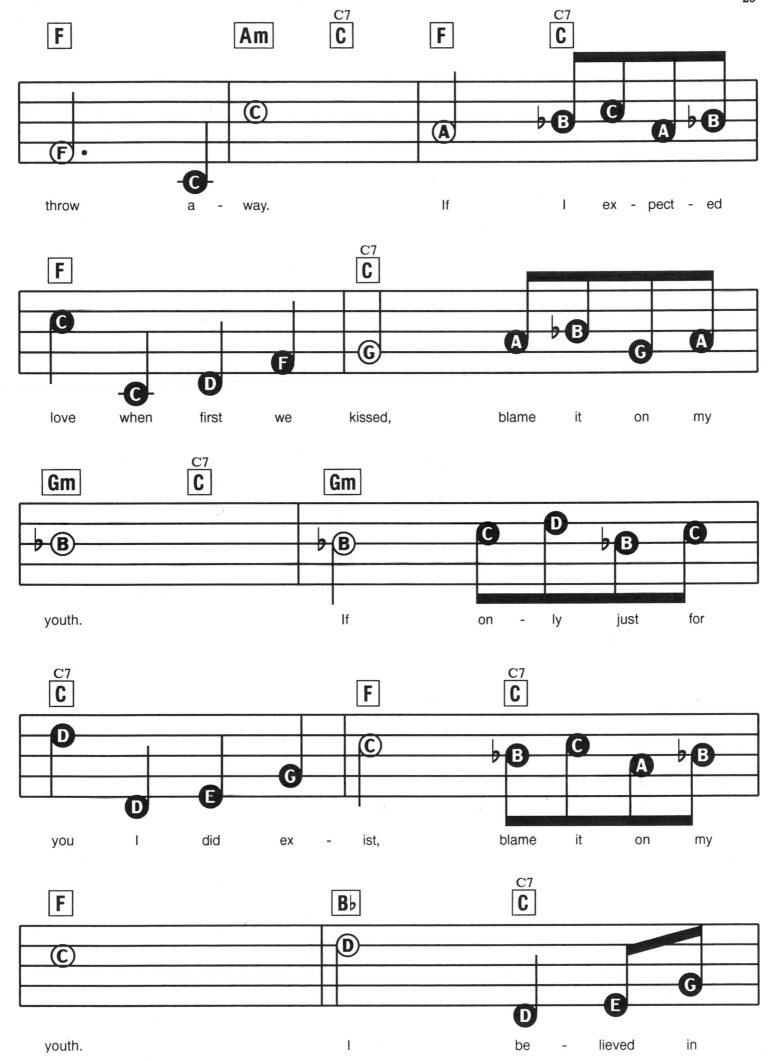

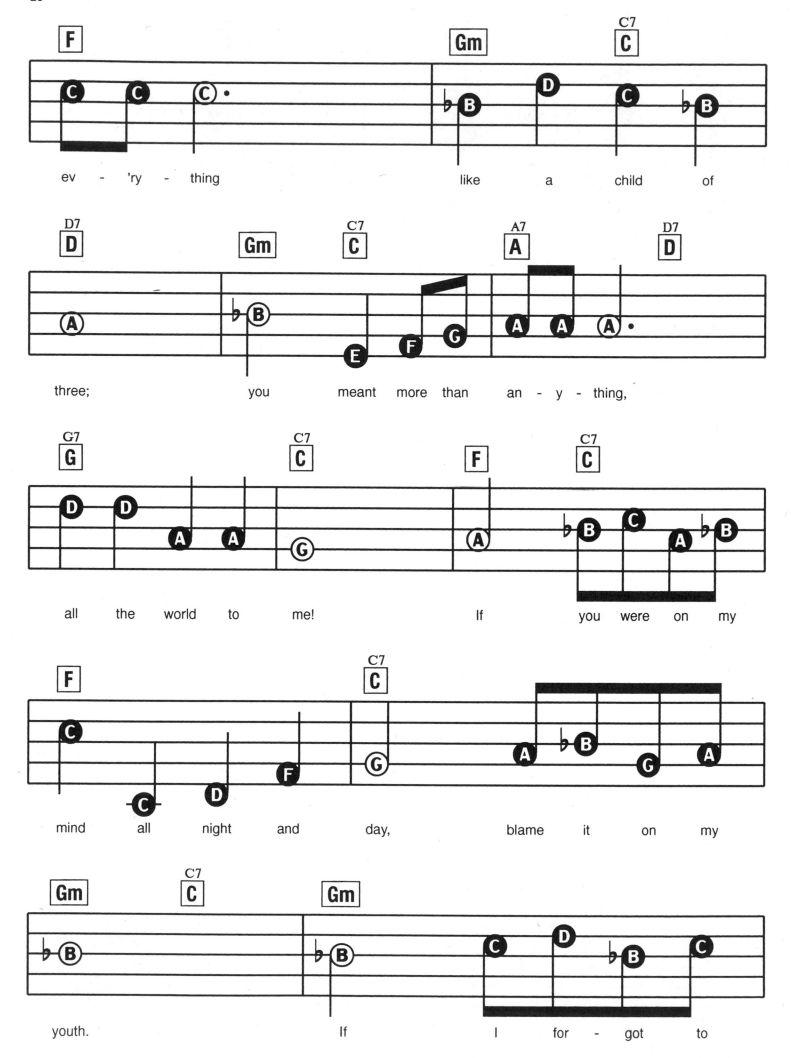

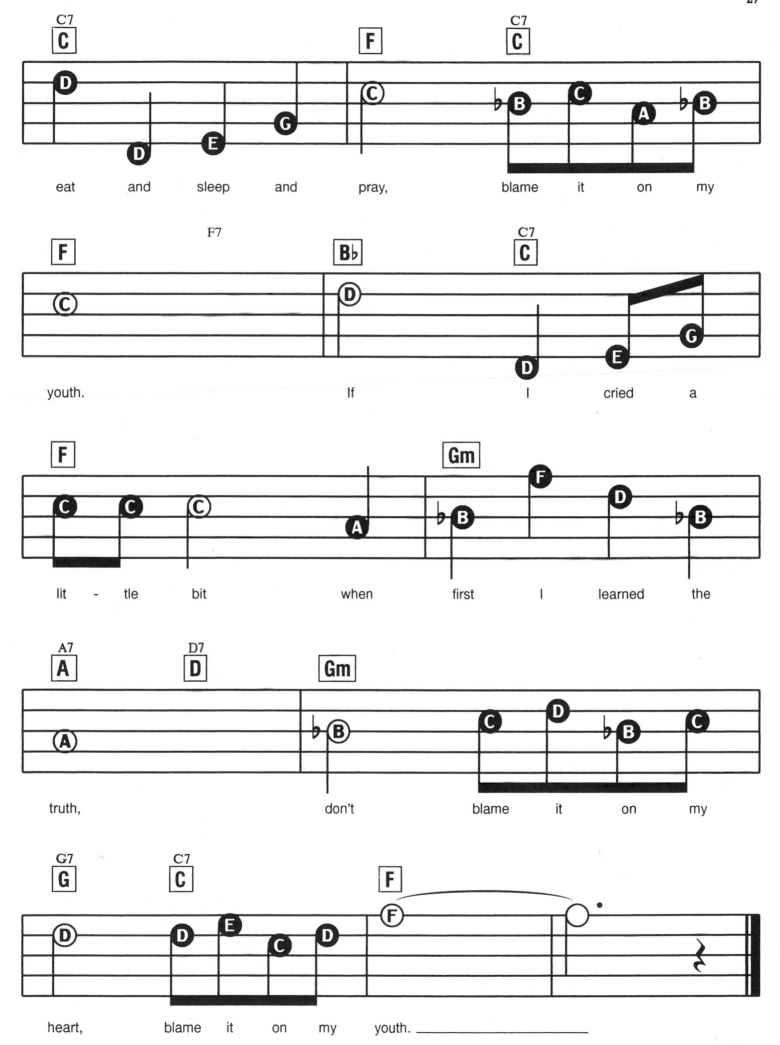

Blue Moon

Registration 8
Rhythm: Swing

Music by Richard Rodgers
Lyrics by Lorenz Hart

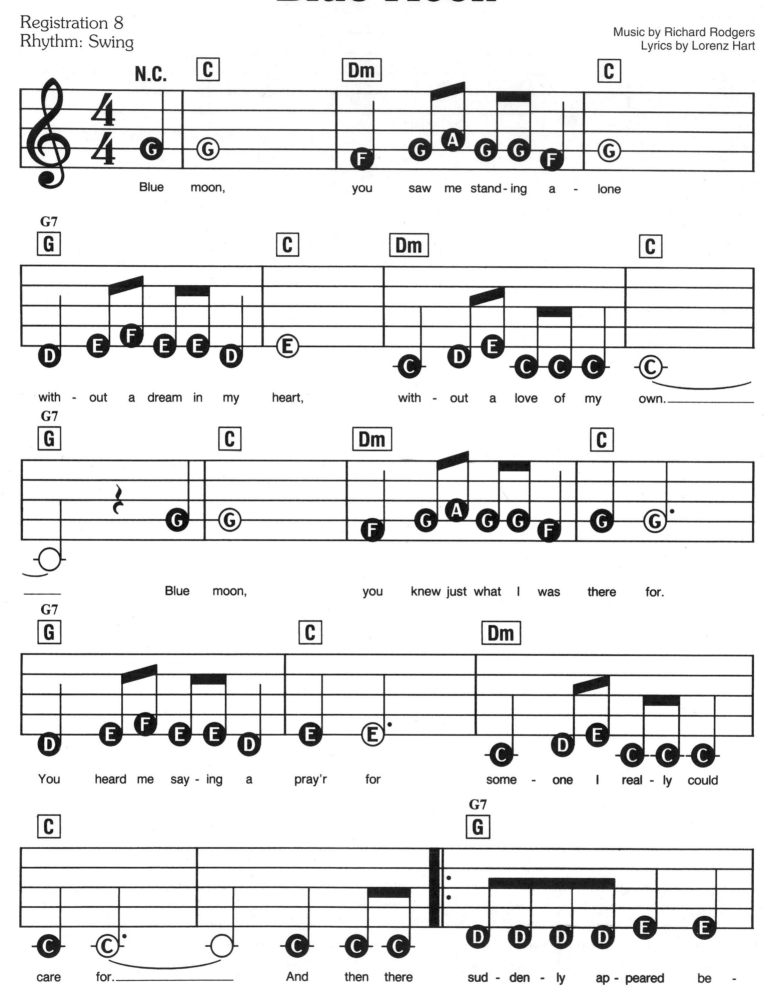

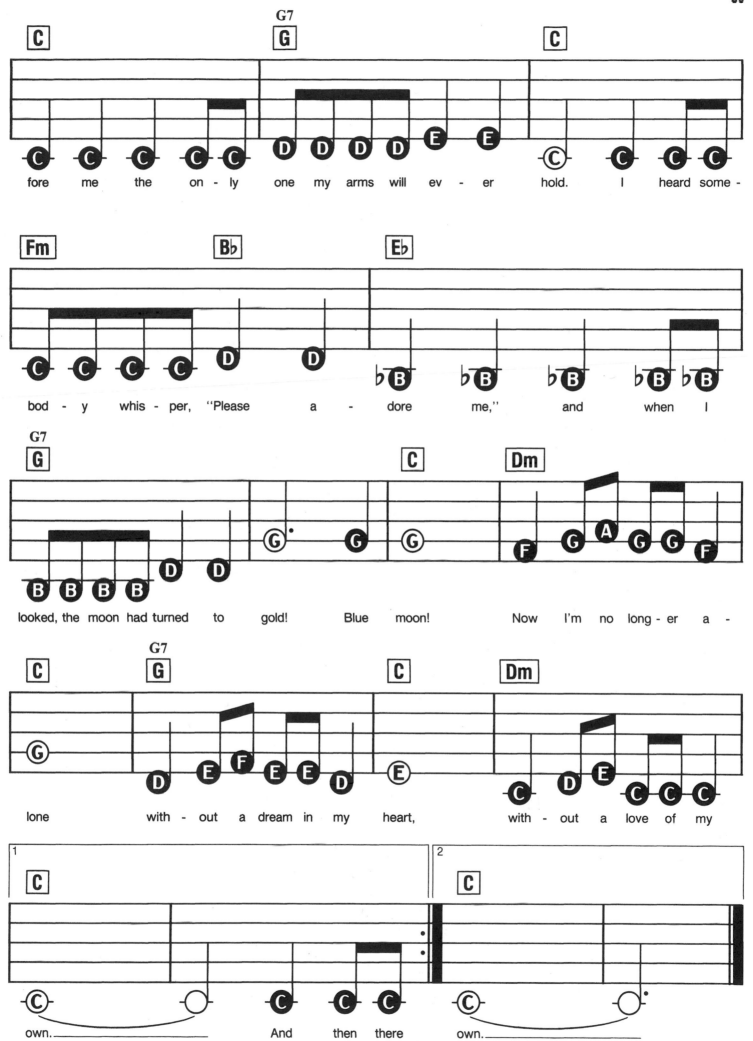

Body and Soul
from THREE'S A CROWD

Registration 8
Rhythm: Ballad

Words by Edward Heyman,
Robert Sour and Frank Eyton
Music by John Green

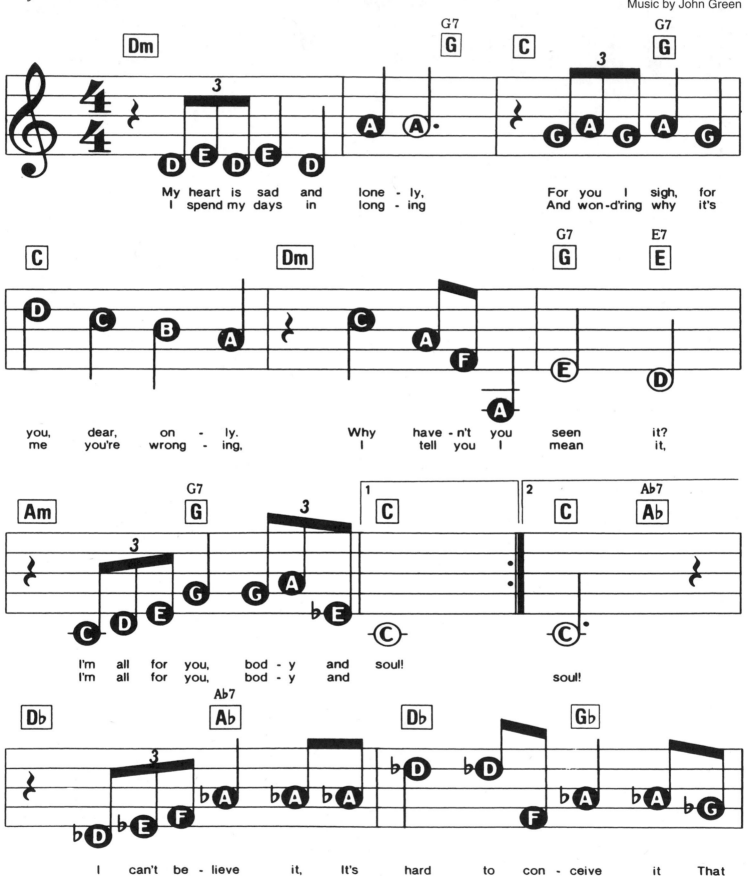

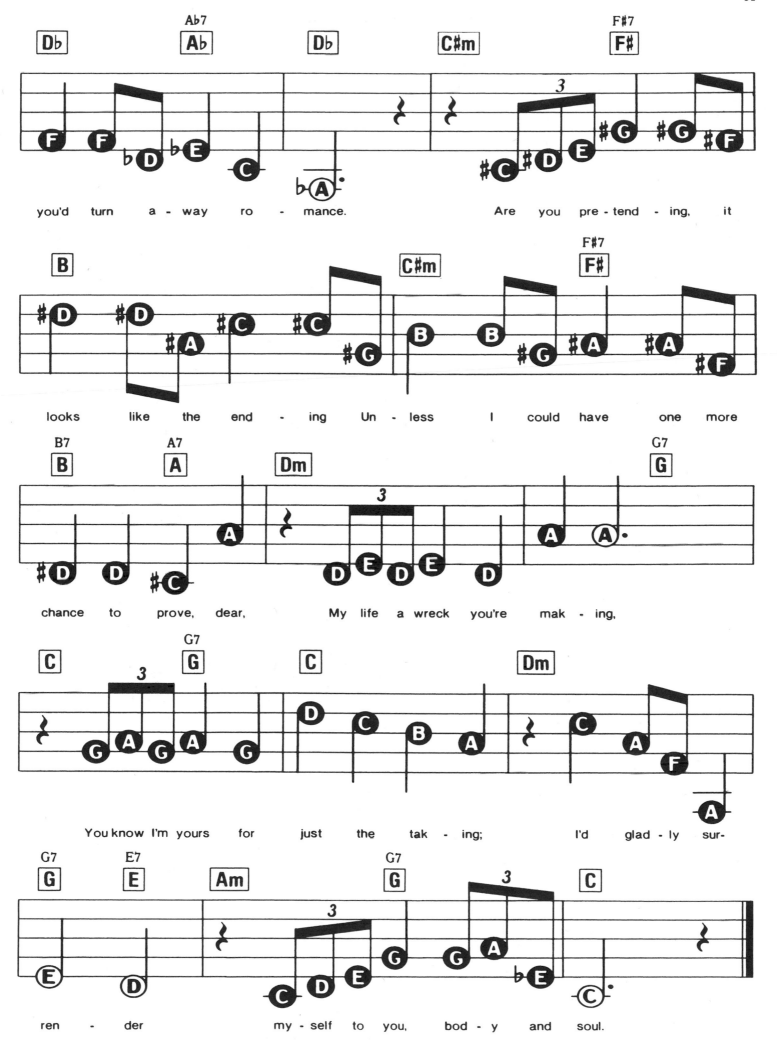

Caravan

Registration 7
Rhythm: Ballad or Fox Trot

Words and Music by Duke Ellington,
Irving Mills and Juan Tizol

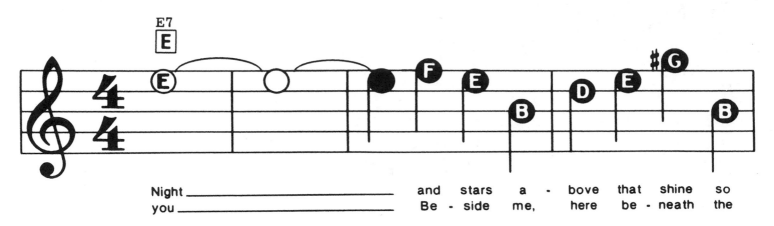

Night _____ and stars a - bove that shine so
you _____ Be - side me, here be - neath the

bright _____ The mys - t'ry of their fad - ing
blue _____ My dream of love is com - ing

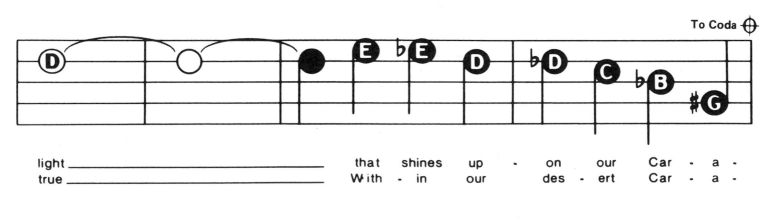

To Coda

light _____ that shines up - on our Car - a -
true _____ With - in our des - ert Car - a -

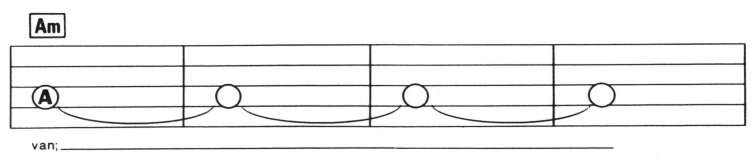

van; _____

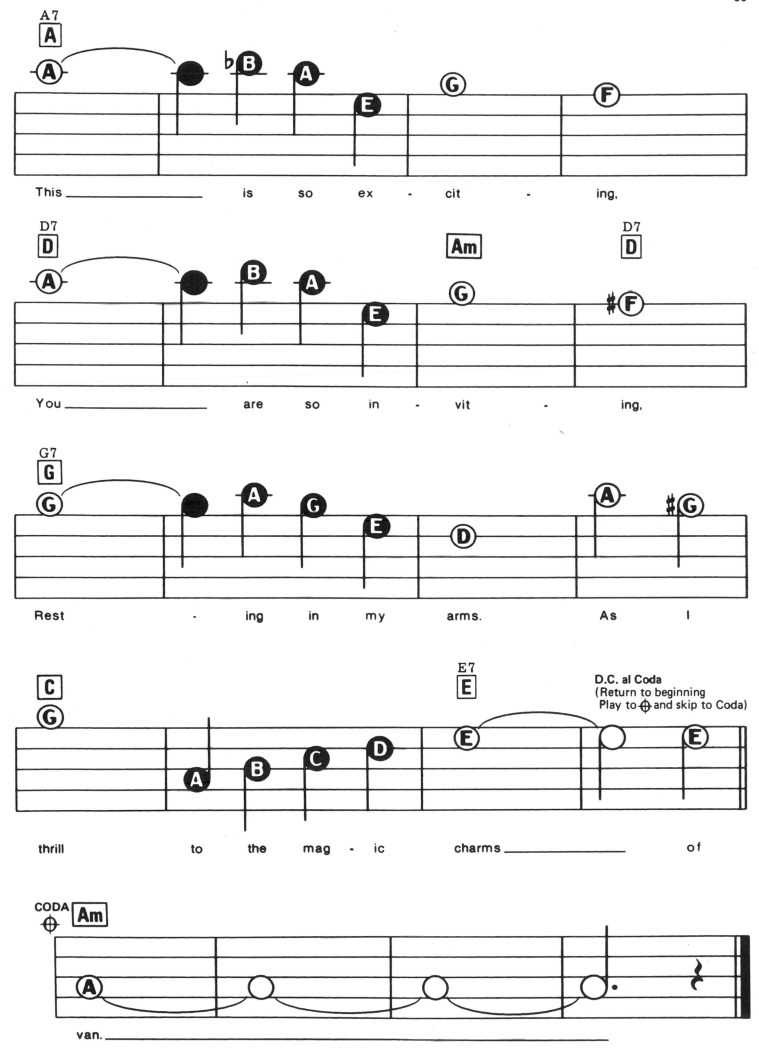

Change Partners
from the RKO Radio Motion Picture CAREFREE

Registration 2
Rhythm: Swing

Words and Music by
Irving Berlin

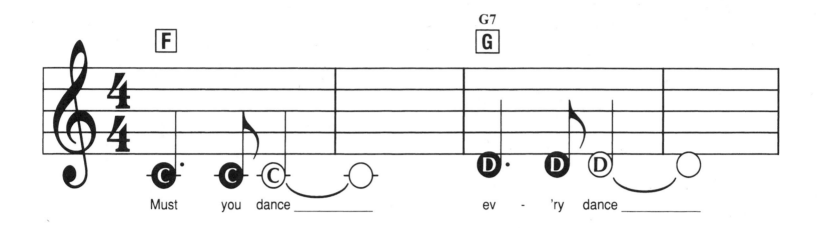

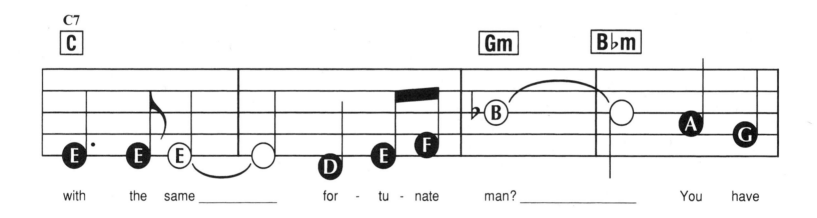

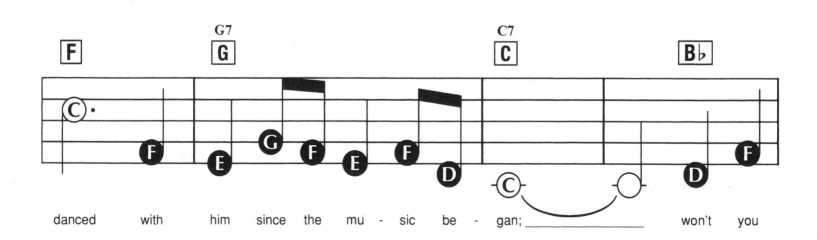

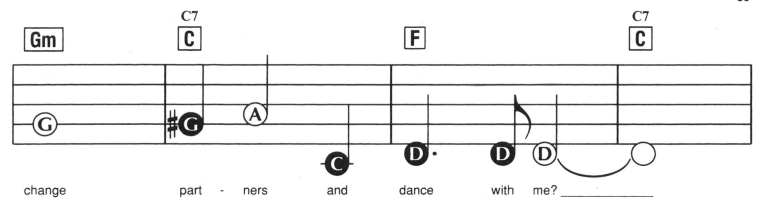

change ... part - ners ... and ... dance ... with me? _____

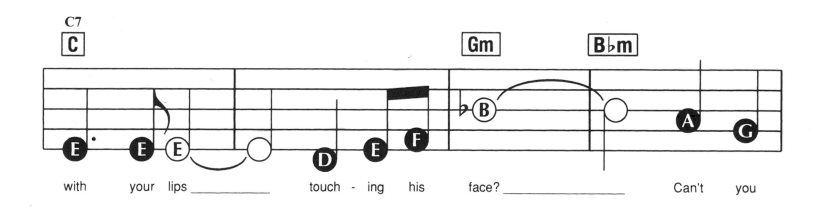

Must ... you dance _____ ... quite ... so close, _____

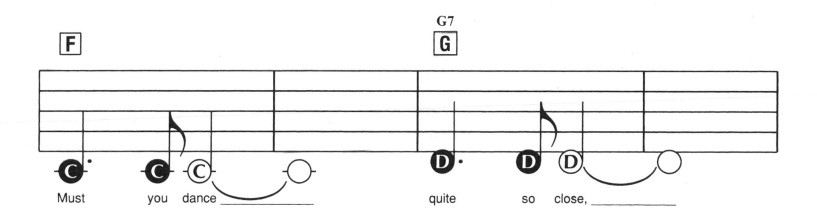

with ... your lips _____ ... touch - ing his ... face? _____ Can't you

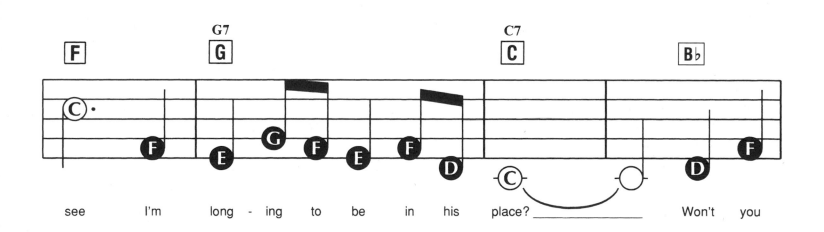

see ... I'm ... long - ing ... to ... be ... in ... his ... place? _____ Won't you

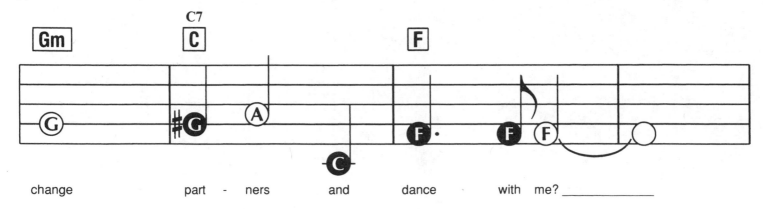

change part - ners and dance with me? _____

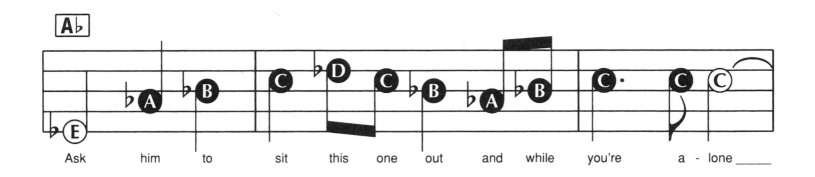

Ask him to sit this one out and while you're a - lone ____

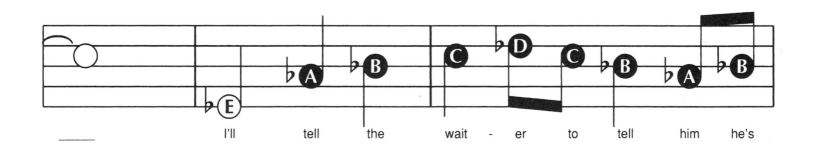

____ I'll tell the wait - er to tell him he's

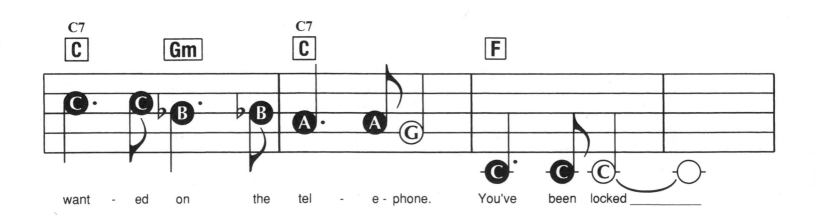

want - ed on the tel - e - phone. You've been locked _____

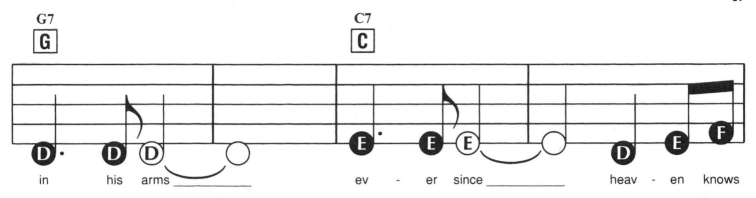

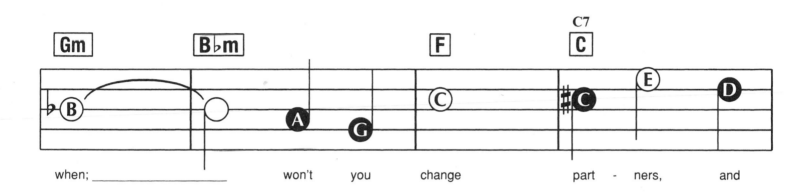

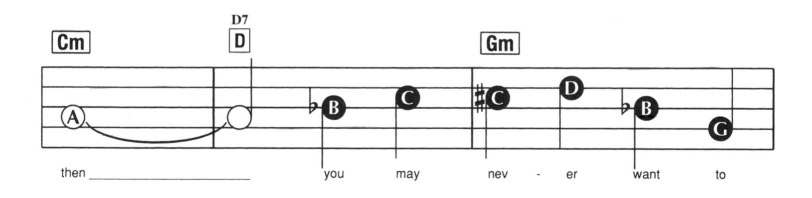

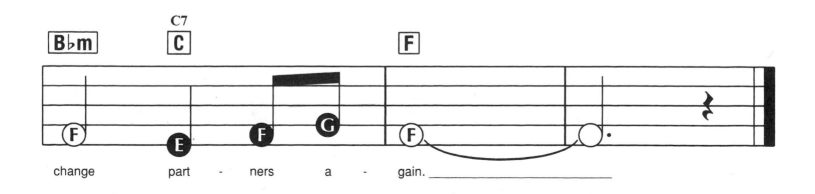

Cheek to Cheek
from the RKO Radio Motion Picture TOP HAT

Registration 1
Rhythm: Fox Trot or Swing

Words and Music by
Irving Berlin

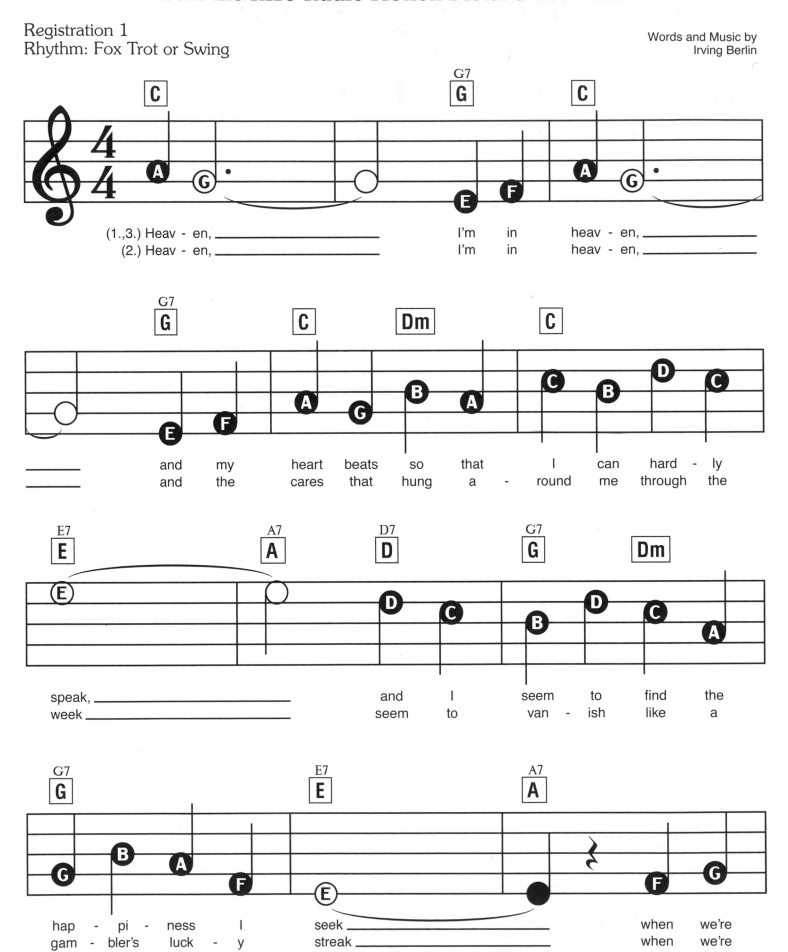

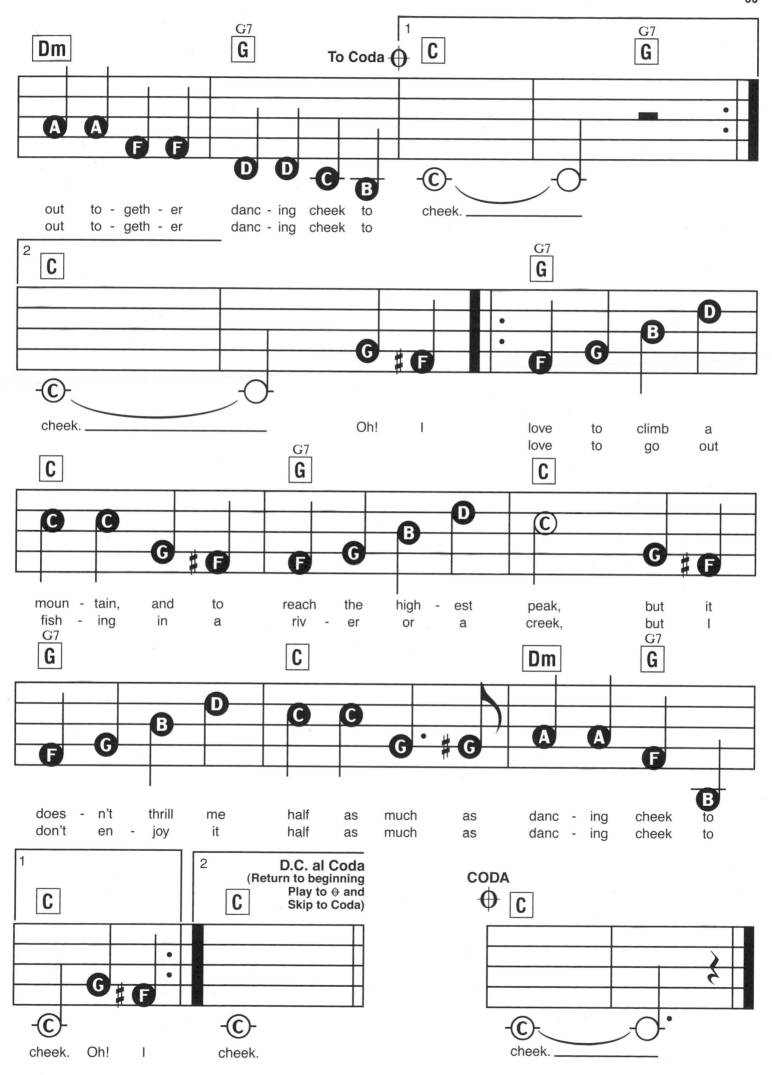

Dancing in the Dark
from THE BAND WAGON and DANCING IN THE DARK

Registration 3
Rhythm: Fox Trot or Swing

Words by Howard Dietz
Music by Arthur Schwartz

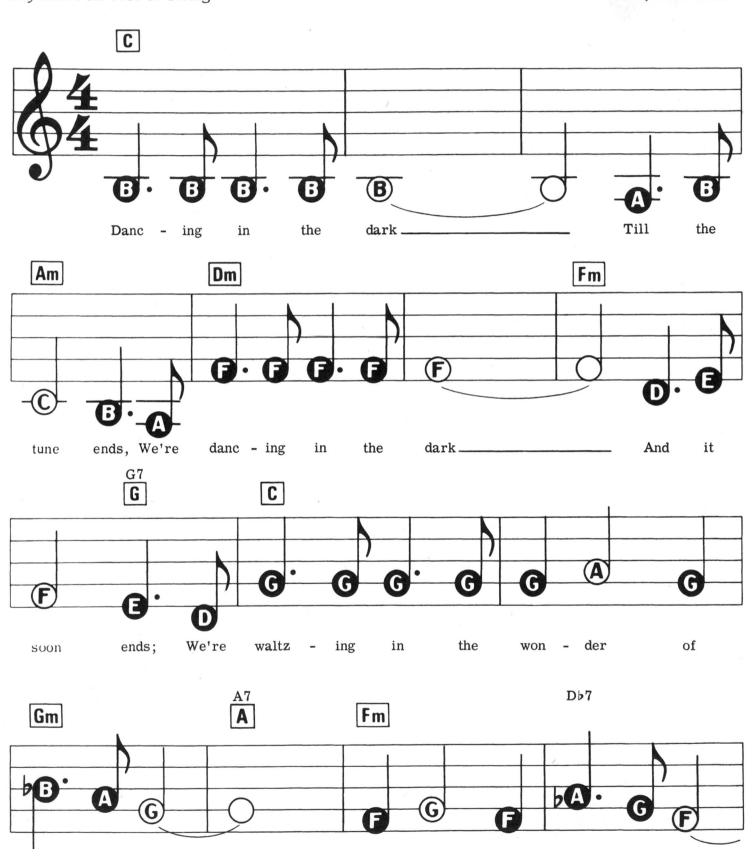

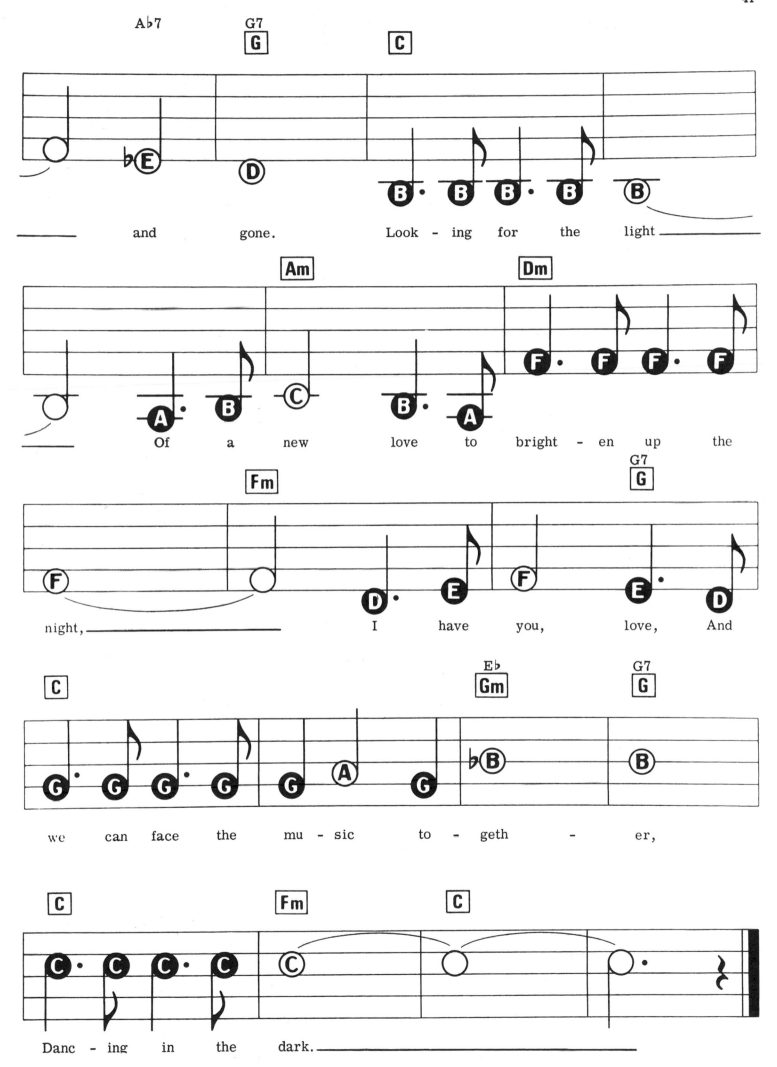

Dancing on the Ceiling
from SIMPLE SIMON

Registration 5
Rhythm: Swing

Words by Howard Dietz
Music by Arthur Schwartz

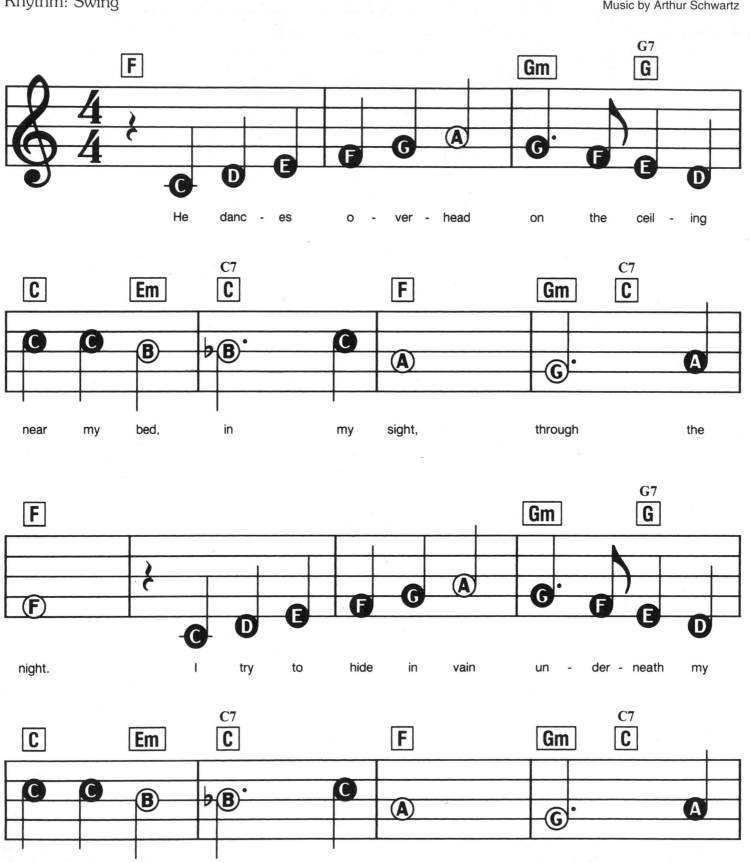

He danc - es o - ver - head on the ceil - ing near my bed, in my sight, through the night. I try to hide in vain un - der - neath my coun - ter - pane. There's my love up a -

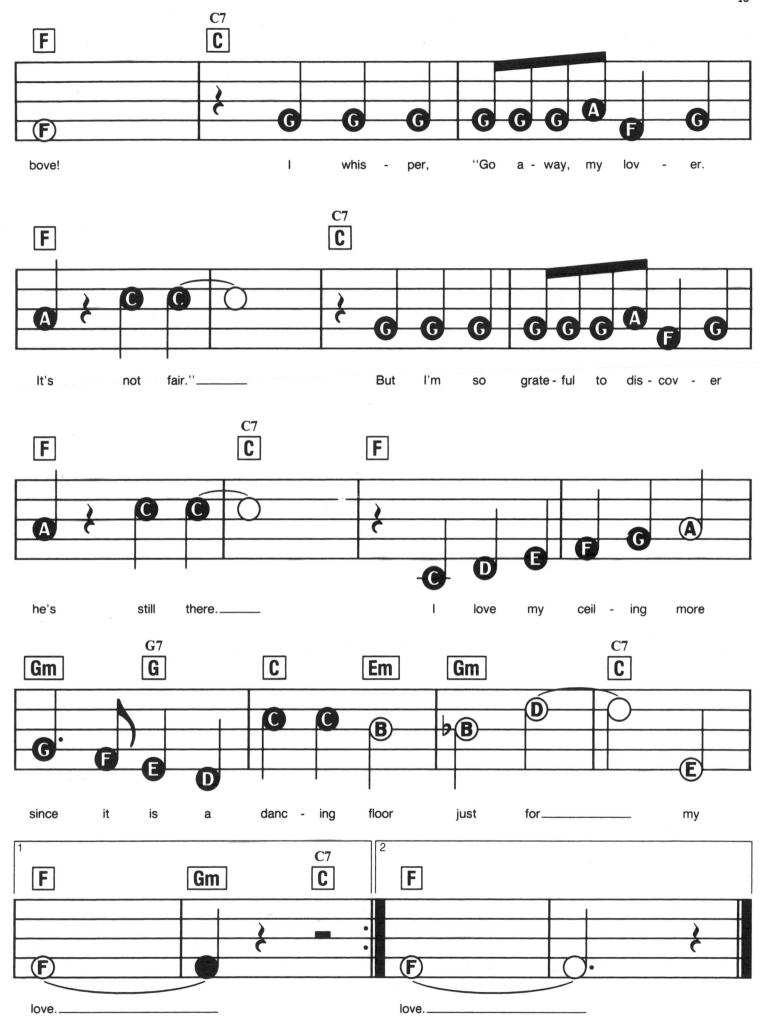

Deep Purple

Registration 1
Rhythm: Ballad or Swing

Words by Mitchell Parish
Music by Peter De Rose

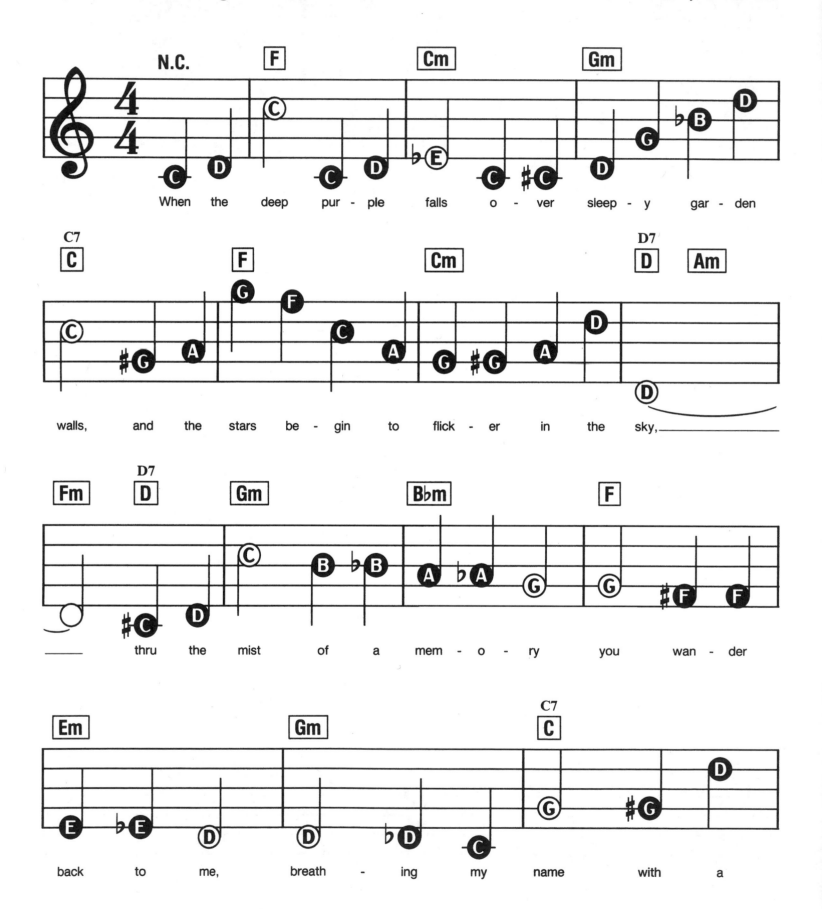

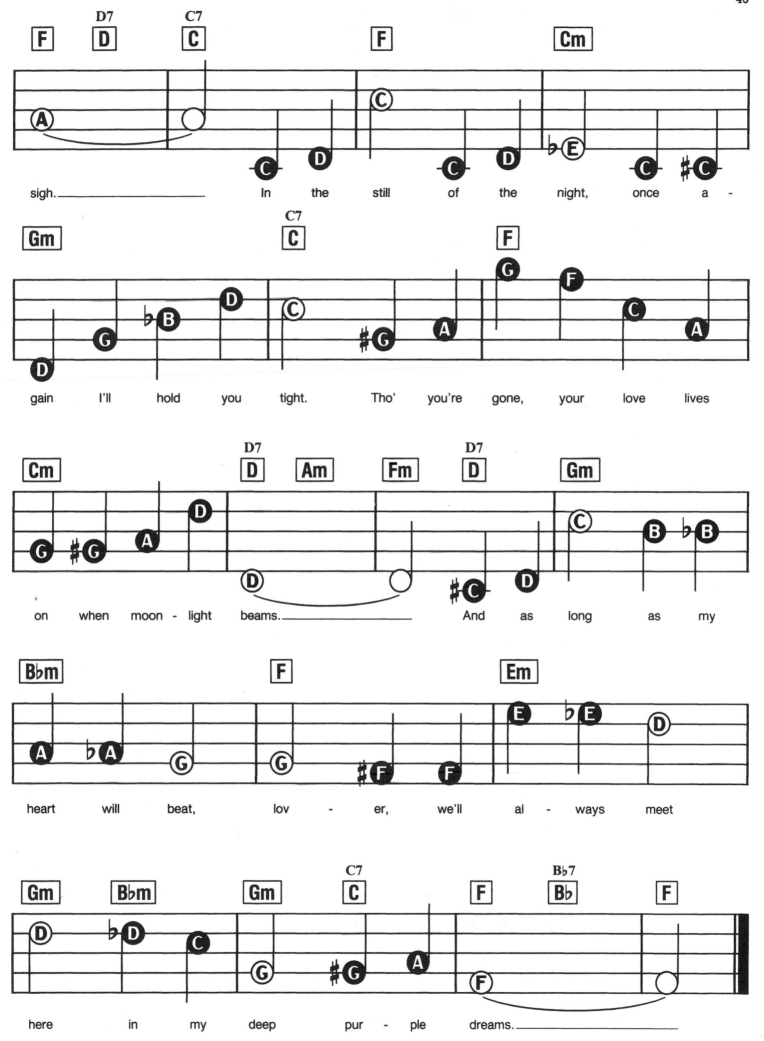

East of the Sun
(And West of the Moon)

Registration 2
Rhythm: Swing or Jazz

Words and Music by
Brooks Bowman

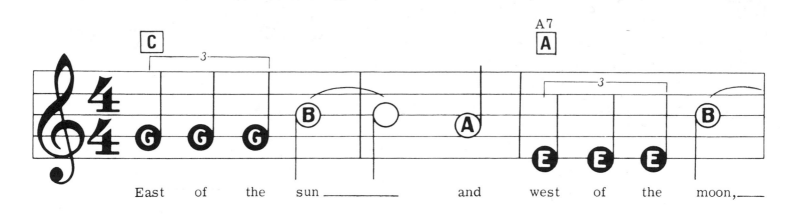

East of the sun _____ and west of the moon, ____

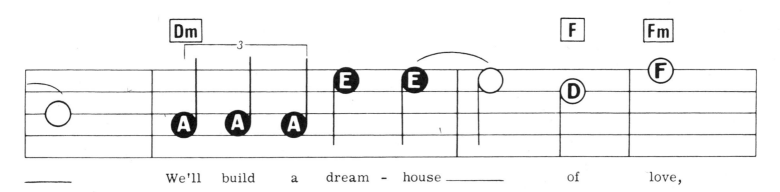

____ We'll build a dream - house _____ of love,

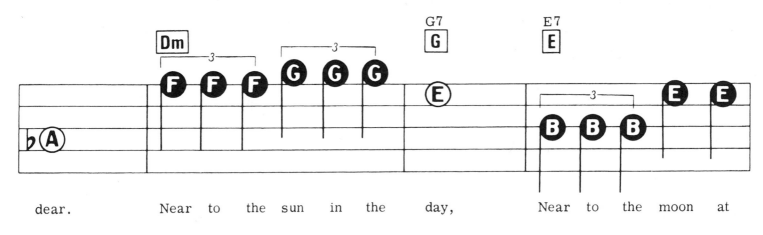

dear. Near to the sun in the day, Near to the moon at

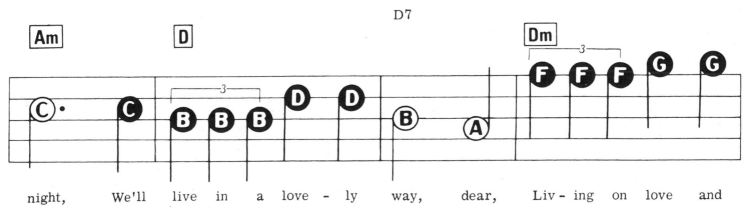

night, We'll live in a love - ly way, dear, Liv - ing on love and

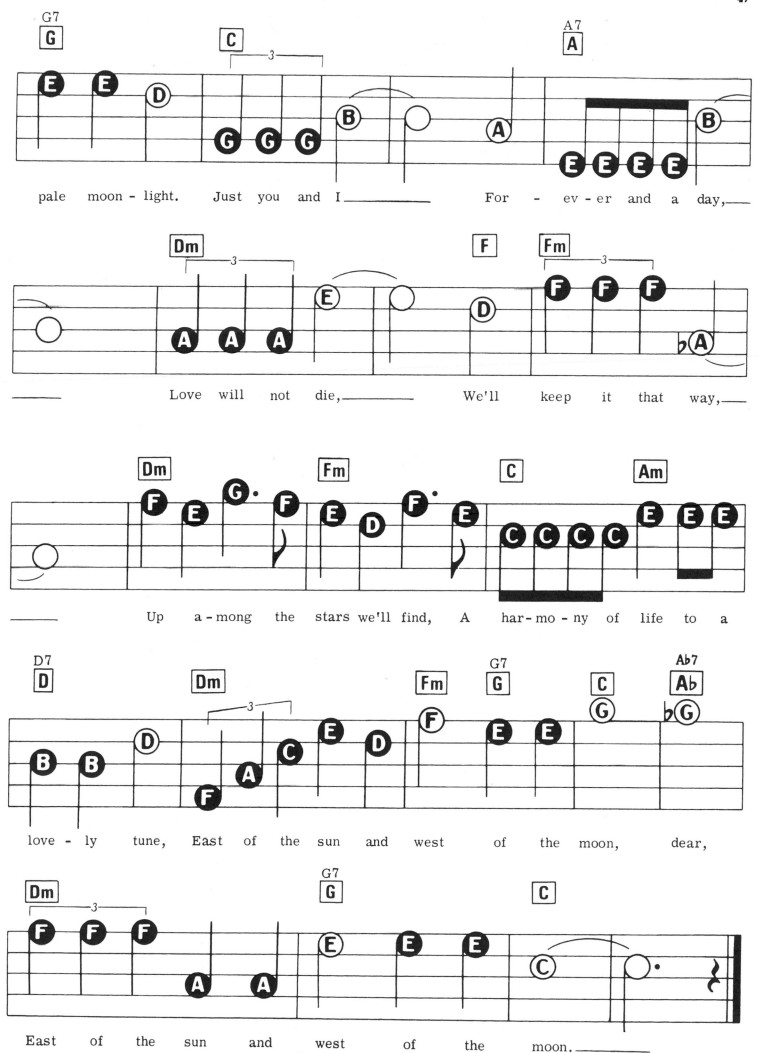

Easy Living
Theme from the Paramount Picture EASY LIVING

Registration 8
Rhythm: Fox Trot or Swing

Words and Music by Leo Robin and
Ralph Rainger

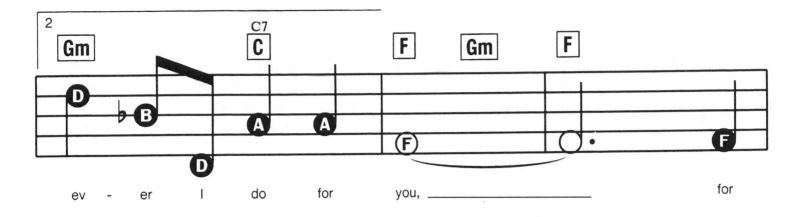

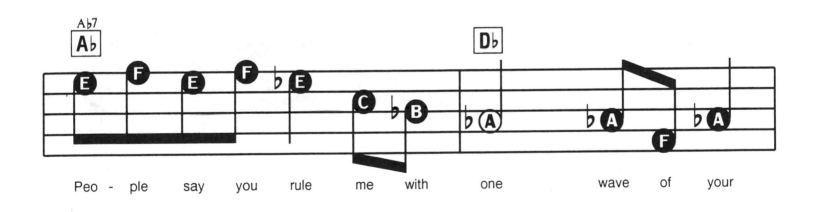

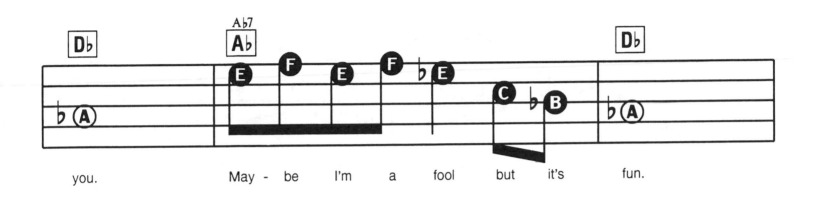

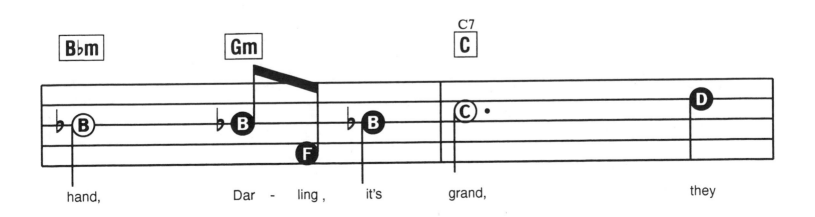

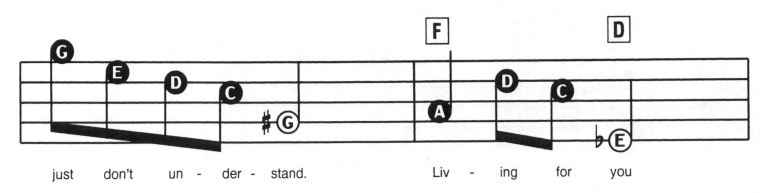

just don't un - der - stand. Liv - ing for you

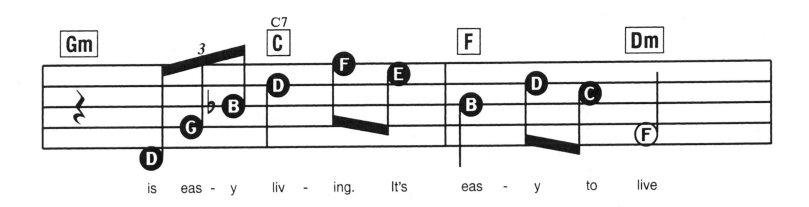

is eas - y liv - ing. It's eas - y to live

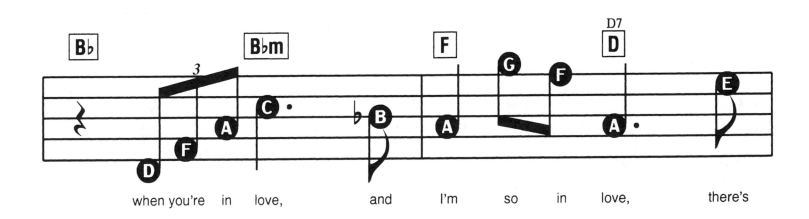

when you're in love, and I'm so in love, there's

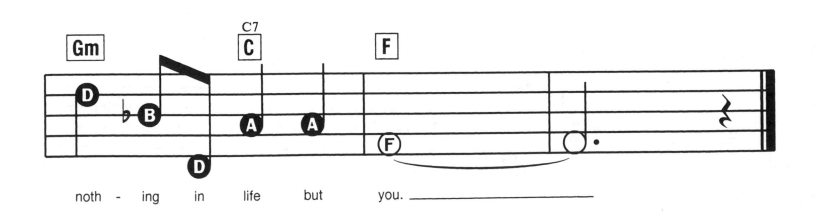

noth - ing in life but you.

The Folks Who Live on the Hill
from HIGH, WIDE AND HANDSOME

Registration 3
Rhythm: Fox Trot or Swing

Lyrics by Oscar Hammerstein II
Music by Jerome Kern

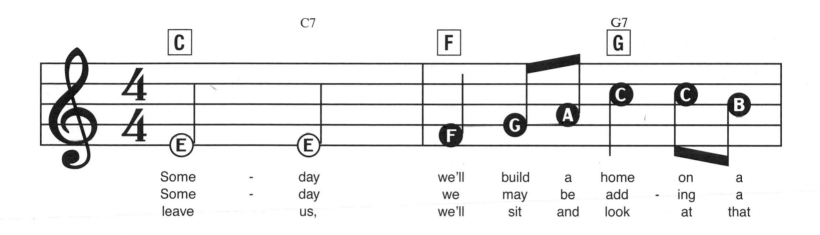

Some	-	day		we'll	build	a	home	on	a
Some	-	day		we	may	be	add	-	ing	a
leave		us,		we'll	sit	and	look	at	that

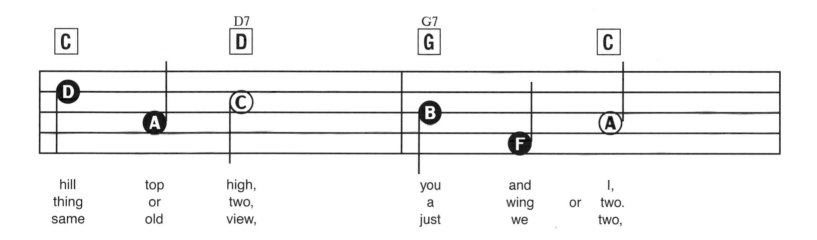

hill	top	high,	you	and	I,
thing	or	two,	a	wing	or	two.
same	old	view,	just	we	two,

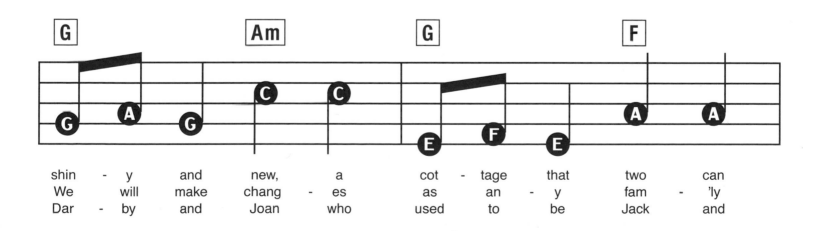

shin	-	y	and	new,	a	cot	-	tage	that	two	can
We	will	make	chang	-	es	as	an	-	y	fam	-	'ly
Dar	-	by	and	Joan	who	used	to	be	Jack	and

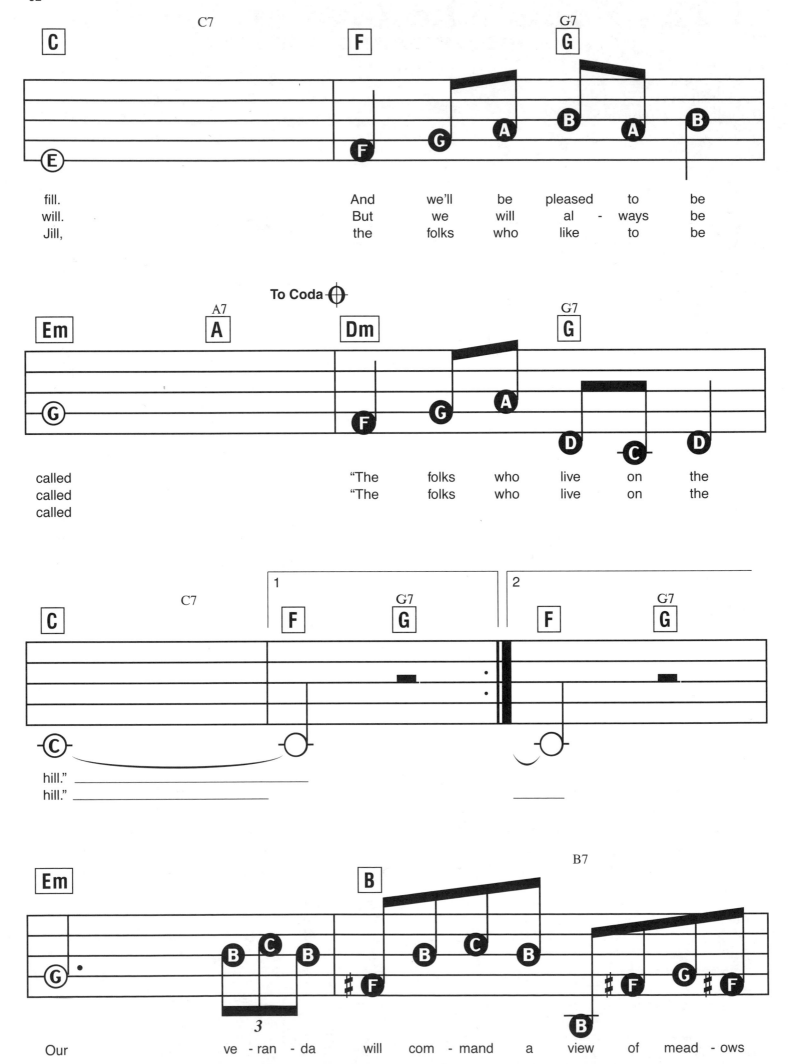

52

green,   the sort of view that seems to want to be

D.C. al Coda
(Return to beginning
Play to ⊕ and
Skip to Coda)

seen,   And when the kids grow up and

CODA

what they have al - ways been called,

"The folks who live on the hill." _____

Easy to Love
(You'd Be So Easy to Love)
from BORN TO DANCE

Registration 3
Rhythm: Swing or Fox Trot

Words and Music by
Cole Porter

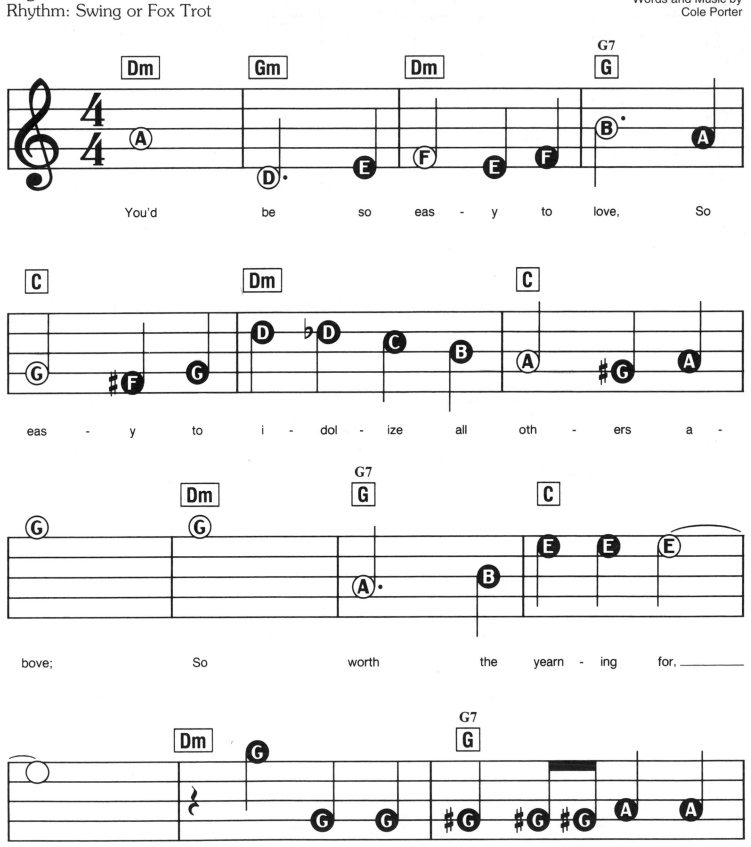

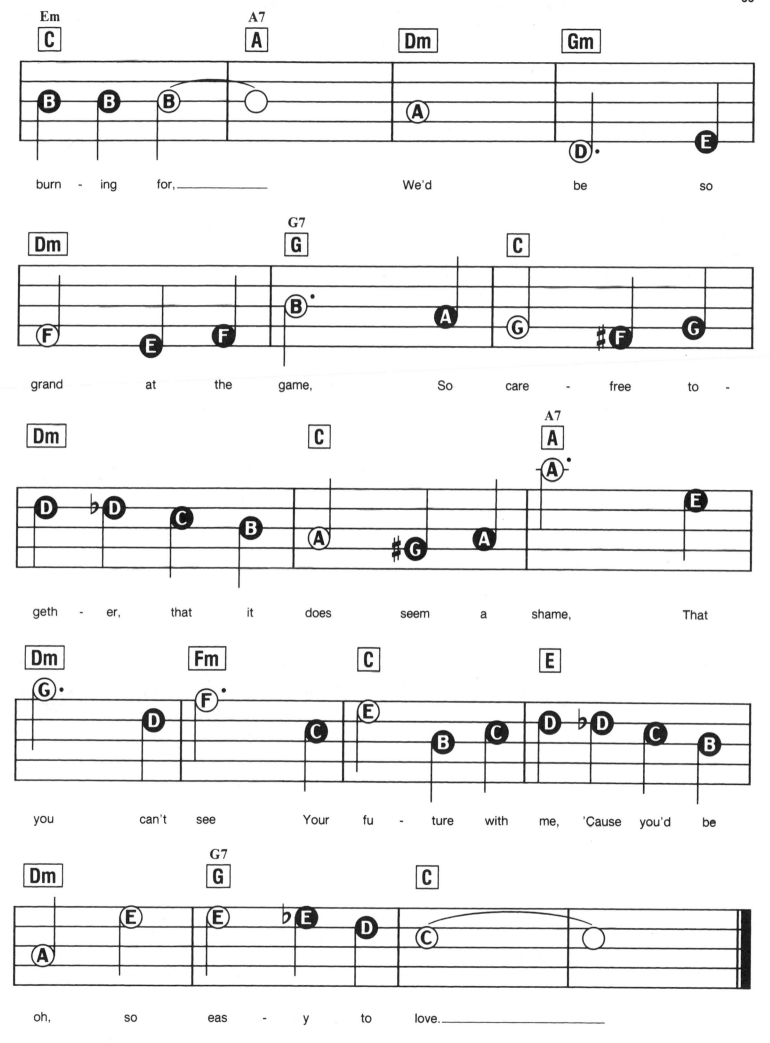

Embraceable You
from CRAZY FOR YOU

Registration 5
Rhythm: Fox Trot or Ballad

Music and Lyrics by George Gershwin
and Ira Gershwin

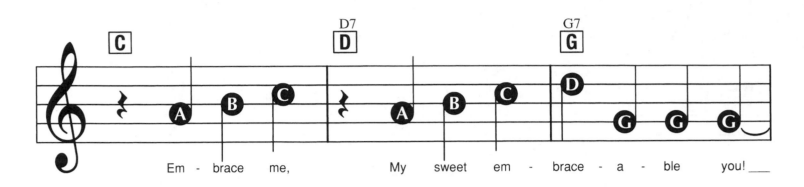

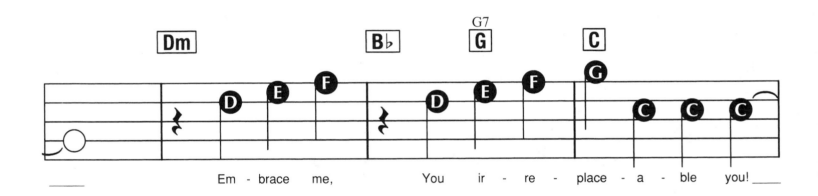

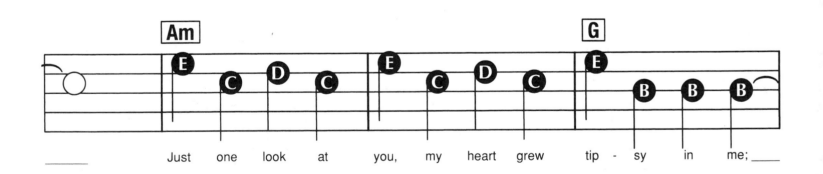

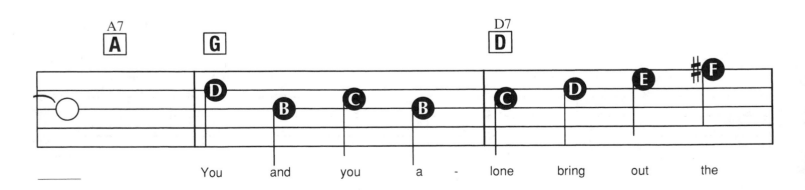

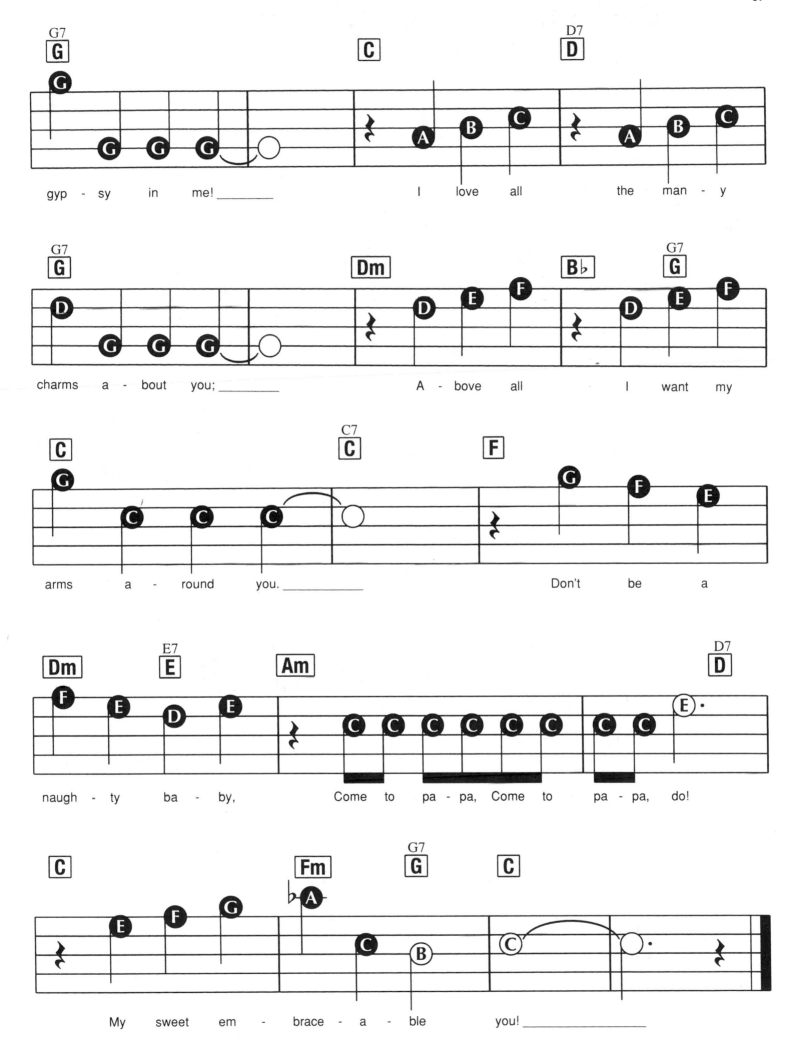

Falling in Love with Love
from THE BOYS FROM SYRACUSE

Registration 5
Rhythm: Waltz

Words by Lorenz Hart
Music by Richard Rodgers

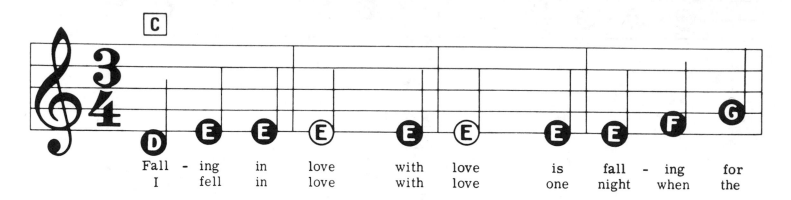

Fall - ing in love with love is fall - ing for
I fell in love love with with love one night when for the

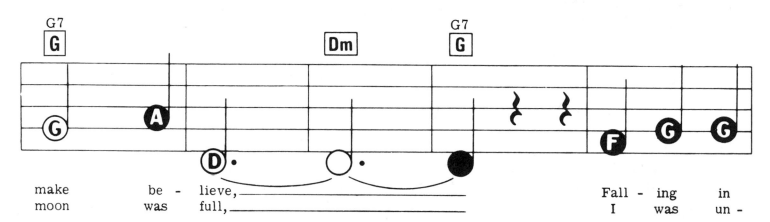

make be - lieve, Fall - ing in
moon was full, I was un -

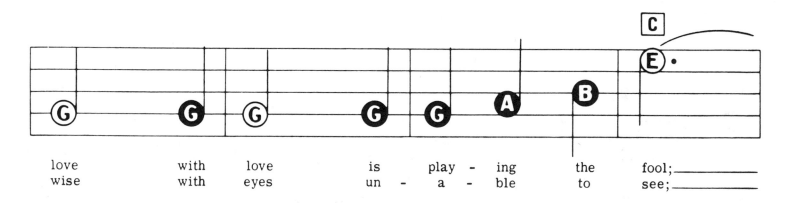

love with love is play - ing the fool;
wise with eyes un - a - ble to see;

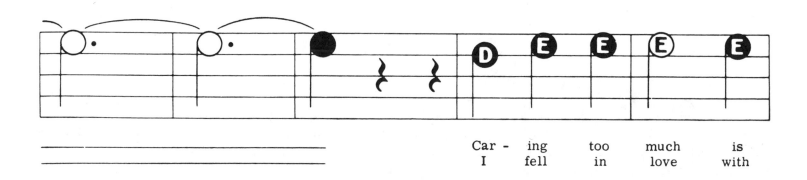

Car - ing too much is
I fell in love with

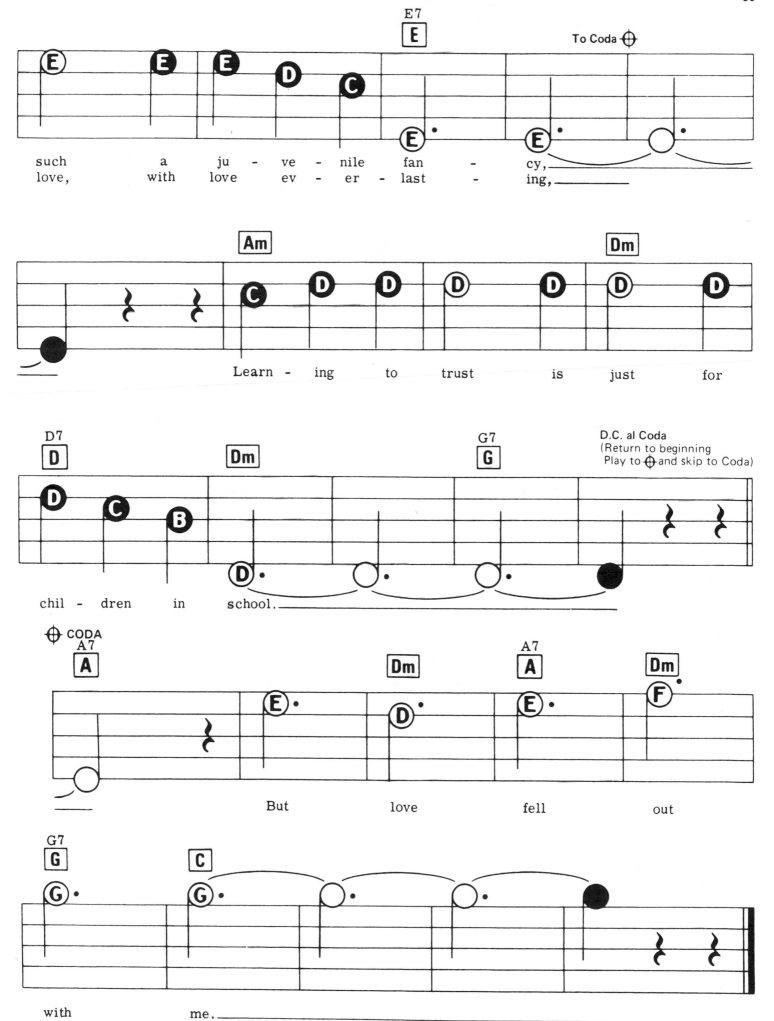

A Fine Romance
from SWING TIME

Registration 2
Rhythm: Ballad or Swing

Words by Dorothy Fields
Music by Jerome Kern

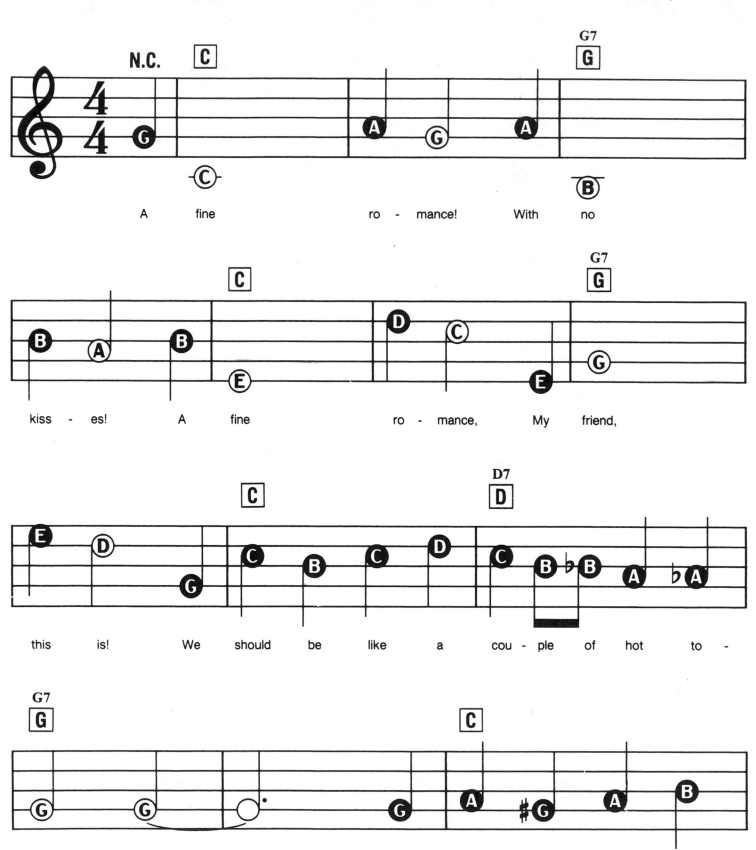

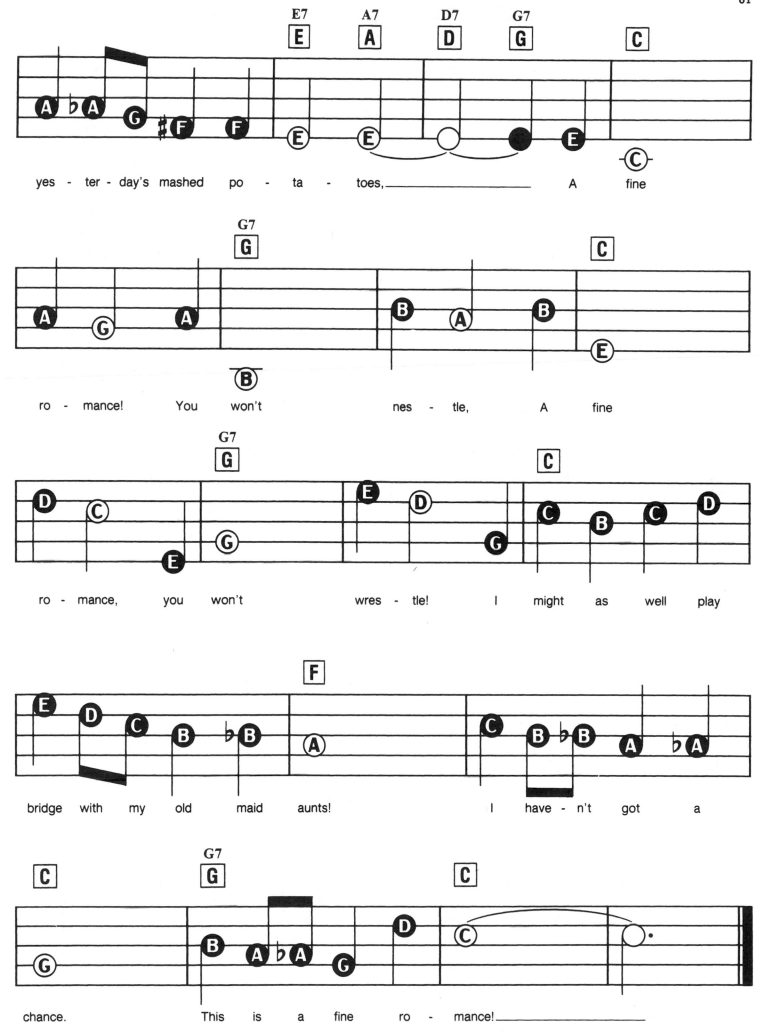

A Foggy Day
(In London Town)
from A DAMSEL IN DISTRESS

Registration 5
Rhythm: Swing or Fox Trot

Music and Lyrics by George Gershwin
and Ira Gershwin

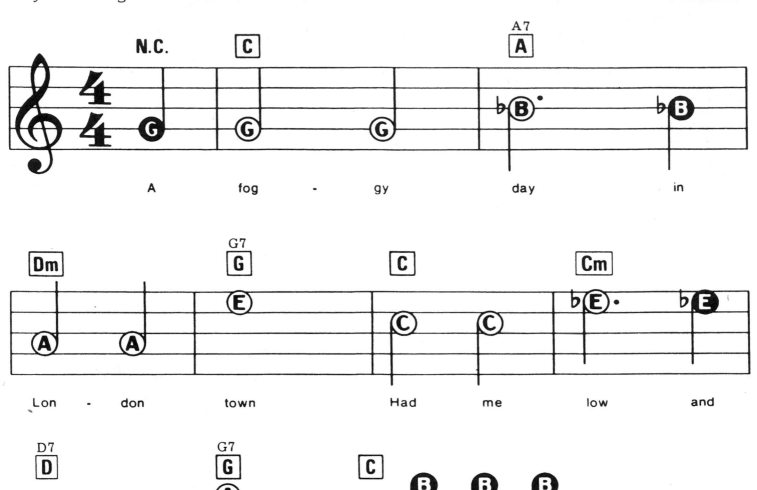

A   fog - gy   day   in

Lon - don   town   Had   me   low   and

had   me   down.   I   viewed   the   morn - ing

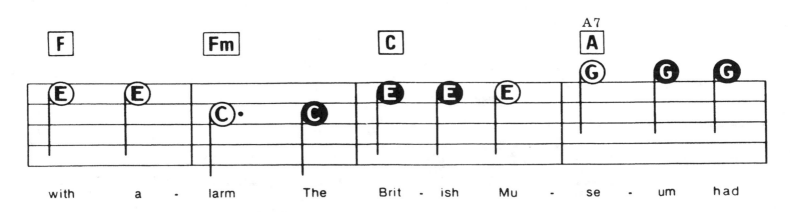

with   a - larm   The   Brit - ish   Mu - se - um   had

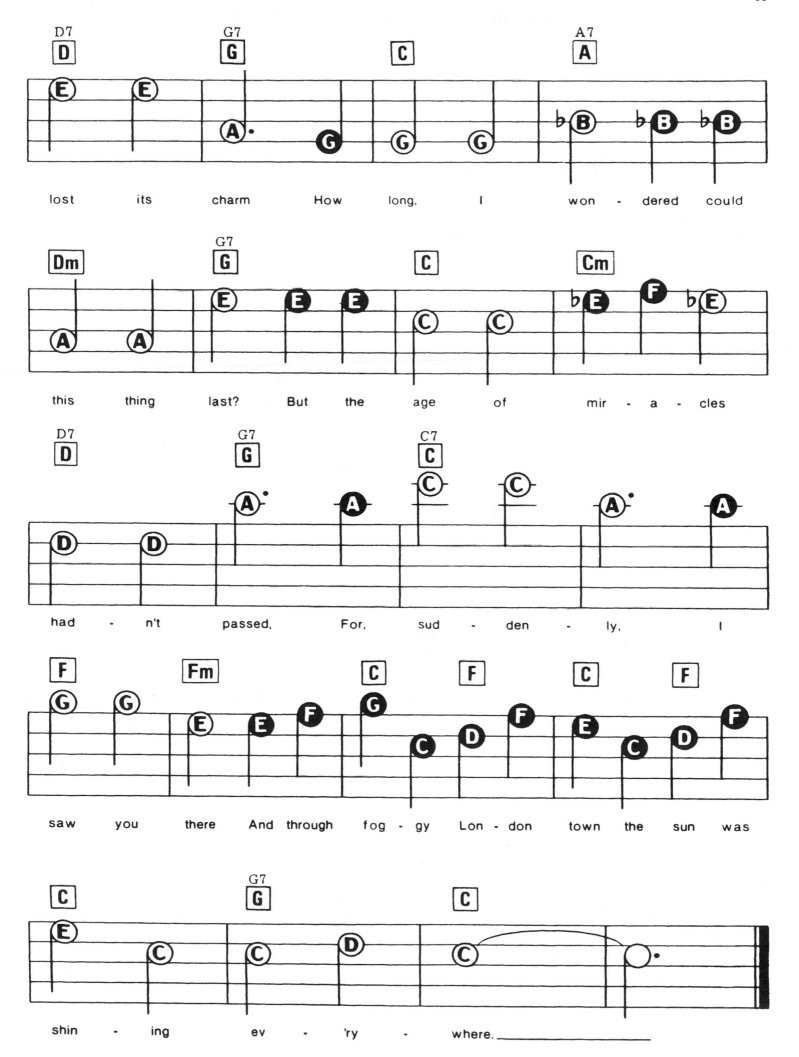

Georgia on My Mind

Registration 4
Rhythm: Swing

Words by Stuart Gorrell
Music by Hoagy Carmichael

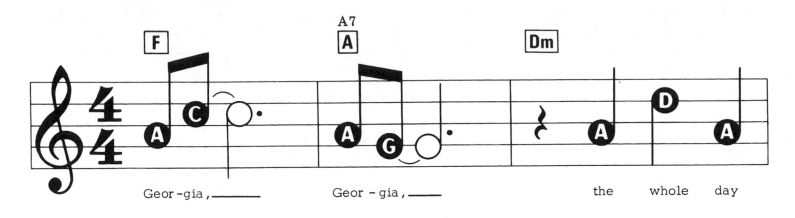

Geor-gia, _____ Geor-gia, _____ the whole day

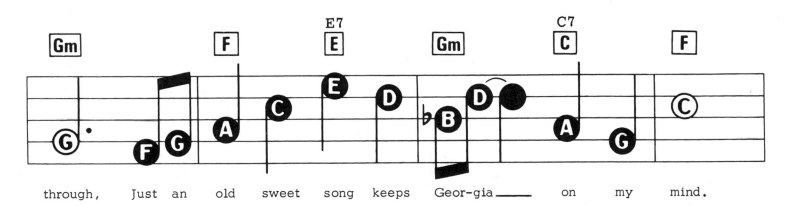

through, Just an old sweet song keeps Geor-gia _____ on my mind.

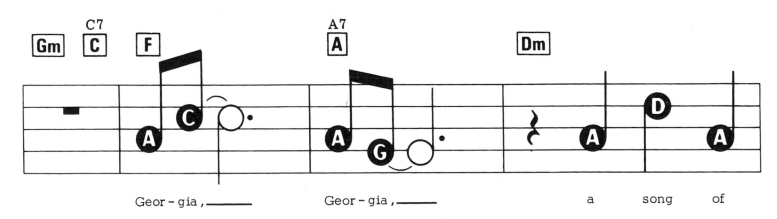

Geor-gia, _____ Geor-gia, _____ a song of

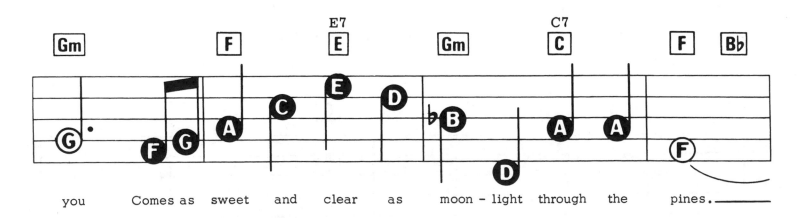

you Comes as sweet and clear as moon-light through the pines. _____

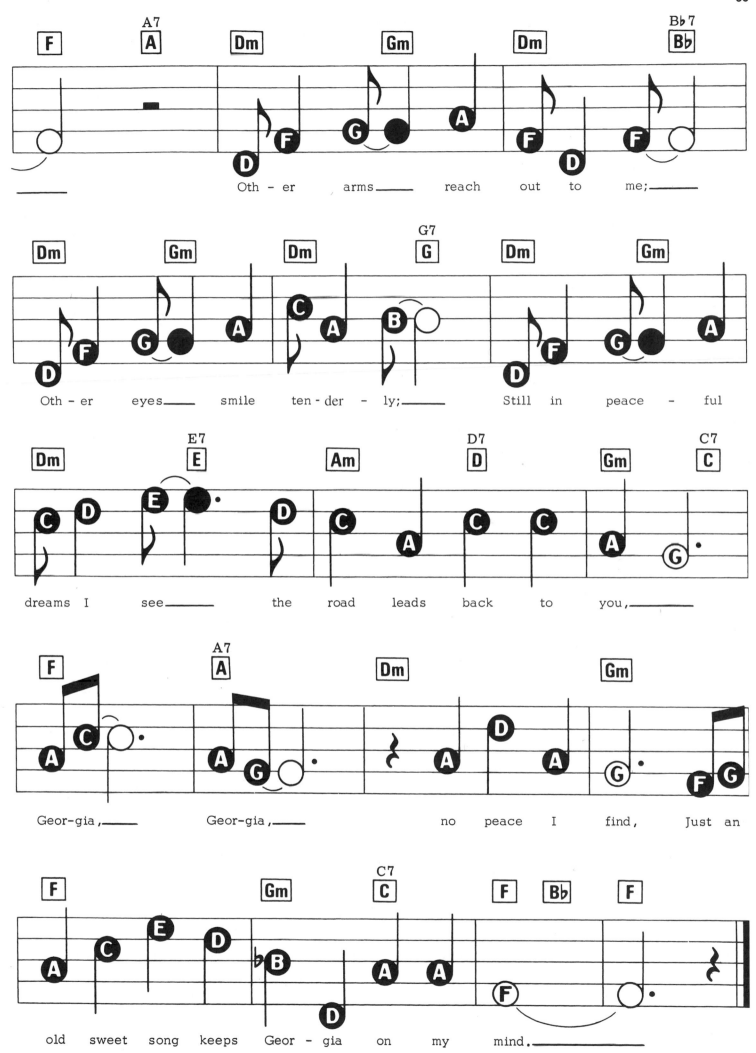

Glad to Be Unhappy
from ON YOUR TOES

Registration 3
Rhythm: Swing

Words by Lorenz Hart
Music by Richard Rodgers

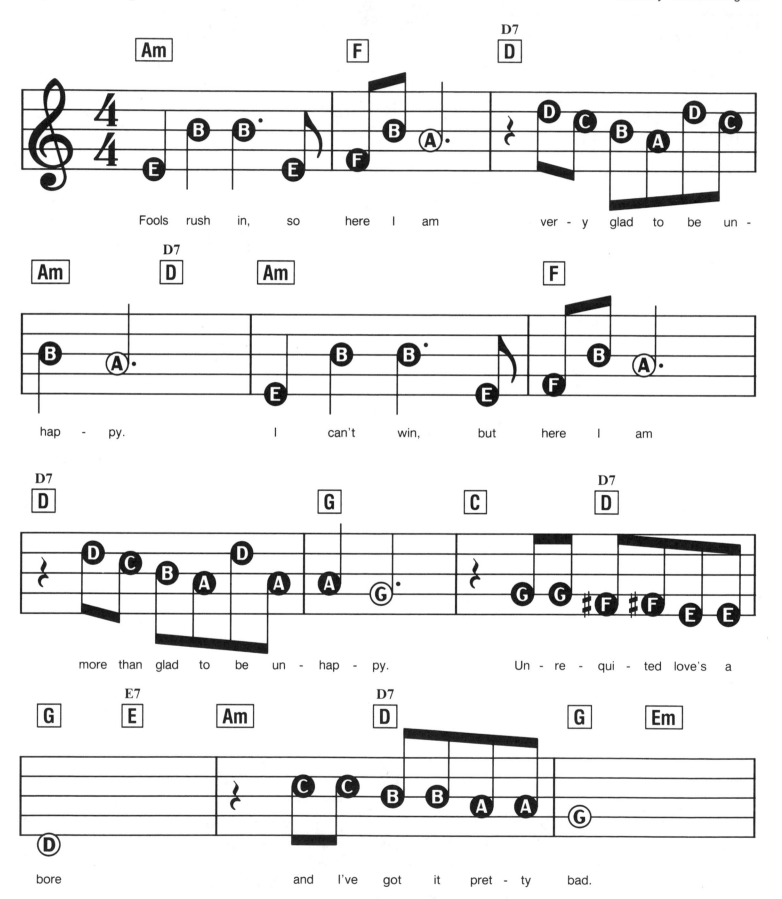

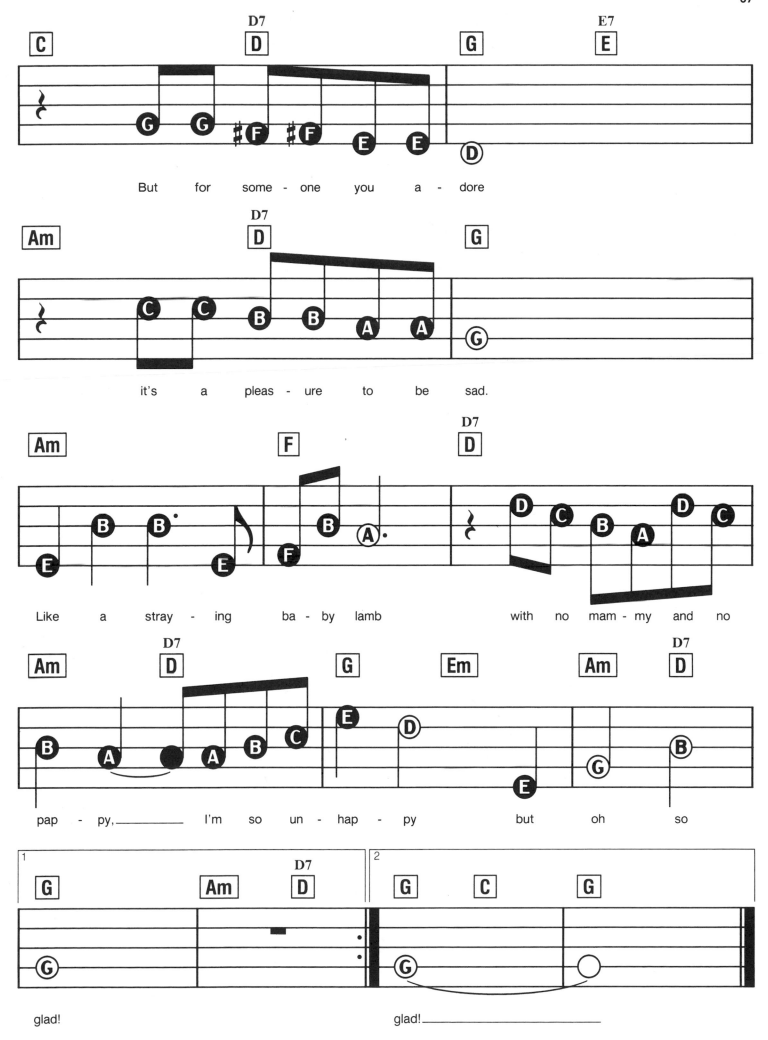

The Glory of Love
featured in GUESS WHO'S COMING TO DINNER

Registration 3
Rhythm: Swing or Ballad

Words and Music by
Billy Hill

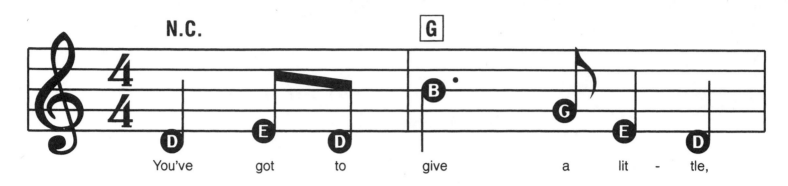

You've got to give a lit - tle,

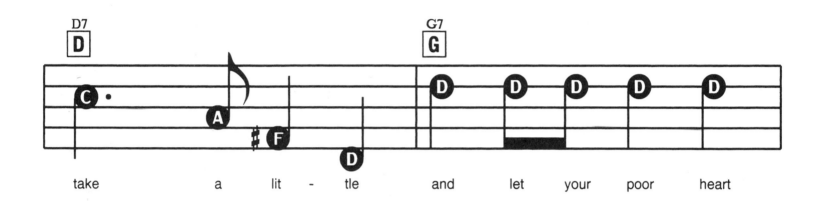

take a lit - tle and let your poor heart

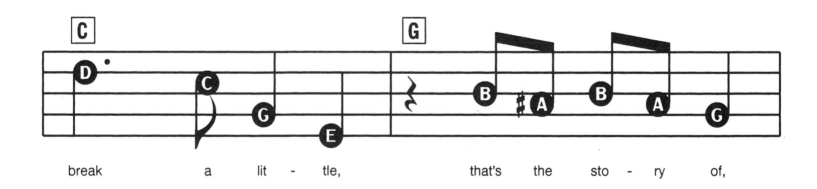

break a lit - tle, that's the sto - ry of,

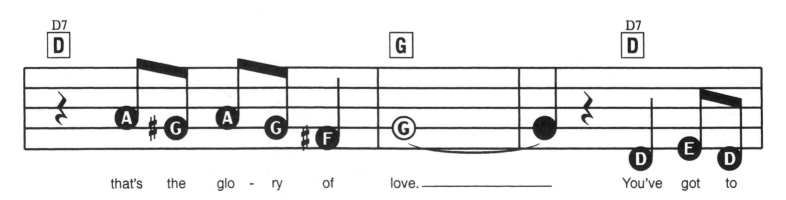

that's the glo - ry of love. _____ You've got to

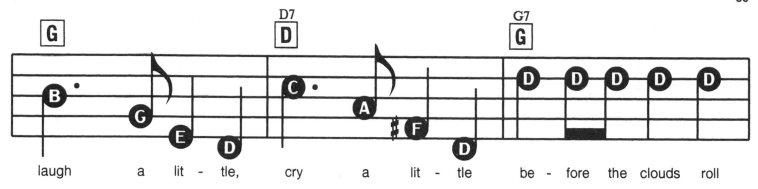

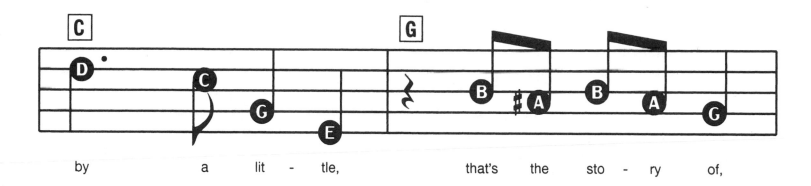

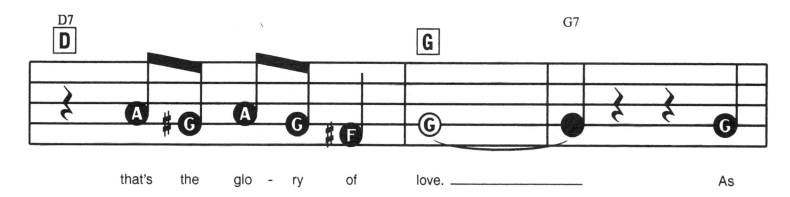

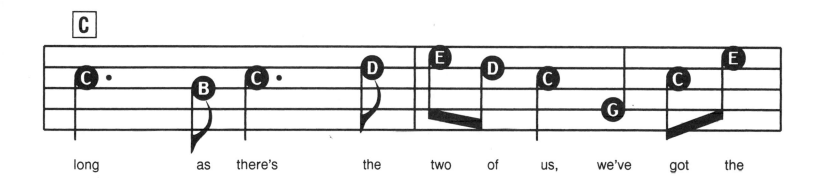

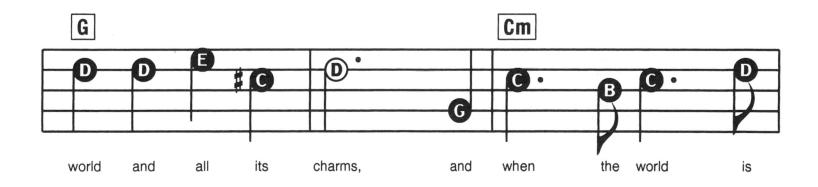

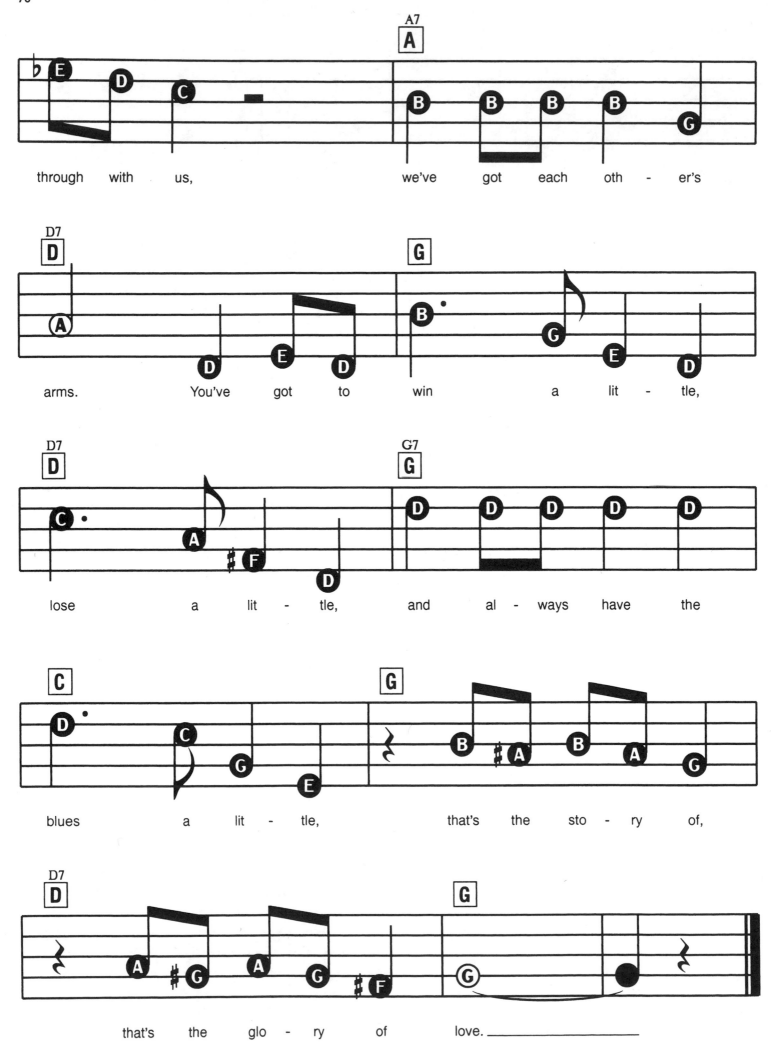

I Can't Get Started
from ZIEGFELD FOLLIES

Registration 2
Rhythm: Fox Trot or Swing

Words by Ira Gershwin
Music by Vernon Duke

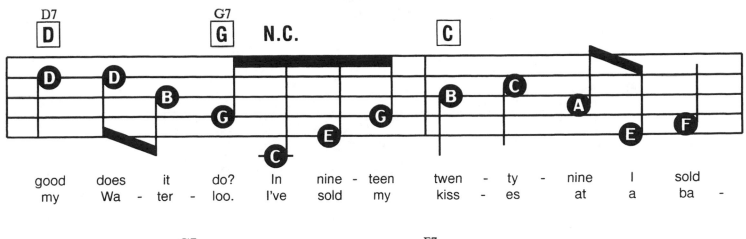

good does it do? In nine-teen twen-ty - nine I sold
my Wa - ter - loo. I've sold my kiss - es at a ba -

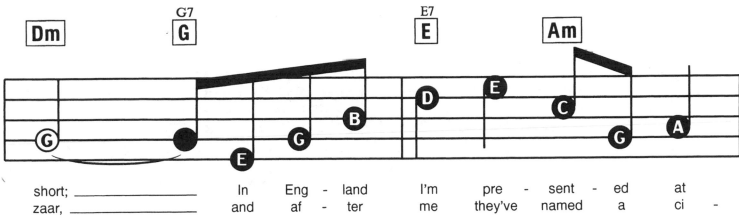

short; _____ In Eng - land I'm pre - sent - ed at
zaar, _____ and af - ter me they've named a ci -

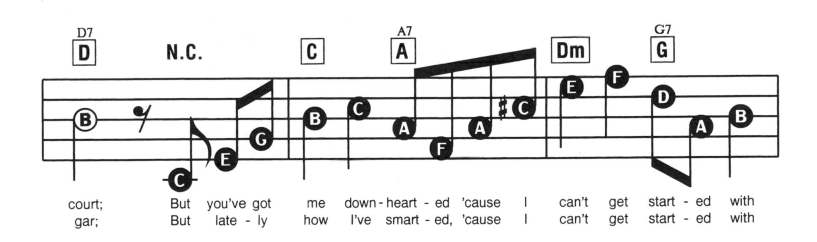

court; But you've got me down-heart - ed 'cause I can't get start - ed with
gar; But late - ly how I've smart - ed, 'cause I can't get start - ed with

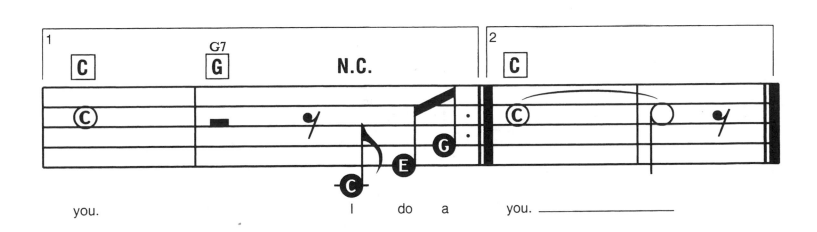

you. I do a you. _____

Goody Goody

Registration 7
Rhythm: Fox Trot or Swing

Words by Johnny Mercer
Music by Matt Malneck

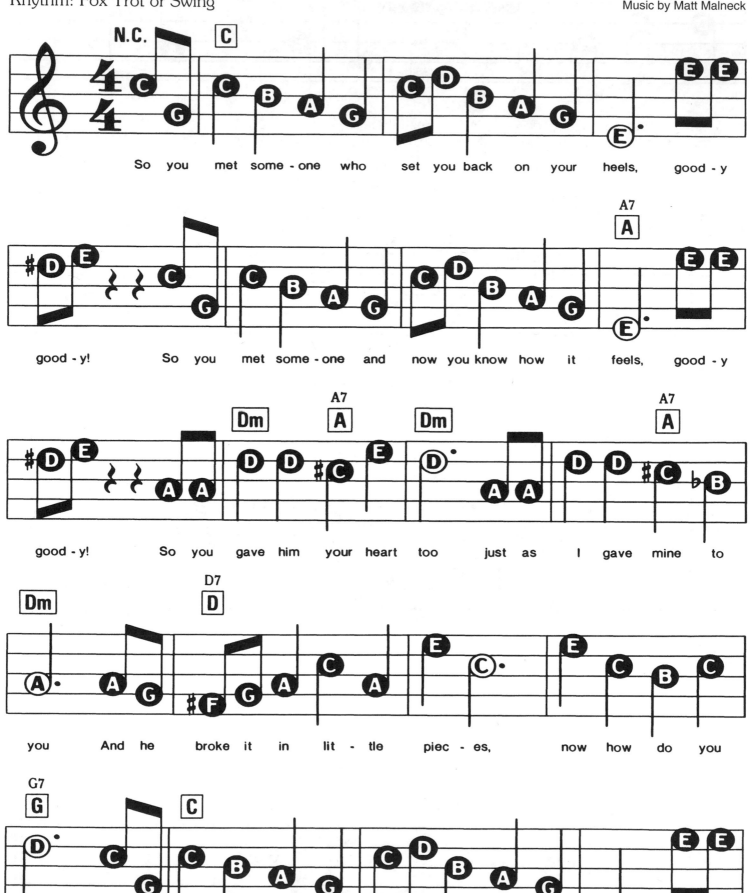

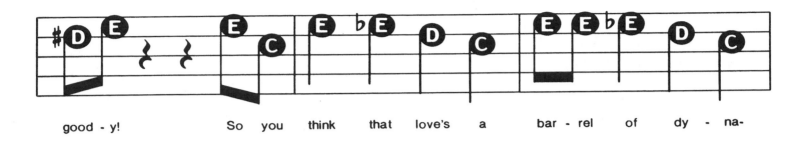

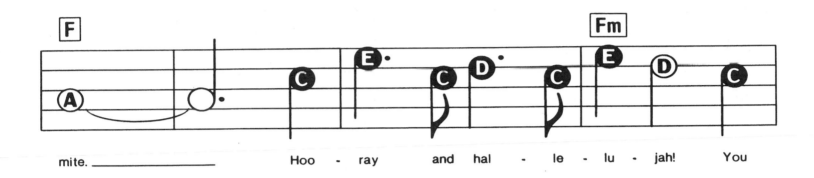

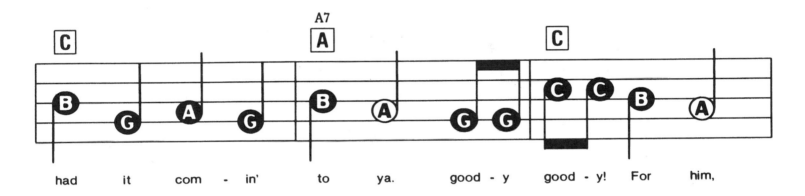

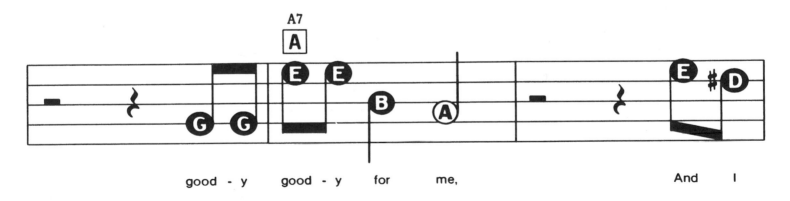

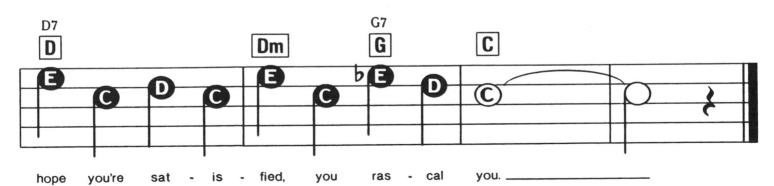

How Deep Is the Ocean
(How High Is the Sky)

Registration 4
Rhythm: Fox Trot or Swing

Words and Music by
Irving Berlin

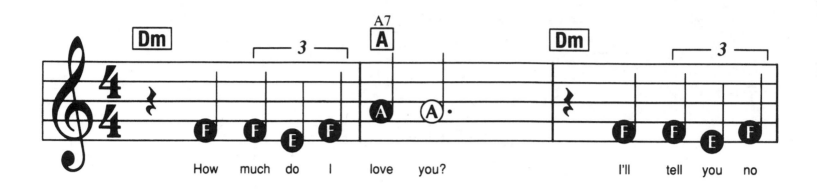

How much do I love you?   I'll tell you no

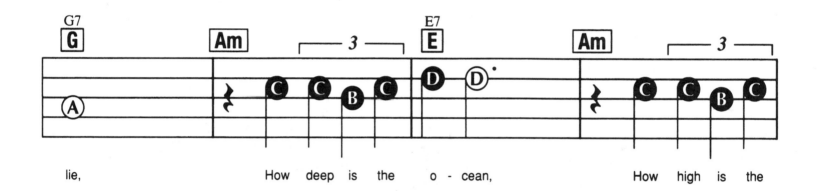

lie,   How deep is the o - cean,   How high is the

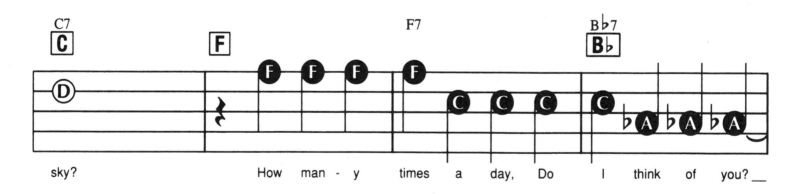

sky?   How man - y times a day, Do I think of you? __

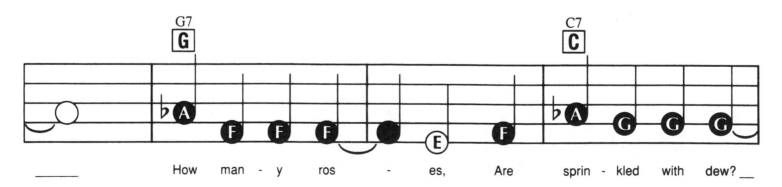

_____   How man - y ros - es, Are sprin - kled with dew? __

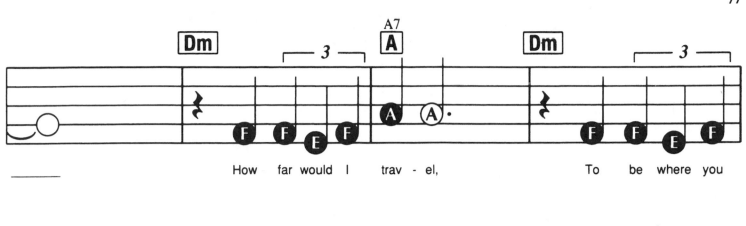

How far would I trav - el, To be where you

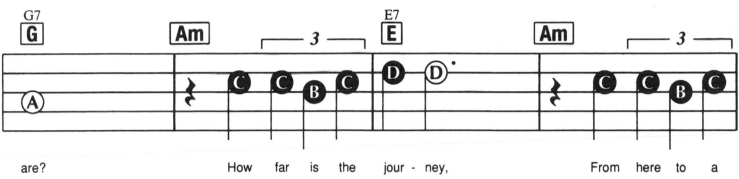

are? How far is the jour - ney, From here to a

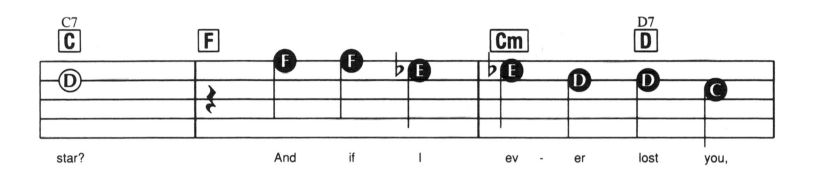

star? And if I ev - er lost you,

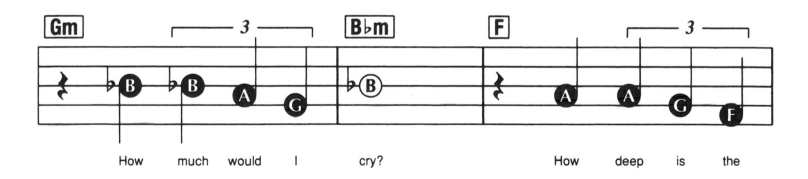

How much would I cry? How deep is the

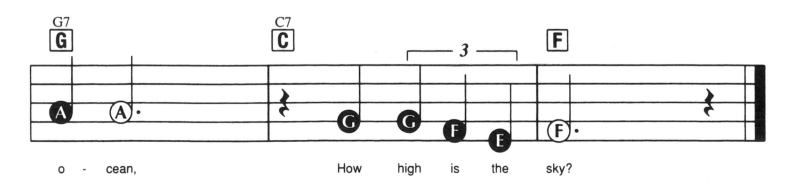

o - cean, How high is the sky?

I Concentrate on You
from BROADWAY MELODY OF 1940

Registration 1
Rhythm: Latin

Words and Music by
Cole Porter

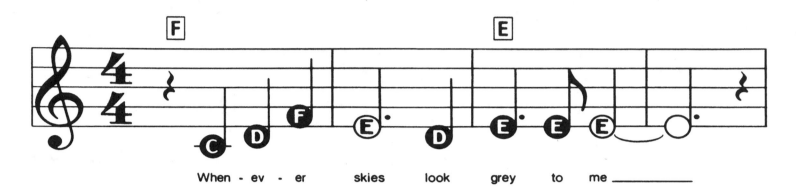

When - ev - er skies look grey to me _____

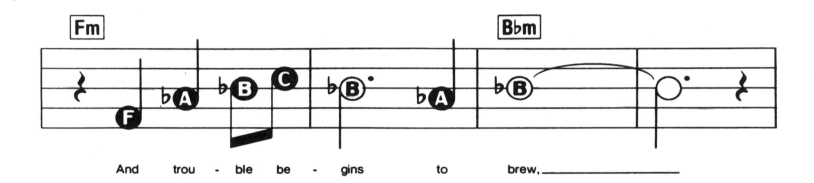

And trou - ble be - gins to brew, _____

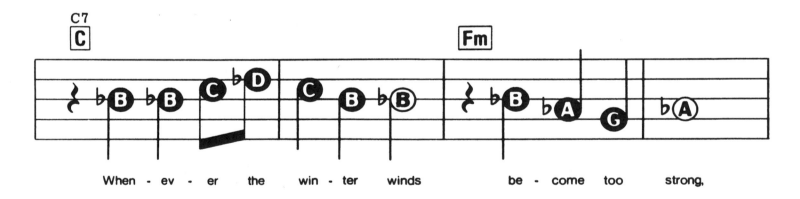

When - ev - er the win - ter winds be - come too strong,

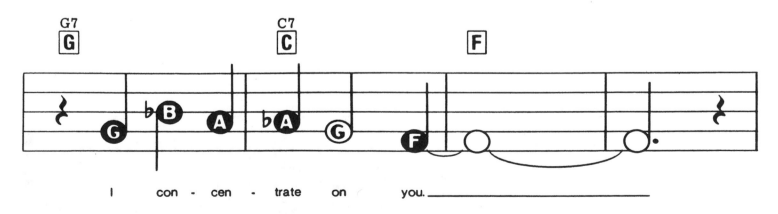

I con - cen - trate on you. _____

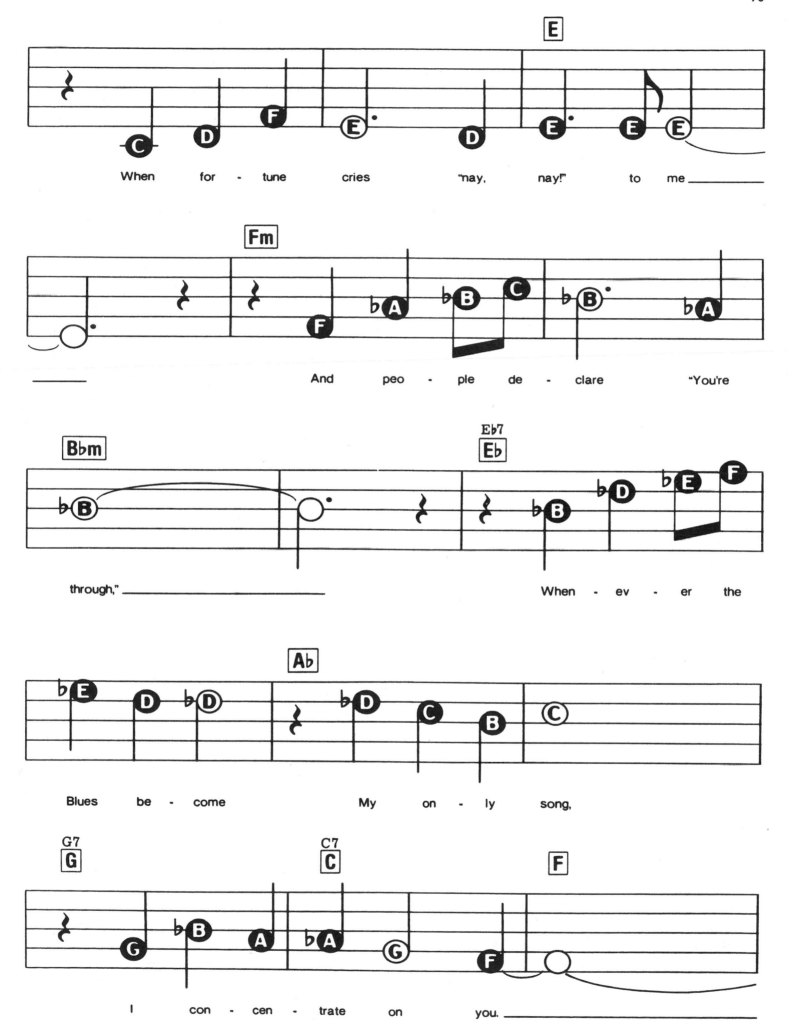

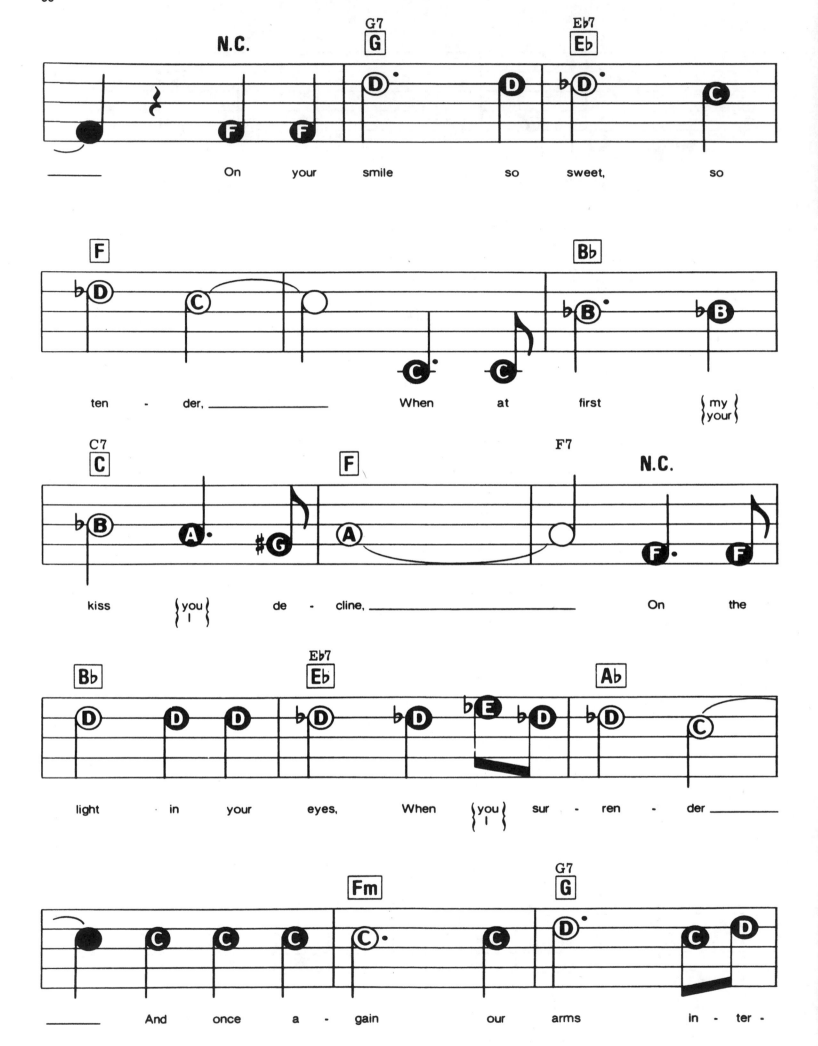

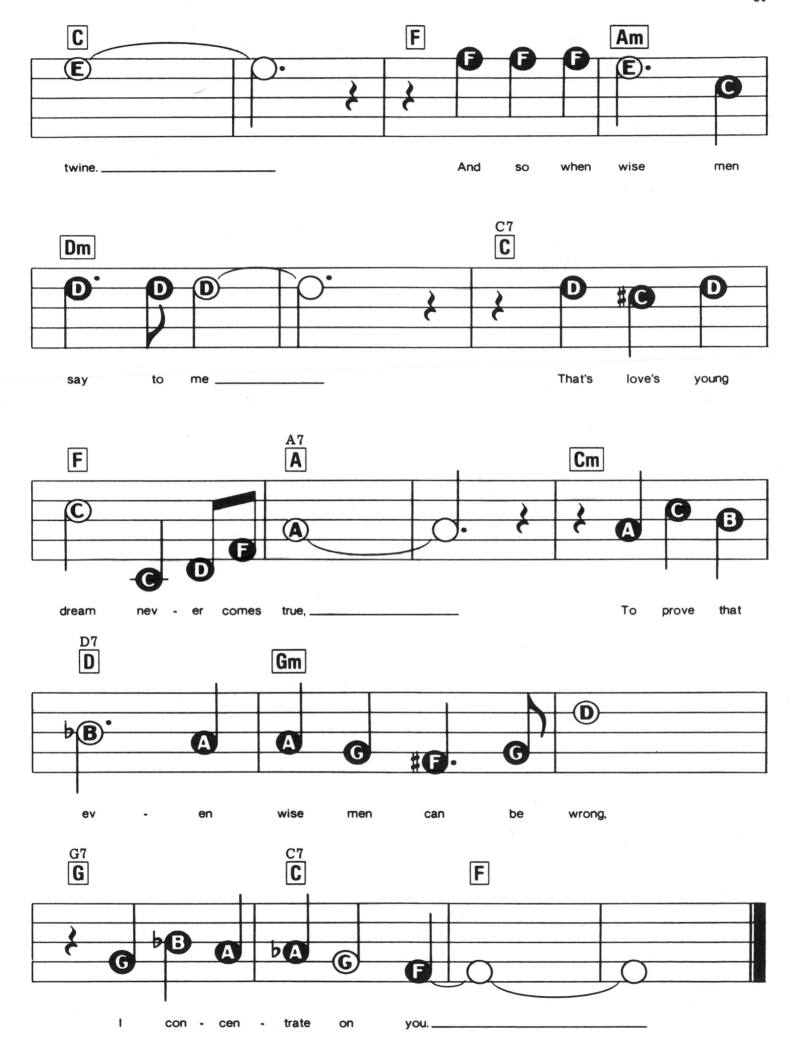

I Don't Know Why

(I Just Do)

Registration 8
Rhythm: Fox Trot or Swing

Lyric by Roy Turk
Music by Fred E. Ahlert

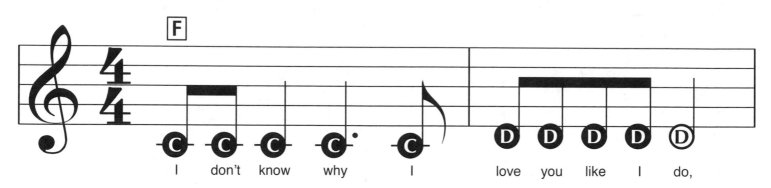

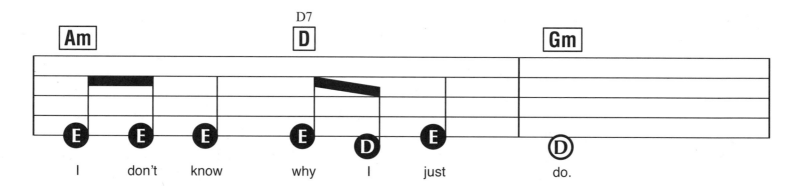

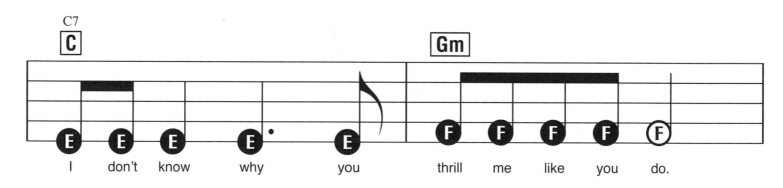

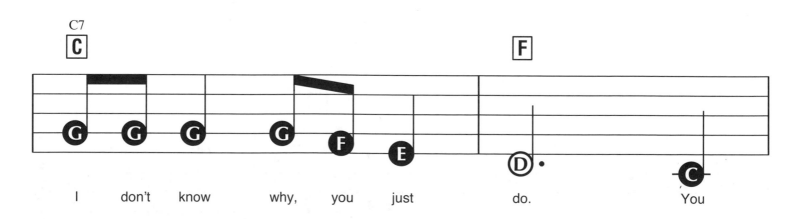

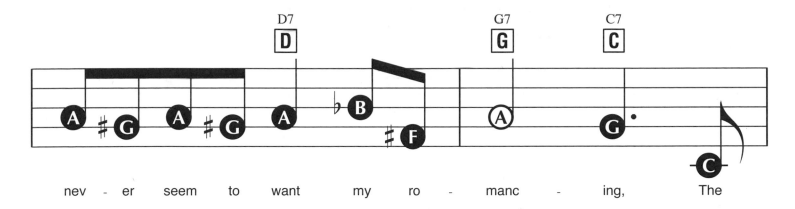

never seem to want my ro - manc - ing, The

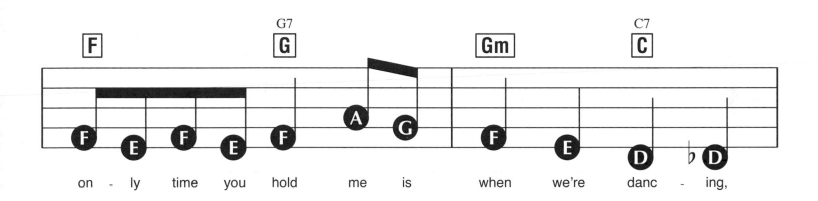

on - ly time you hold me is when we're danc - ing,

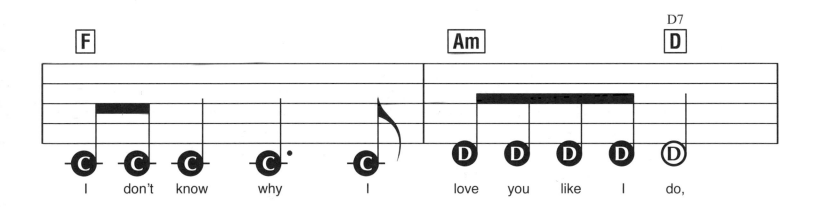

I don't know why I love you like I do,

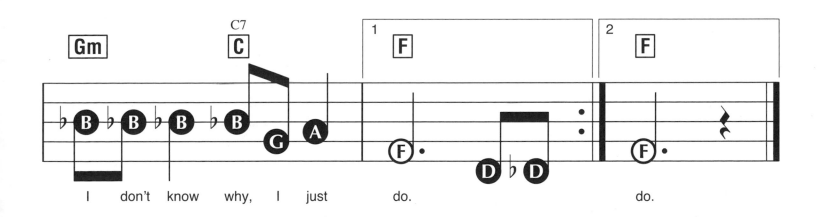

I don't know why, I just do. do.

I Don't Stand a Ghost of a Chance with You

Registration 3
Rhythm: Fox Trot

Words by Bing Crosby and Ned Washington
Music by Victor Young

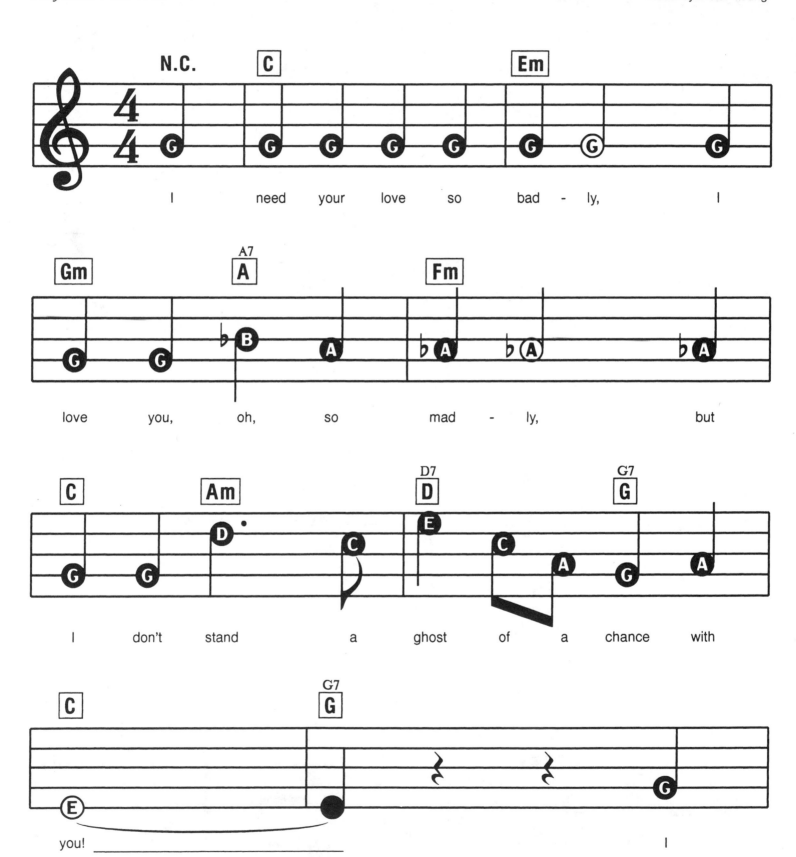

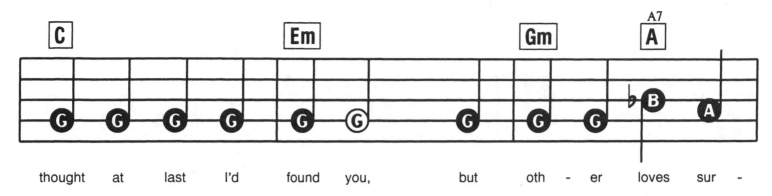

thought at last I'd found you, but oth - er loves sur -

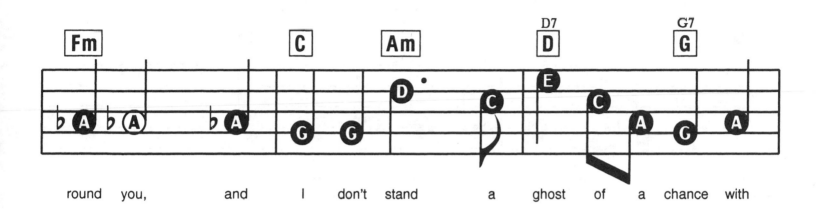

round you, and I don't stand a ghost of a chance with

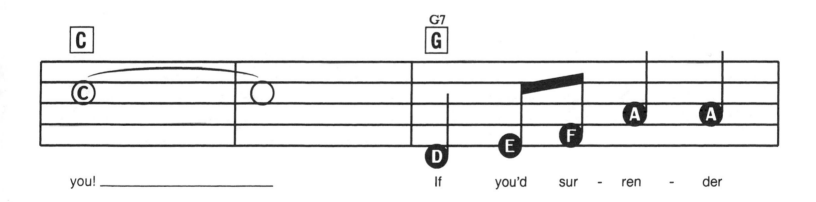

you! _____ If you'd sur - ren - der

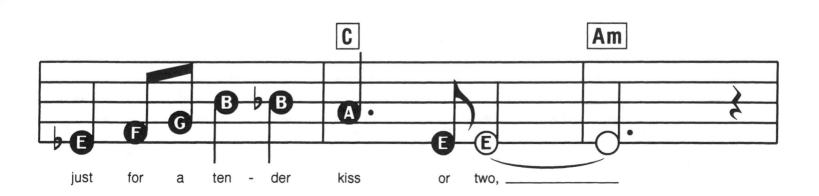

just for a ten - der kiss or two, _____

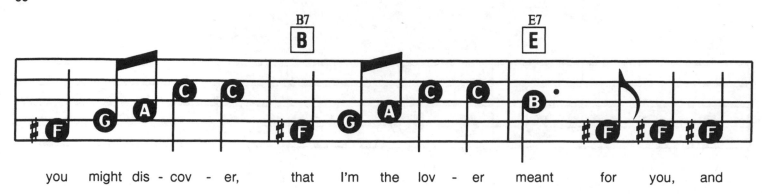

you might dis - cov - er, that I'm the lov - er meant for you, and

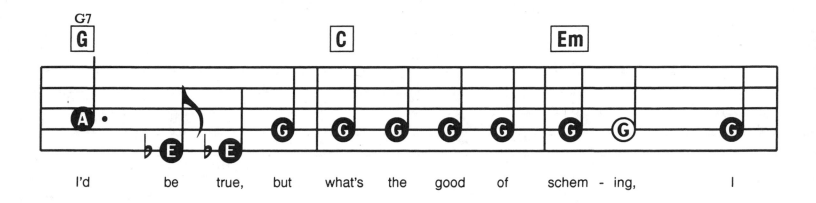

I'd be true, but what's the good of schem - ing, I

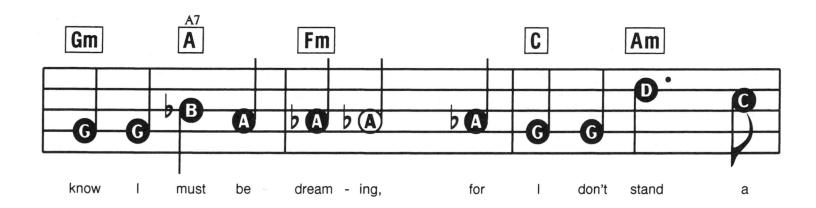

know I must be dream - ing, for I don't stand a

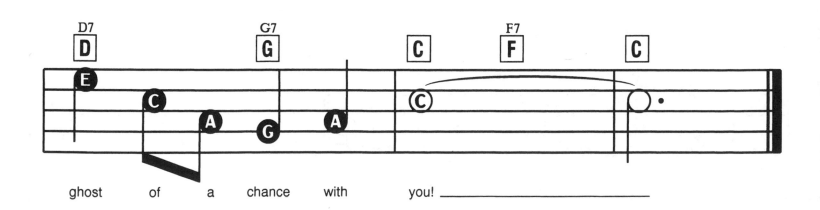

ghost of a chance with you!

I Won't Dance
from ROBERTA

Registration 3
Rhythm: Fox Trot or Swing

Words and Music by Jimmy McHugh,
Dorothy Fields, Jerome Kern,
Oscar Hammerstein II and Otto Harbach

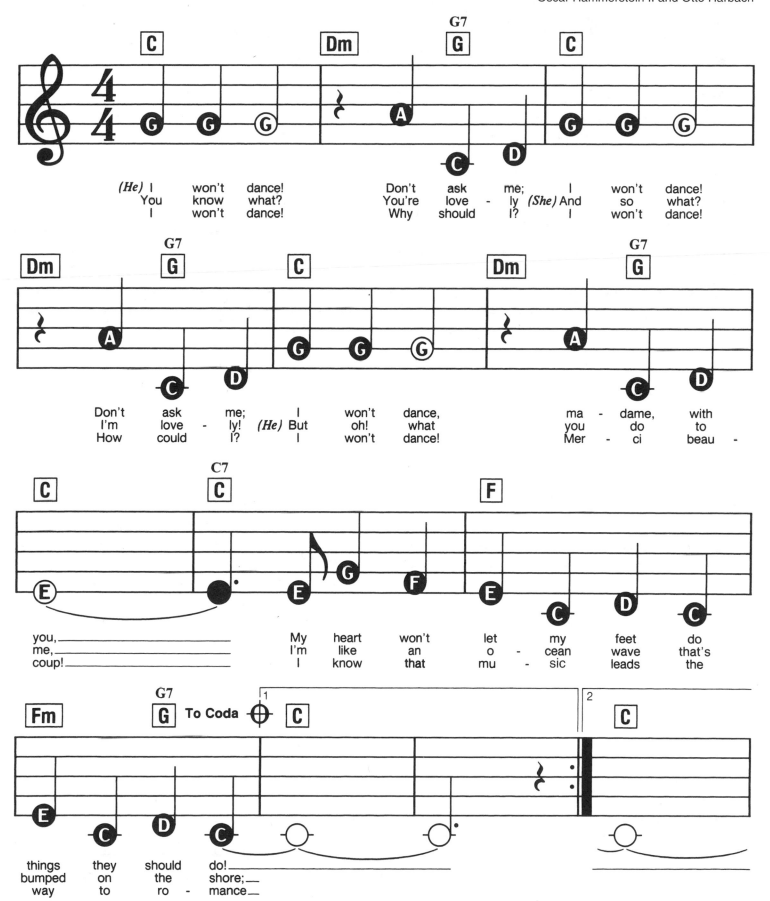

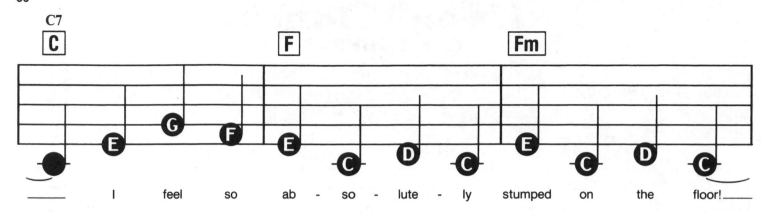

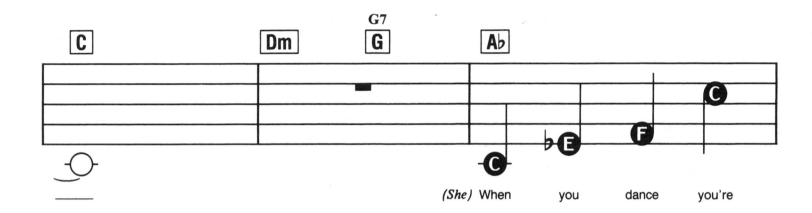

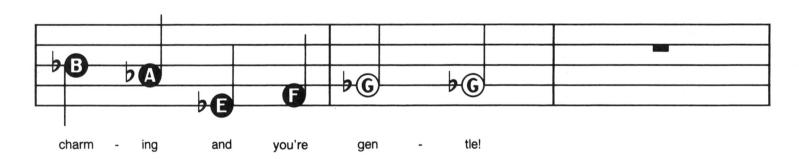

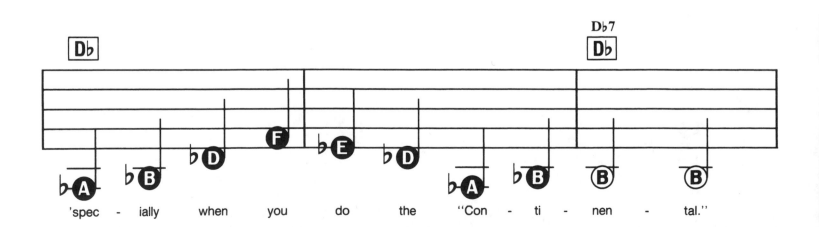

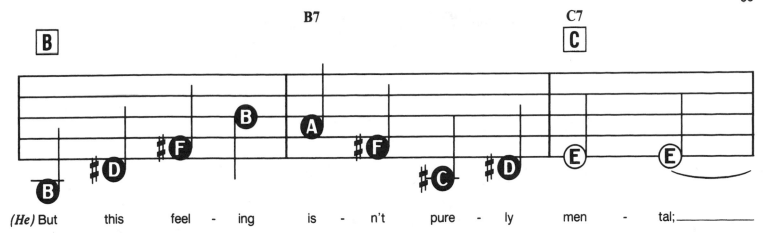

(He) But this feel - ing is - n't pure - ly men - tal;____

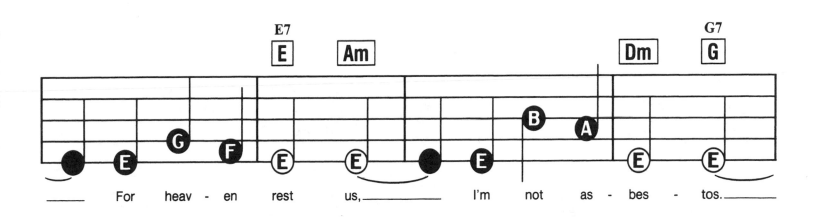

____ For heav - en rest us,____ I'm not as - bes - tos.____

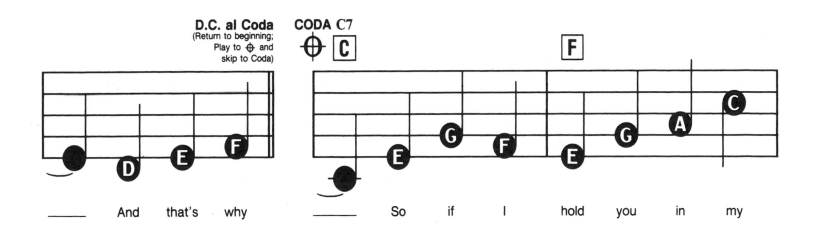

____ And that's why ____ So if I hold you in my

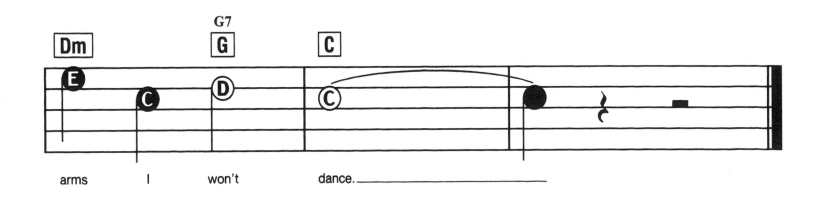

arms I won't dance.____

I Got Rhythm
from AN AMERICAN IN PARIS

Registration 7
Rhythm: Fox Trot or Swing

Music and Lyrics by George Gershwin
and Ira Gershwin

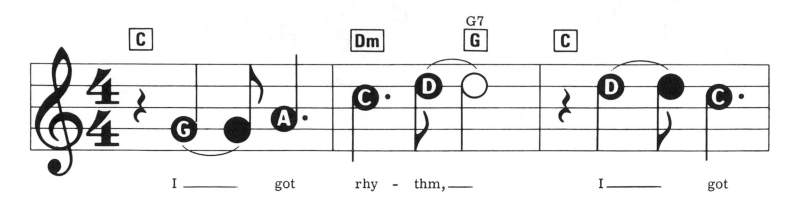

I _____ got rhy - thm, _____ I _____ got

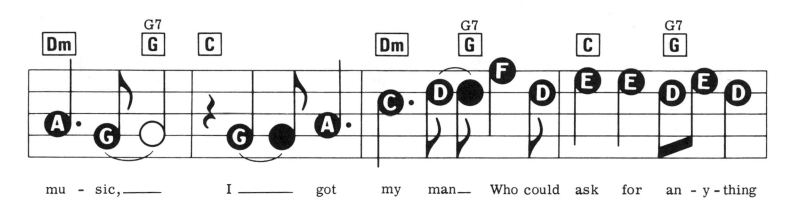

mu - sic, _____ I _____ got my man _____ Who could ask for an - y - thing

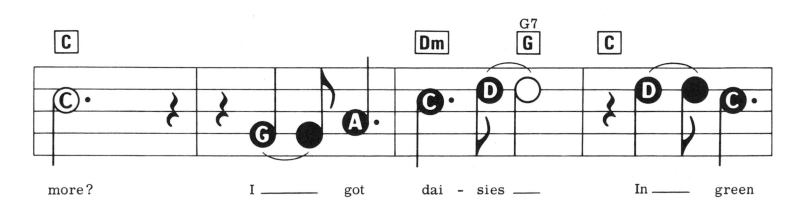

more? I _____ got dai - sies _____ In _____ green

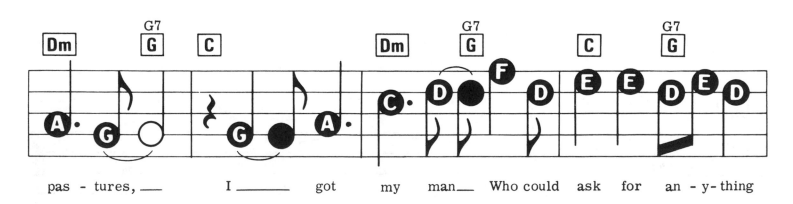

pas - tures, _____ I _____ got my man _____ Who could ask for an - y - thing

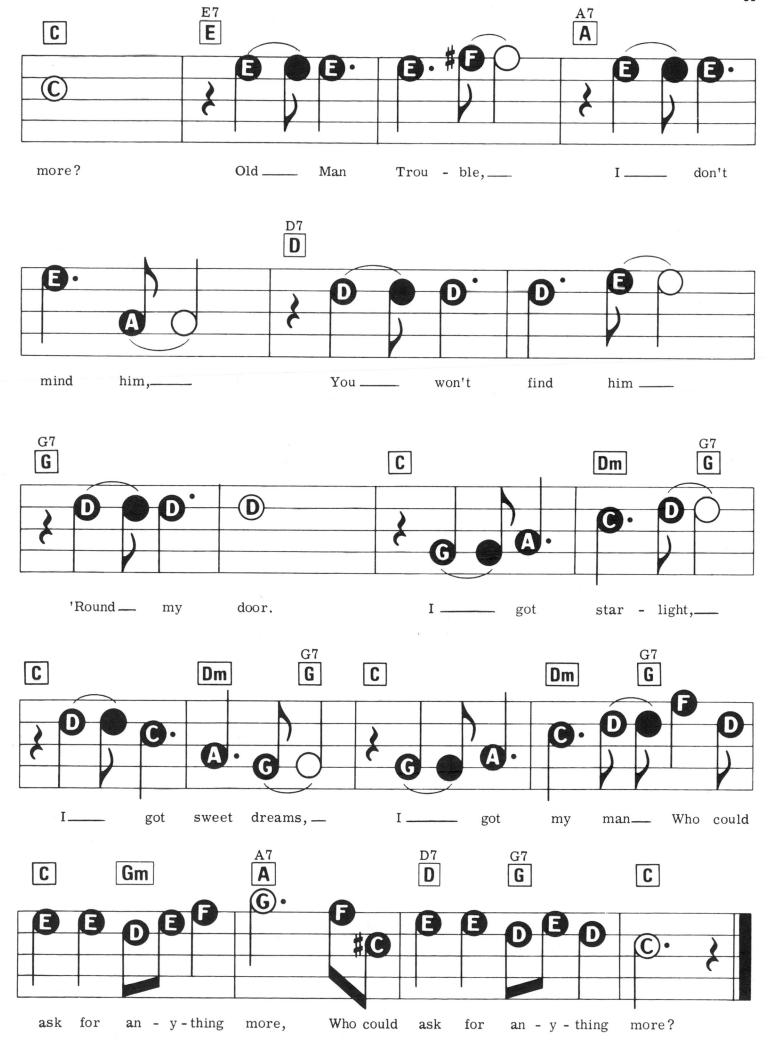

I Only Have Eyes for You

from DAMES

Registration 3
Rhythm: Fox Trot or Swing

Words by Al Dubin
Music by Harry Warren

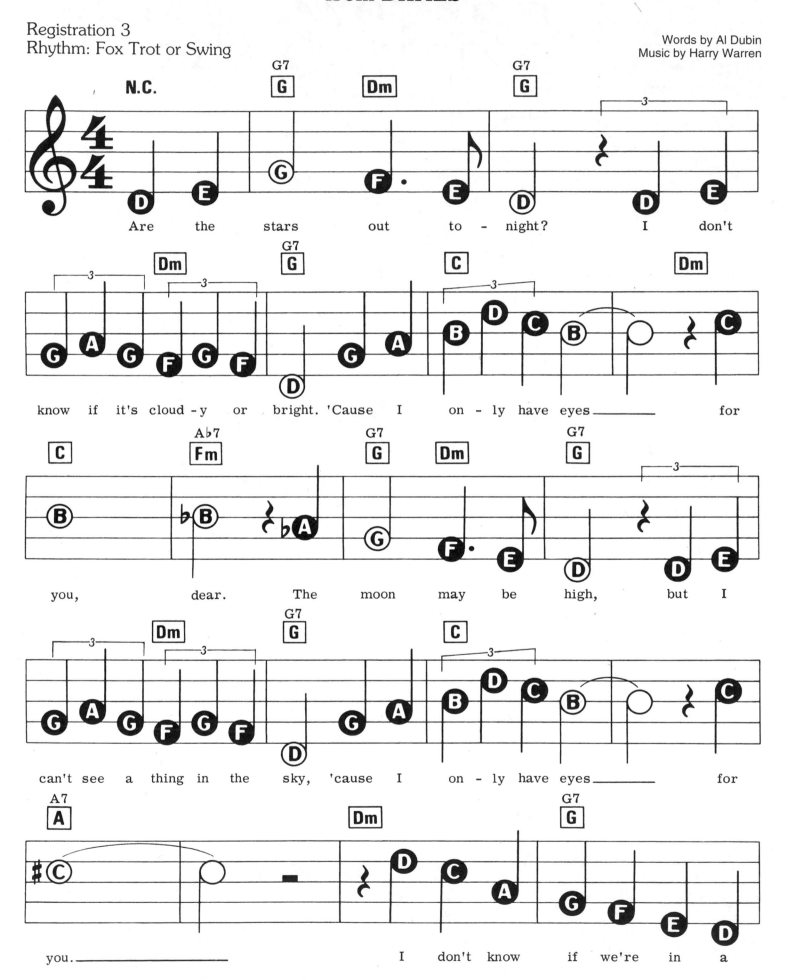

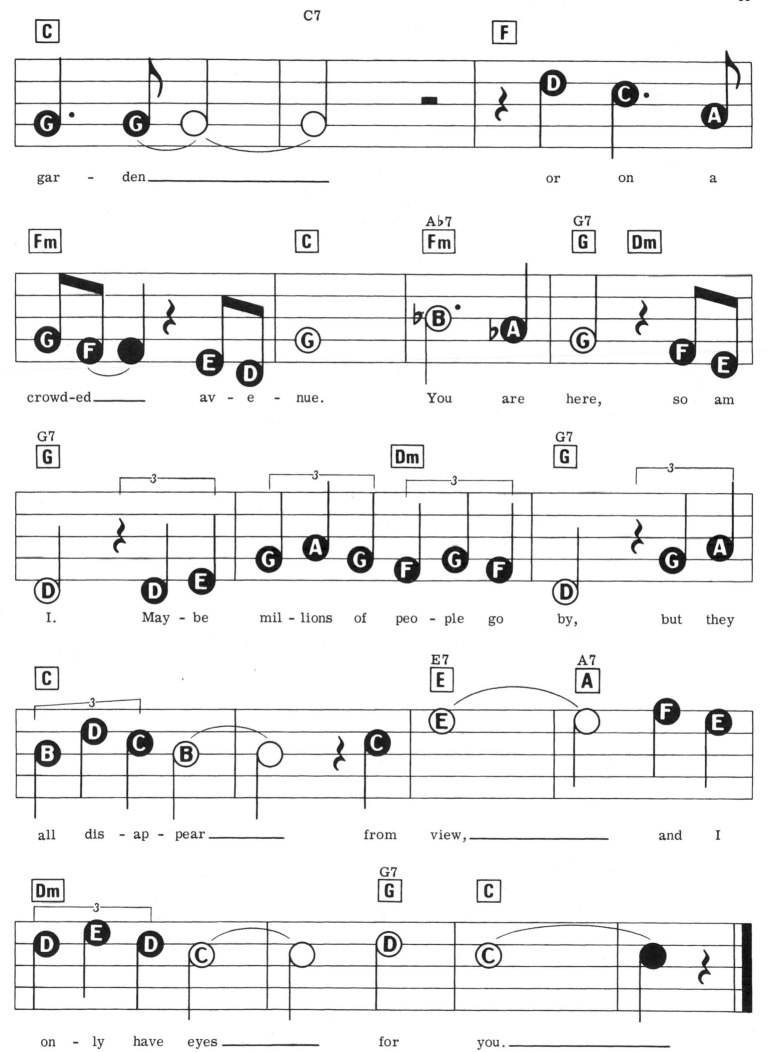

I'll Be Seeing You
from RIGHT THIS WAY

Registration 5
Rhythm: Swing

Written by Irving Kahal
and Sammy Fain

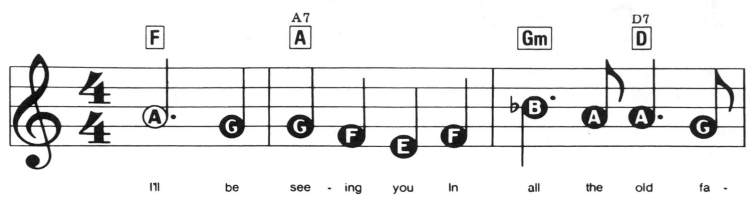

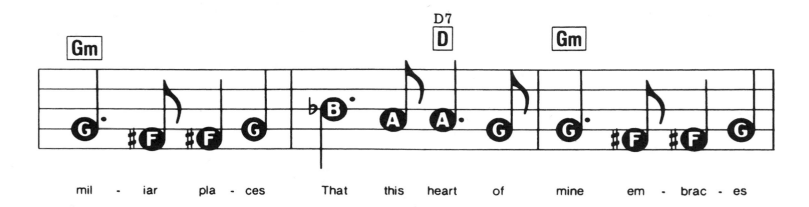

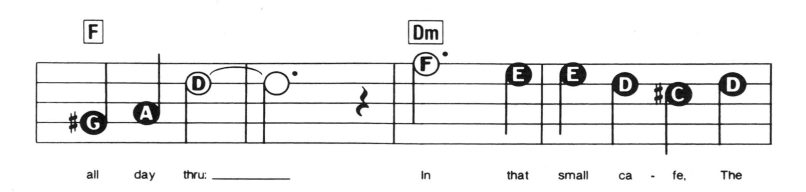

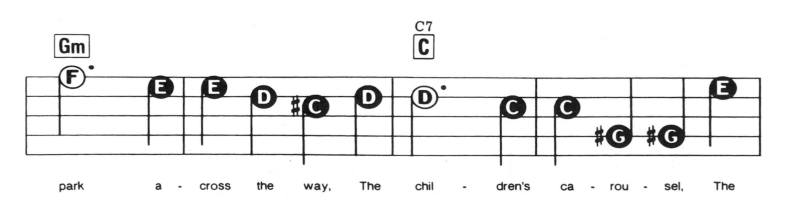

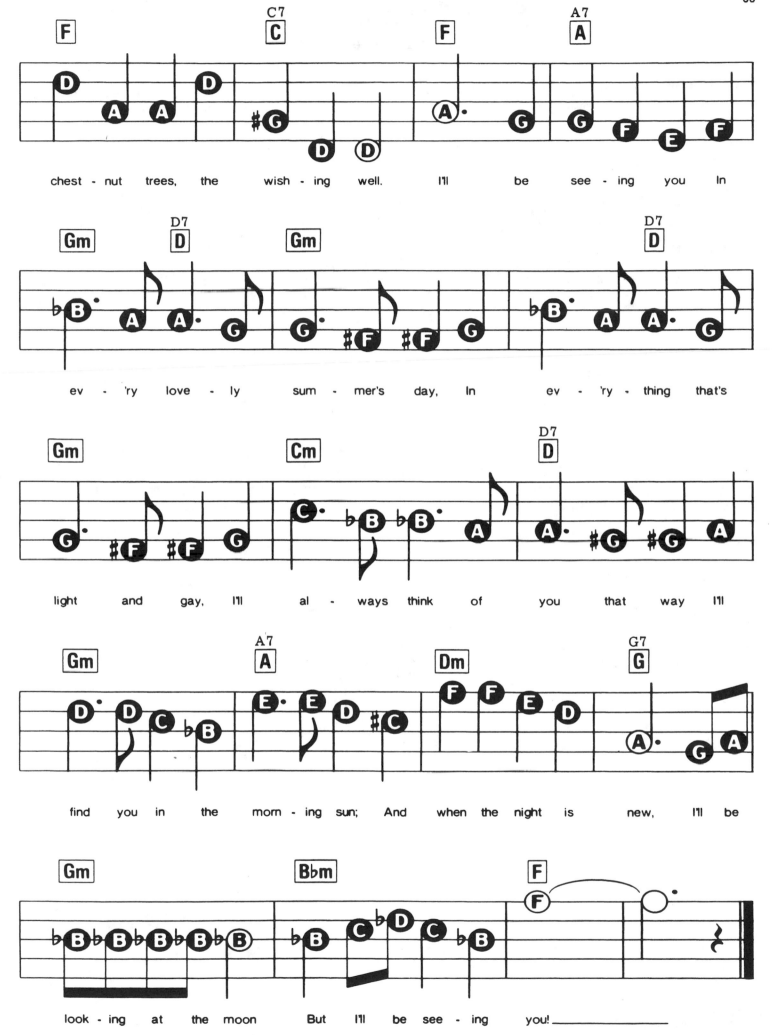

I'm Confessin'
(That I Love You)

Registration 2
Rhythm: Fox Trot or Swing

Words and Music by Al Neiburg,
Doc Daugherty and Ellis Reynolds

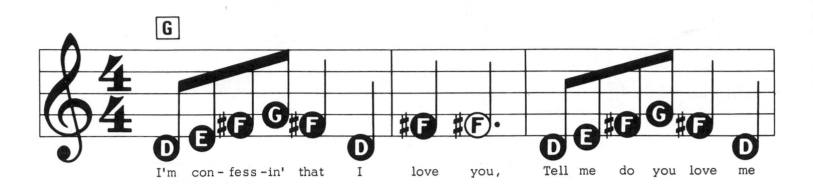

I'm con-fess-in' that I love you, Tell me do you love me

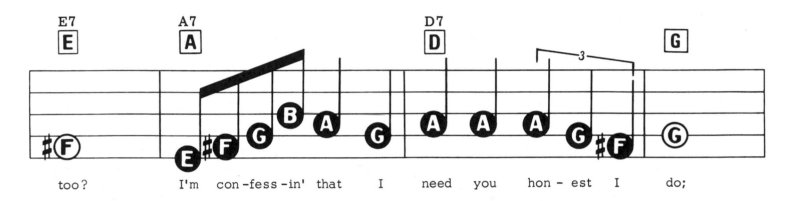

too? I'm con-fess-in' that I need you hon-est I do;

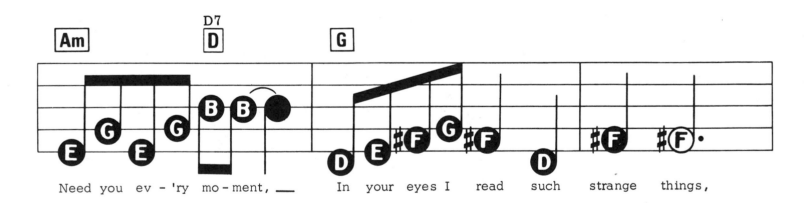

Need you ev-'ry mo-ment, ___ In your eyes I read such strange things,

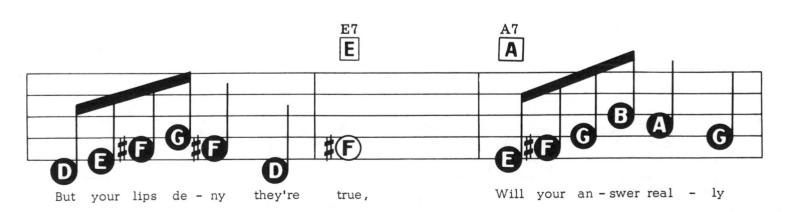

But your lips de-ny they're true, Will your an-swer real-ly

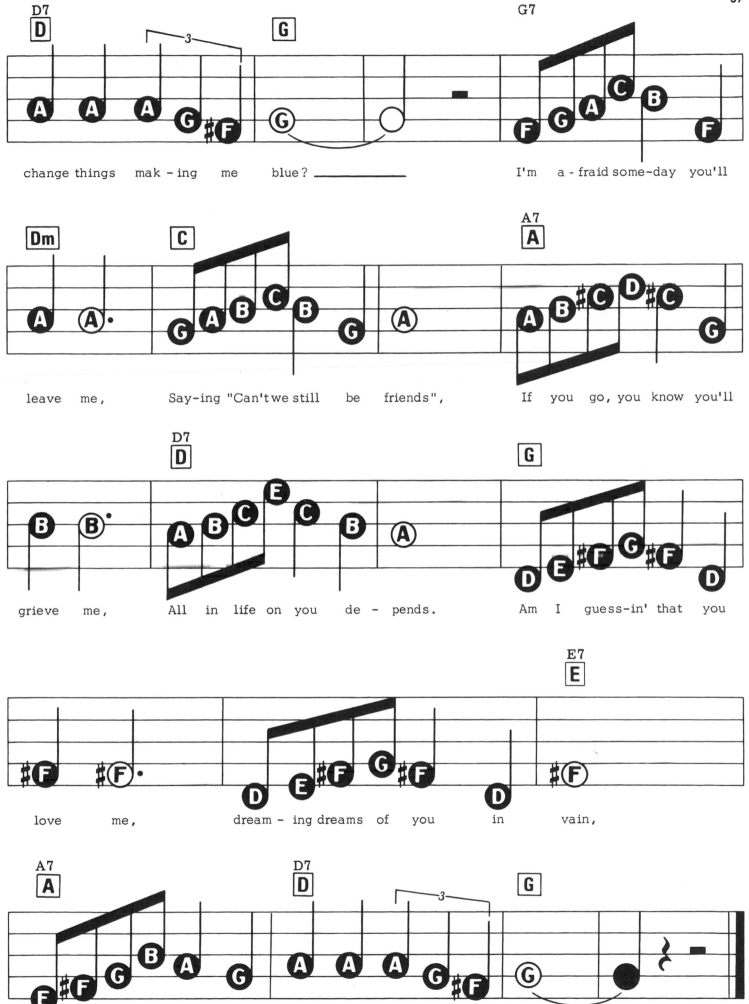

I'm Getting Sentimental Over You

Registration 1
Rhythm: Swing

Words by Ned Washington
Music by George Bassman

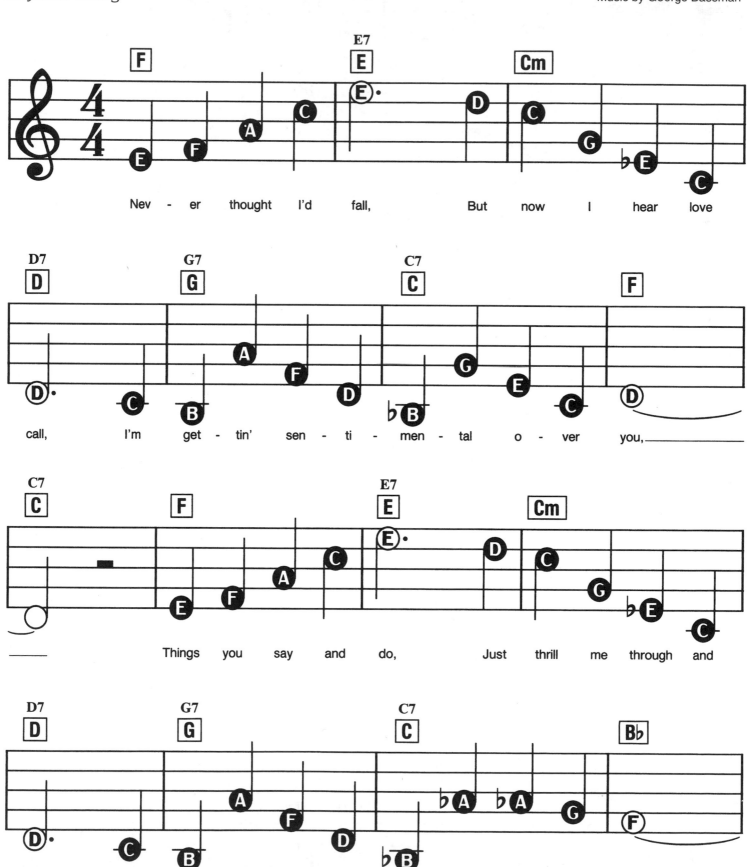

Nev - er thought I'd fall, But now I hear love call, I'm get - tin' sen - ti - men - tal o - ver you,_____ Things you say and do, Just thrill me through and through, I'm get - tin' sen - ti - men - tal o - ver you,_____

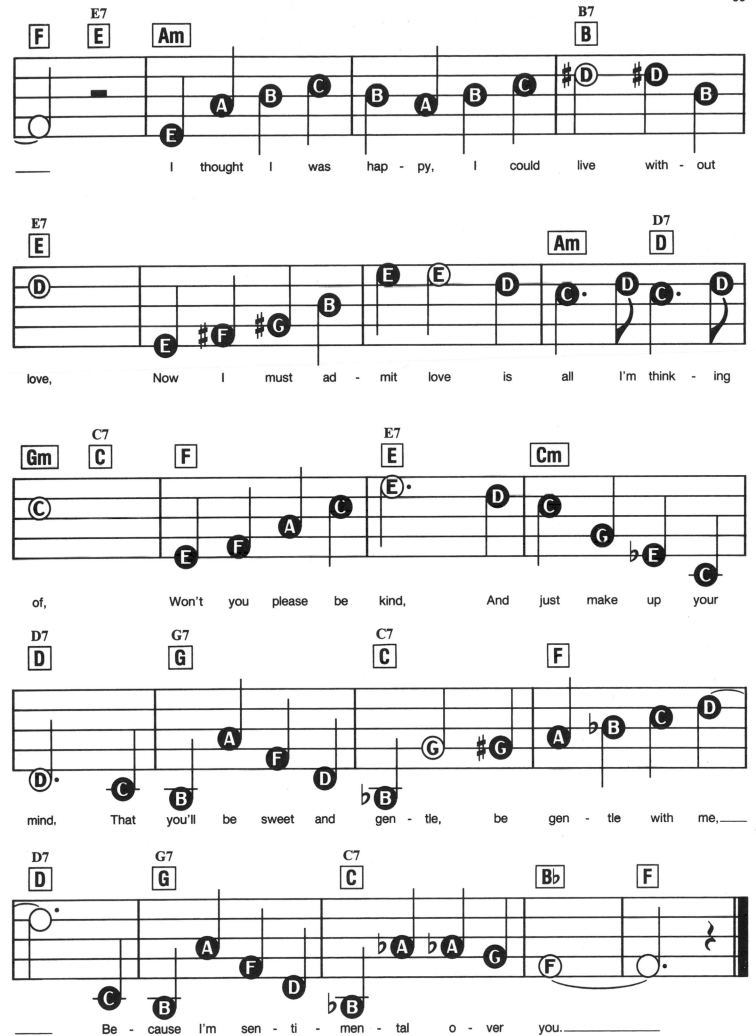

I'm in the Mood for Love
from EVERY NIGHT AT EIGHT

Registration 9
Rhythm: Fox Trot or Pops

Words and Music by Jimmy McHugh
and Dorothy Fields

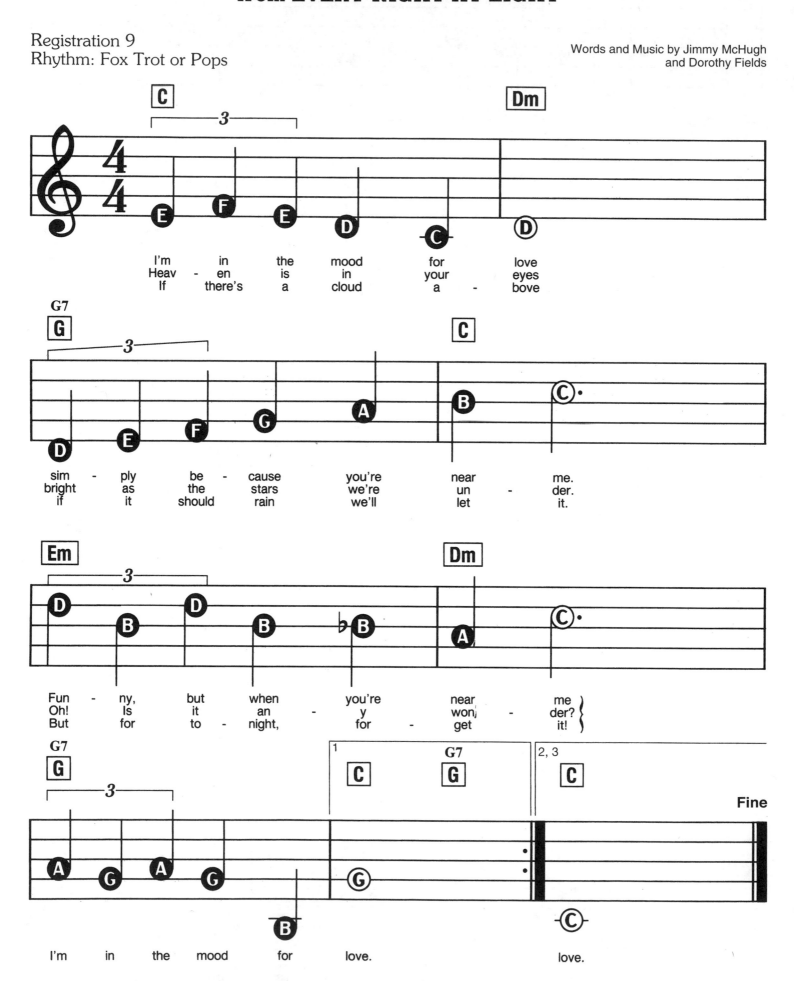

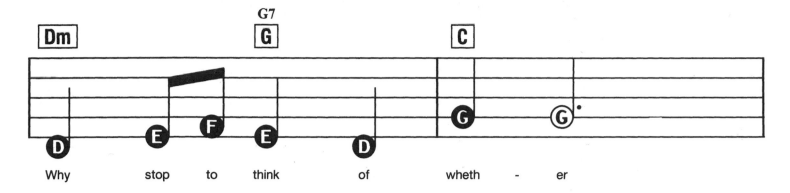

Why stop to think of wheth - er

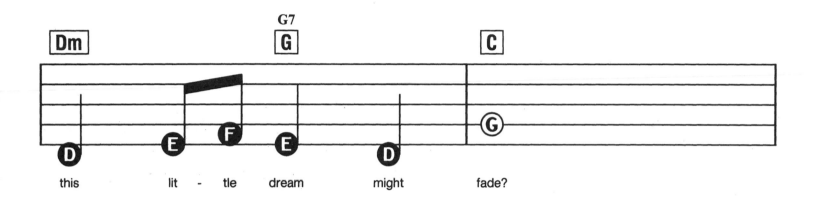

this lit - tle dream might fade?

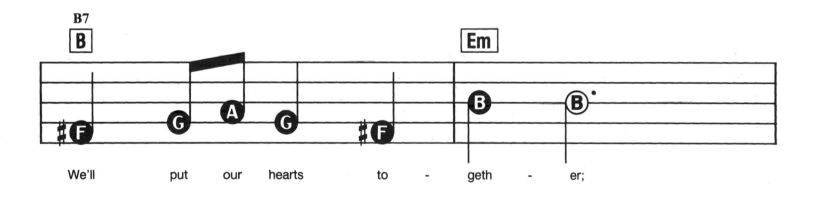

We'll put our hearts to - geth - er;

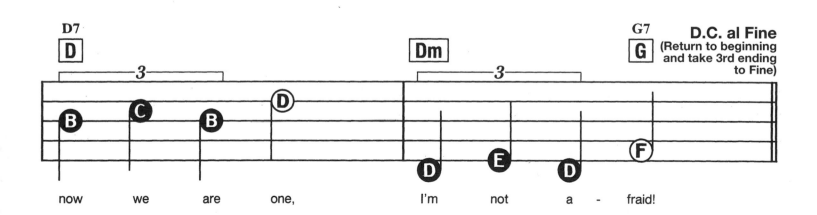

now we are one, I'm not a - fraid!

I've Got My Love to Keep Me Warm
from the 20th Century Fox Motion Picture ON THE AVENUE

Registration 4
Rhythm: Fox Trot or Swing

Words and Music by
Irving Berlin

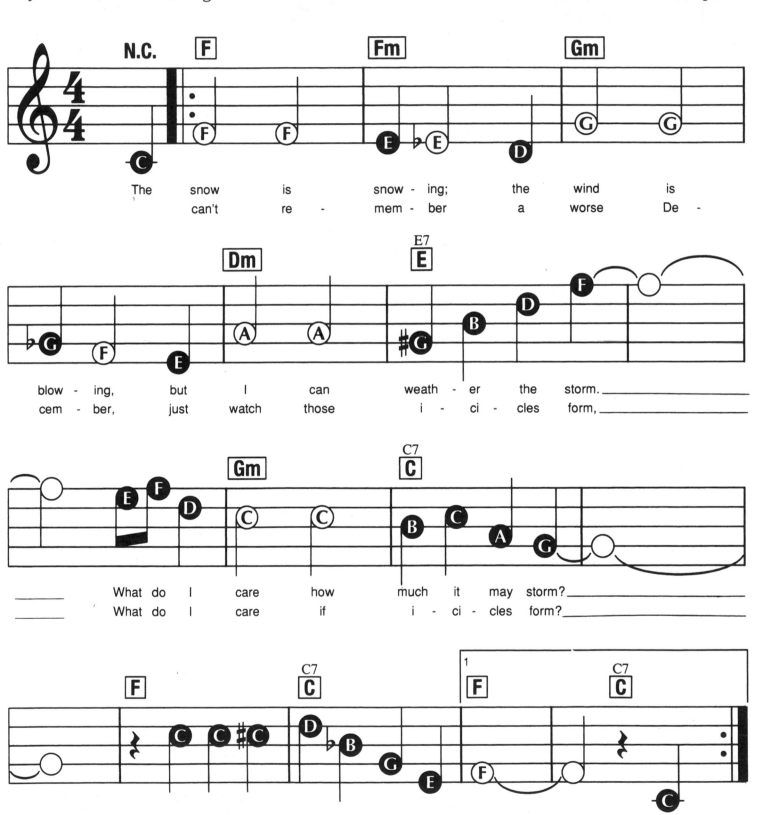

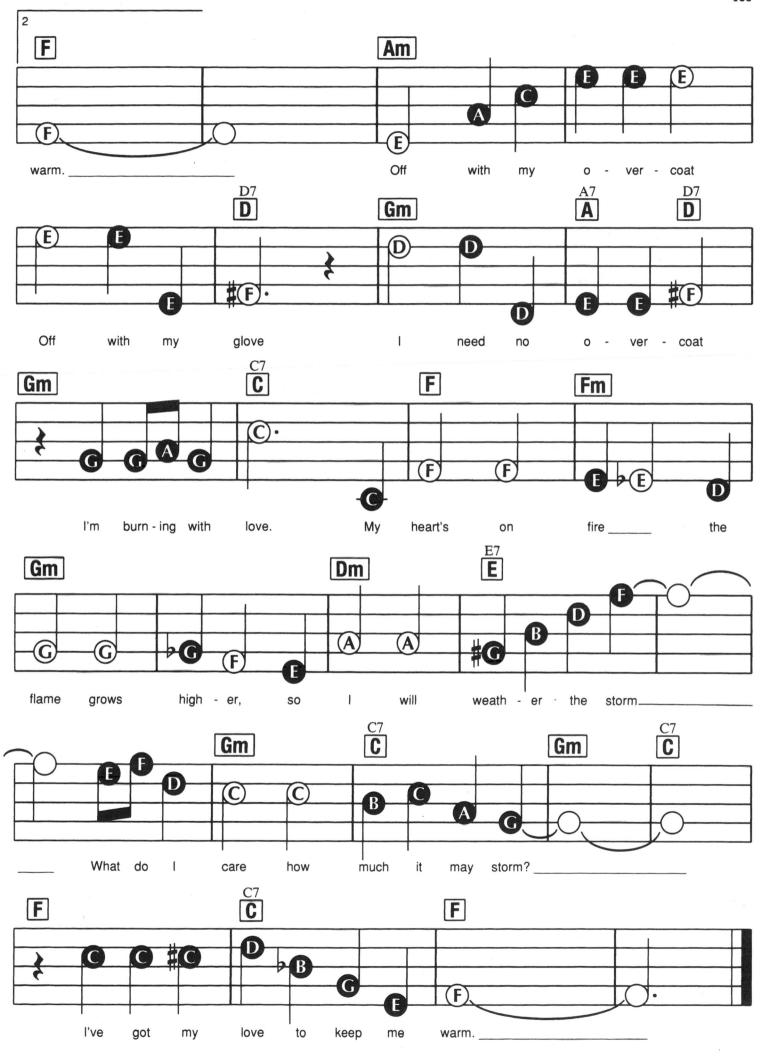

I've Got the World on a String

Registration 1
Rhythm: Swing

Lyric by Ted Koehler
Music by Harold Arlen

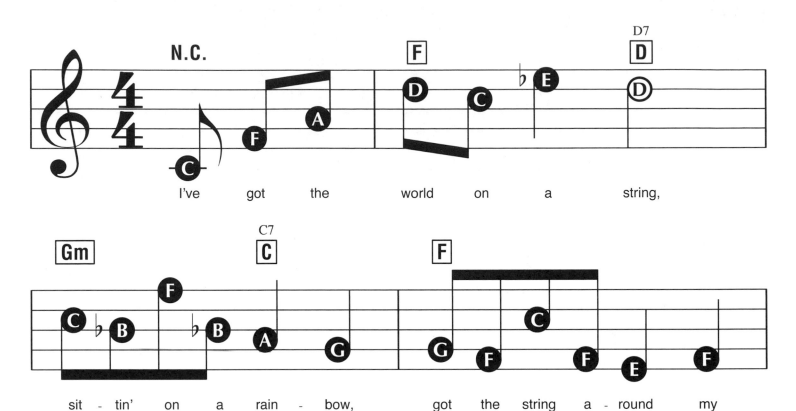

I've got the world on a string, sit-tin' on a rain-bow, got the string a-round my

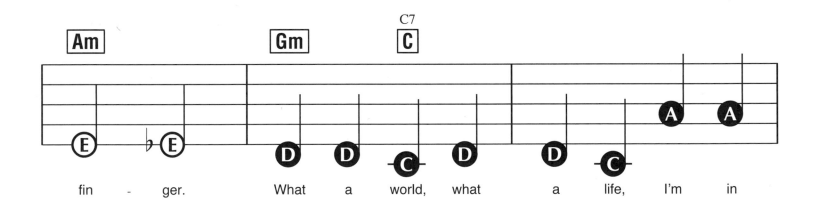

fin - ger. What a world, what a life, I'm in

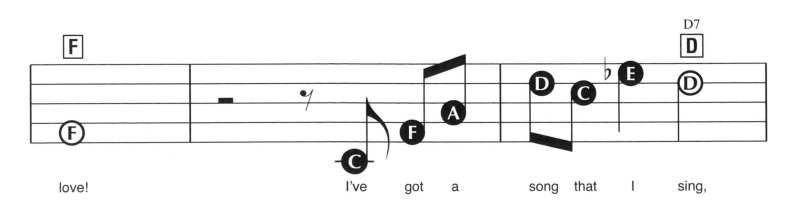

love! I've got a song that I sing,

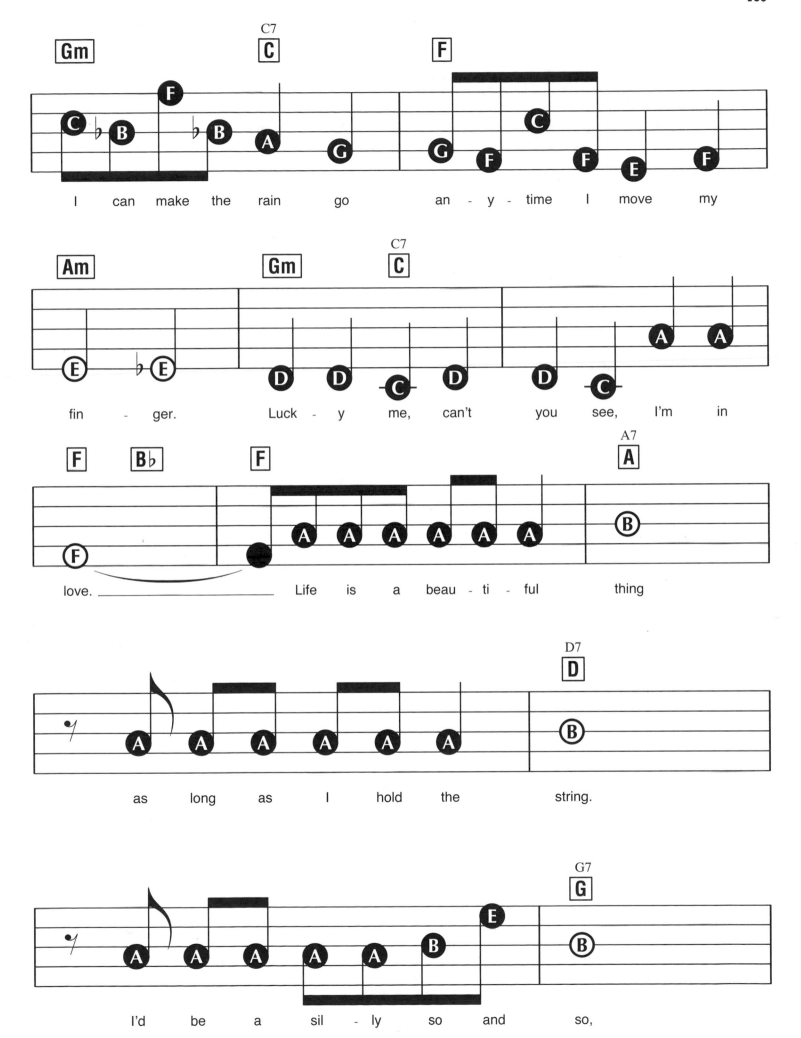

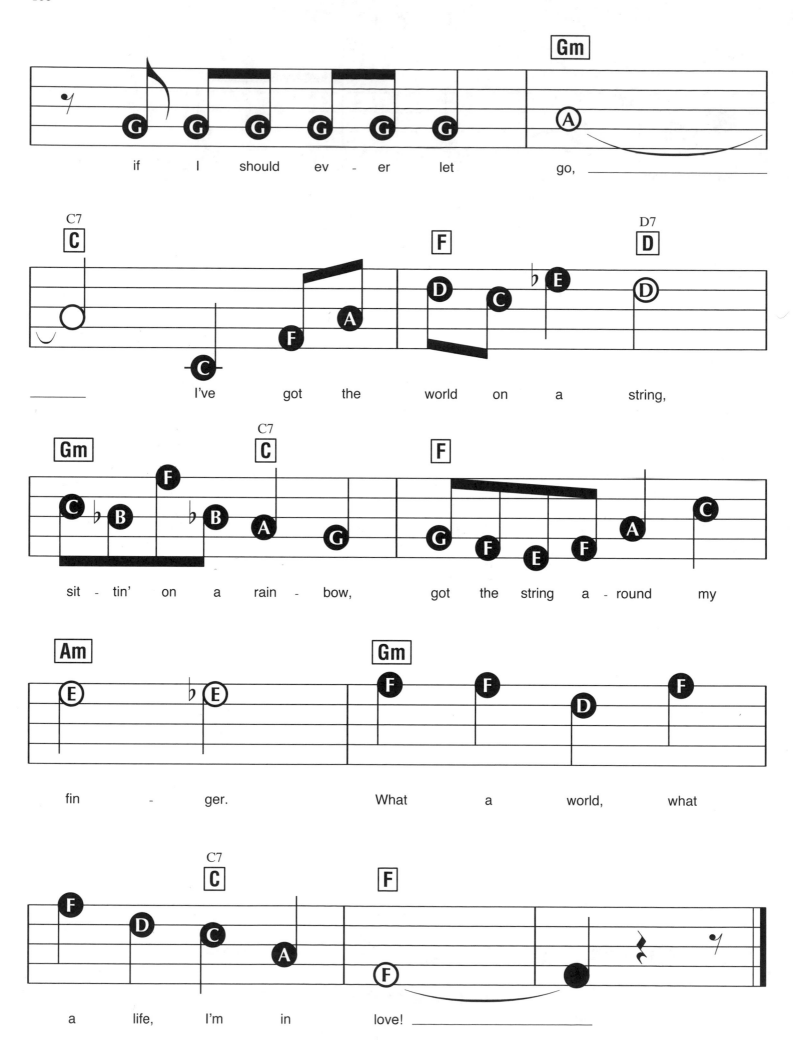

In the Mood

Registration 8
Rhythm: Swing

By Joe Garland

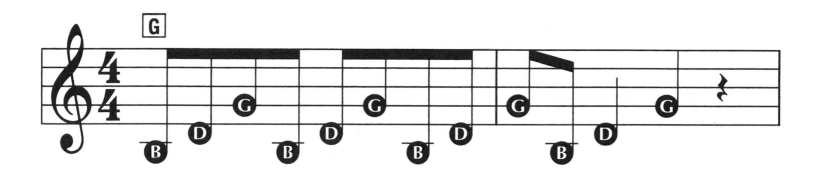

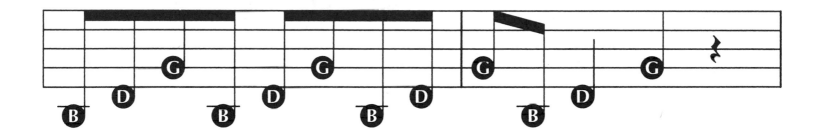

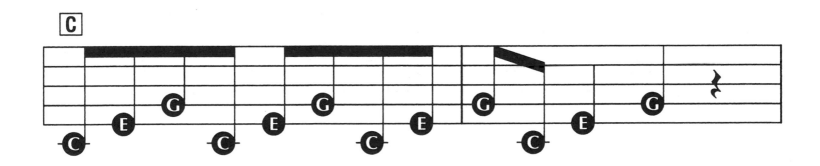

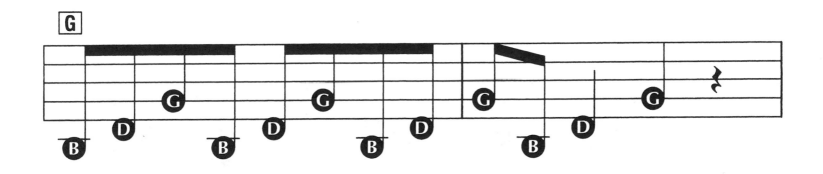

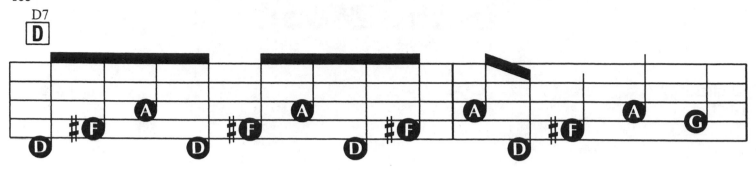

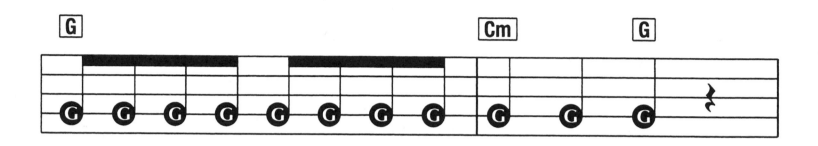

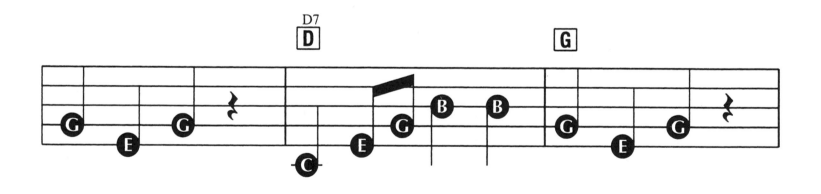

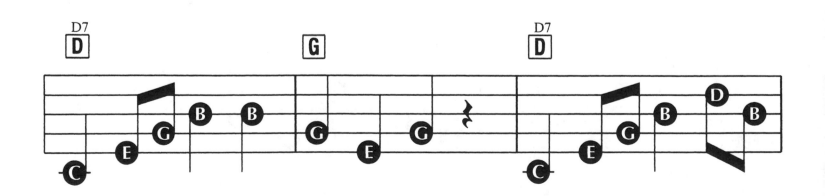

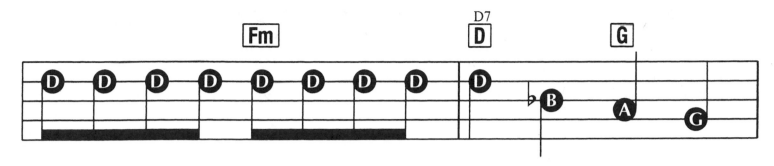

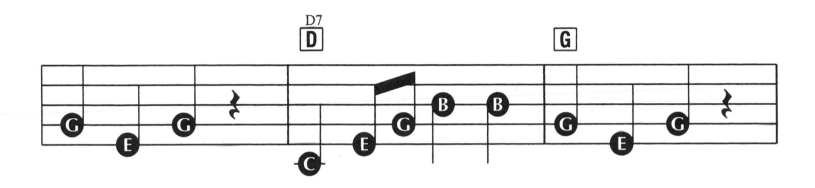

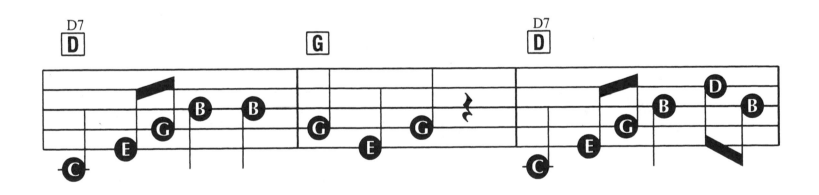

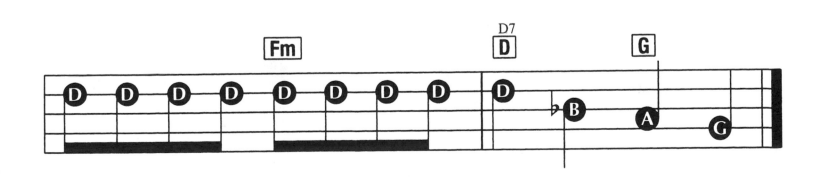

I've Got You Under My Skin
from BORN TO DANCE

Registration 5
Rhythm: Ballad or Fox Trot

Words and Music by
Cole Porter

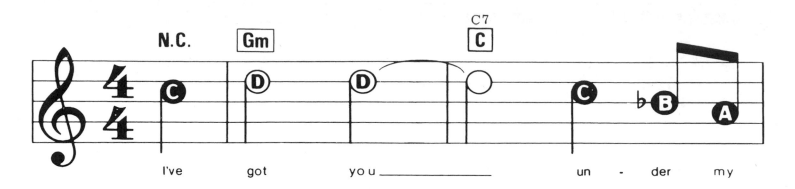

I've got you _____ un - der my

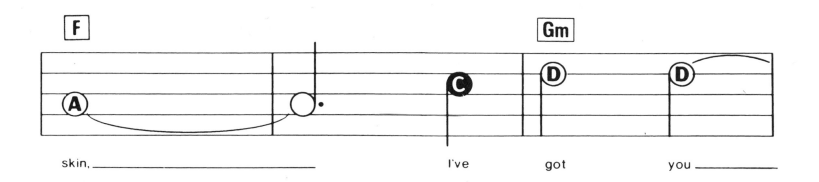

skin, _____ I've got you _____

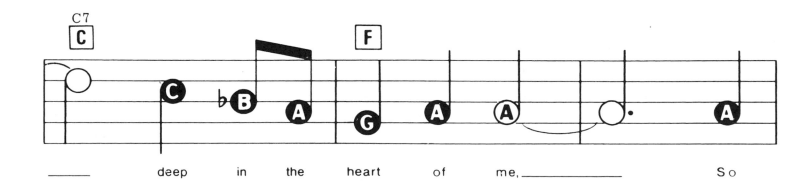

_____ deep in the heart of me, _____ So

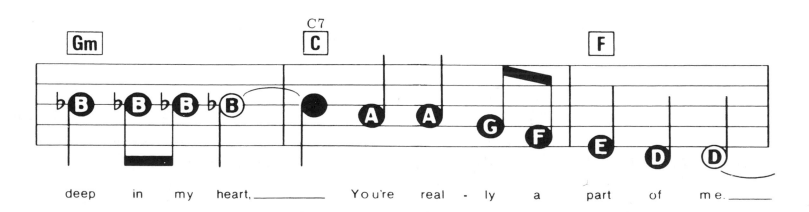

deep in my heart, _____ You're real - ly a part of me. _____

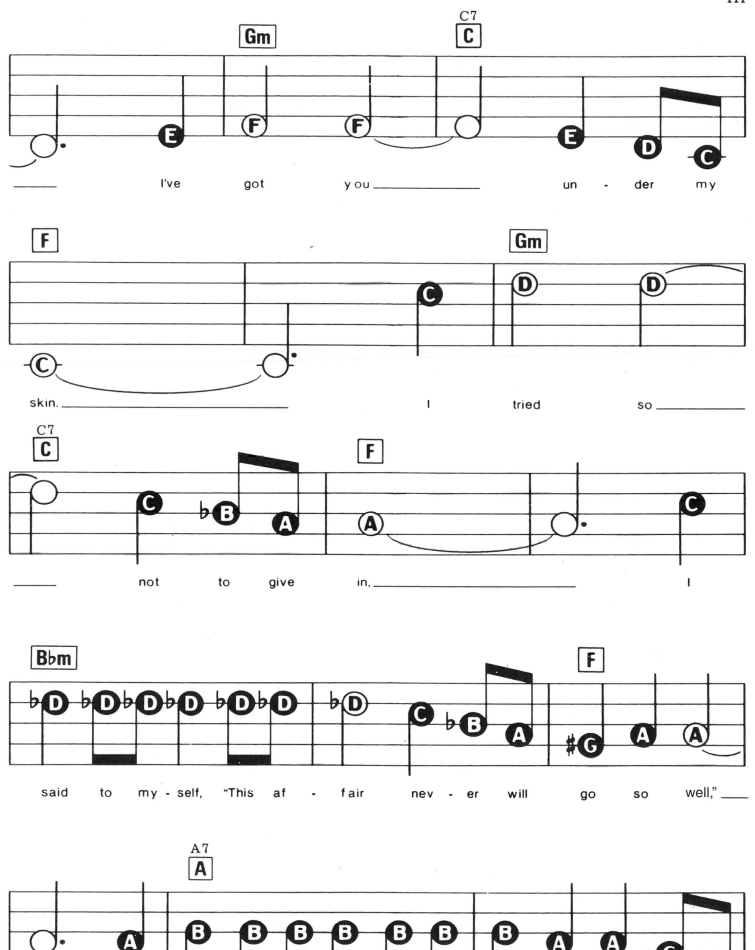

know   so   well _____   I've   got   you _____

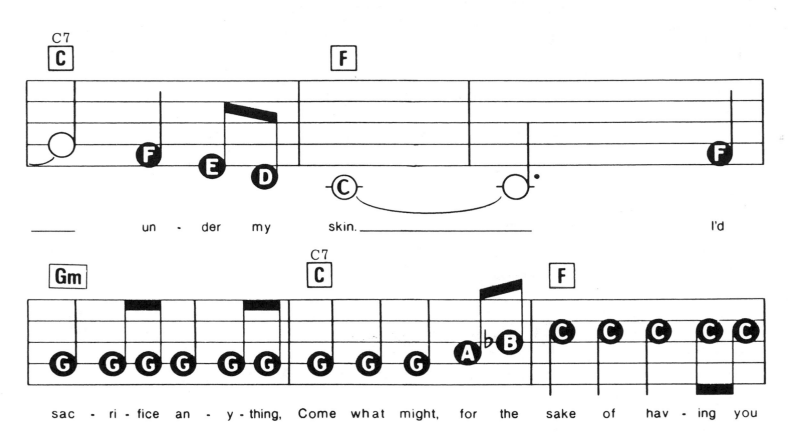

____   un - der   my   skin. _____   I'd

sac - ri - fice an - y - thing, Come what might, for the sake of hav - ing you

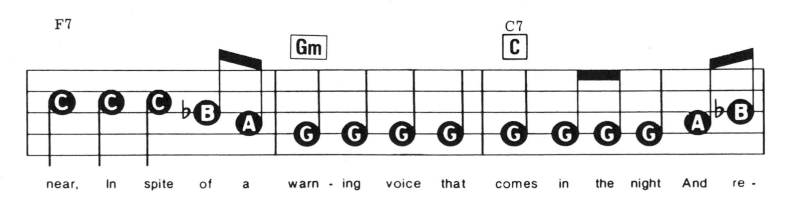

near, In spite of a warn - ing voice that comes in the night And re -

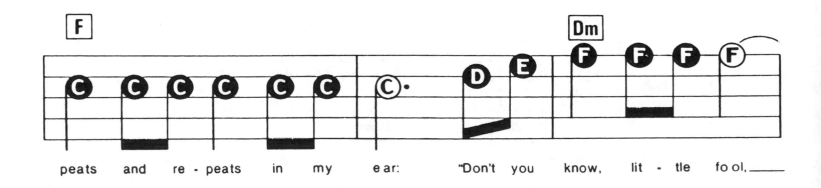

peats and re - peats in my ear: "Don't you know, lit - tle fool, ____

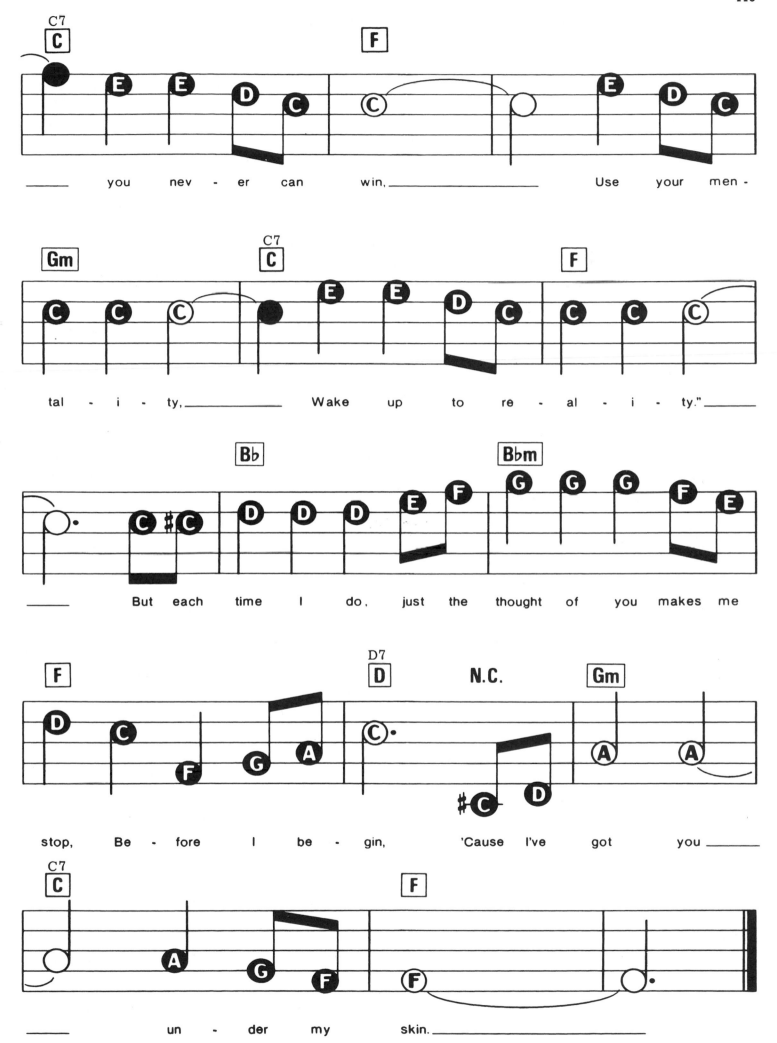

In a Sentimental Mood

Registration 1
Rhythm: Swing

Words and Music by Duke Ellington,
Irving Mills and Manny Kurtz

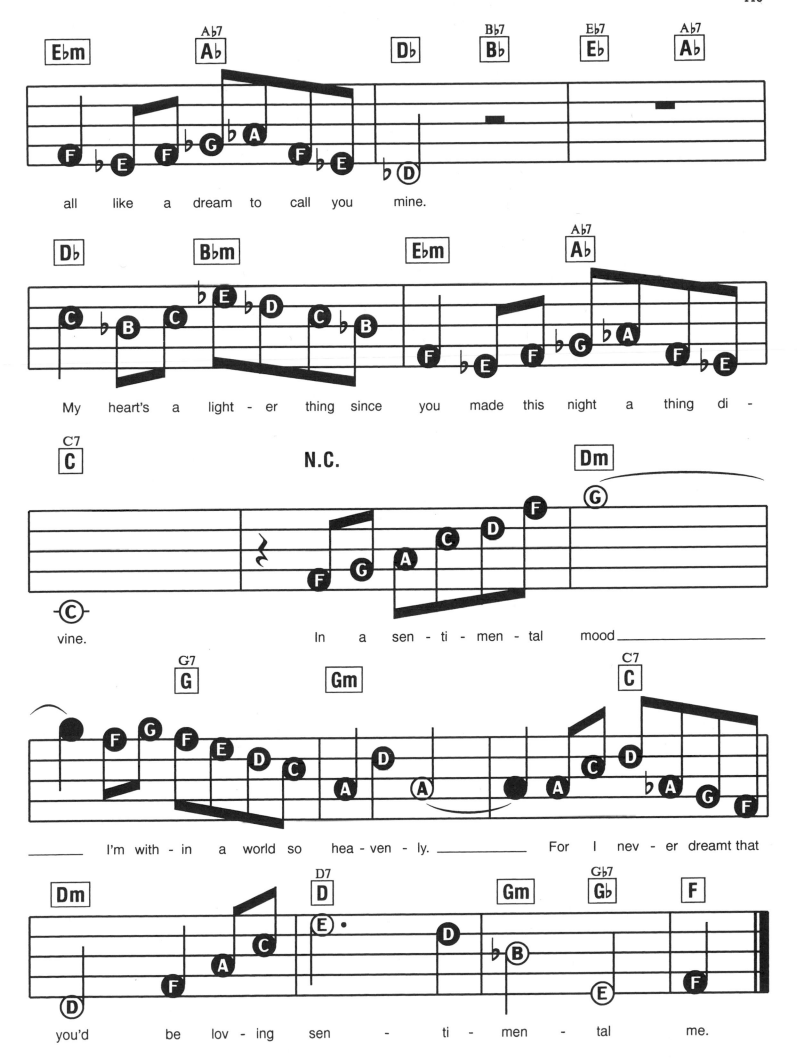

In the Still of the Night
from ROSALIE

Registration 2
Rhythm: Latin

Words and Music by
Cole Porter

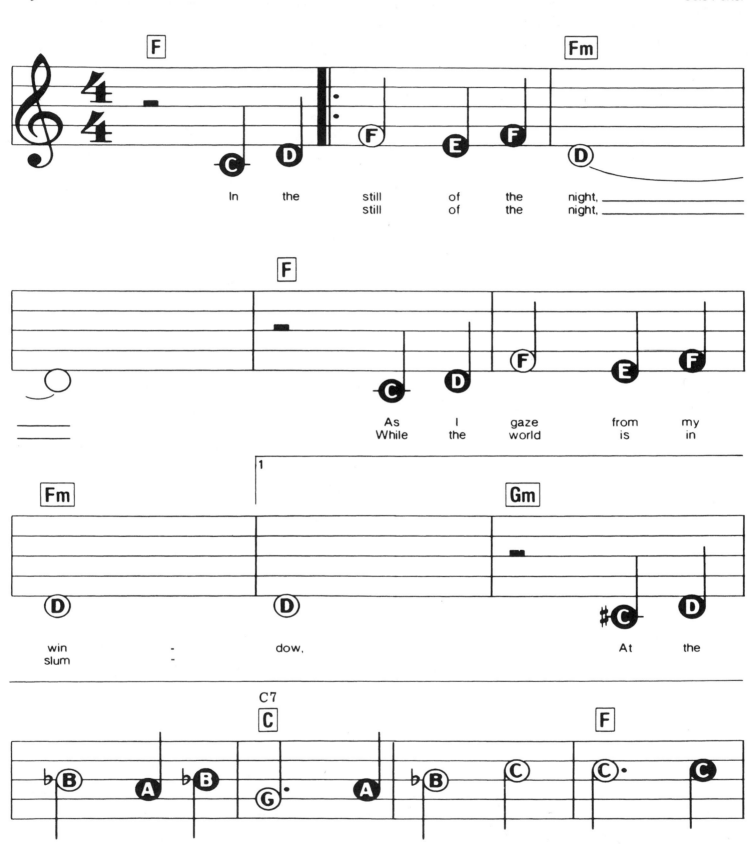

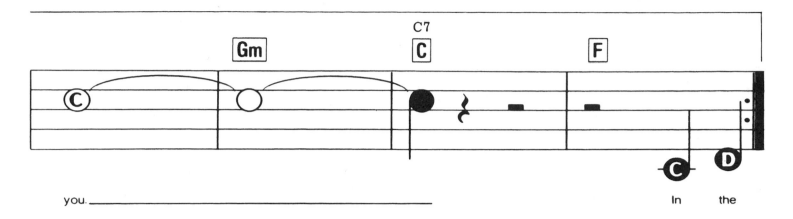

you._____ In the

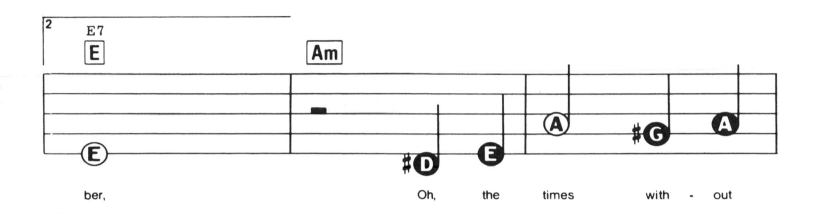

ber, Oh, the times with - out

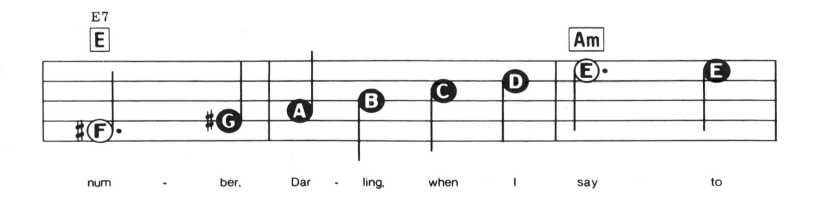

num - ber, Dar - ling, when I say to

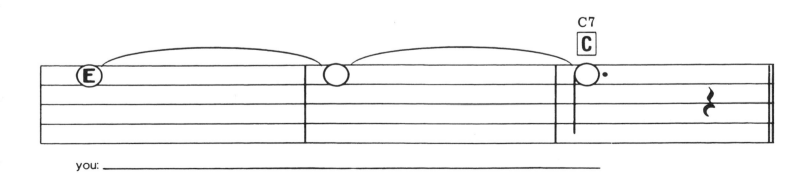

you:_____

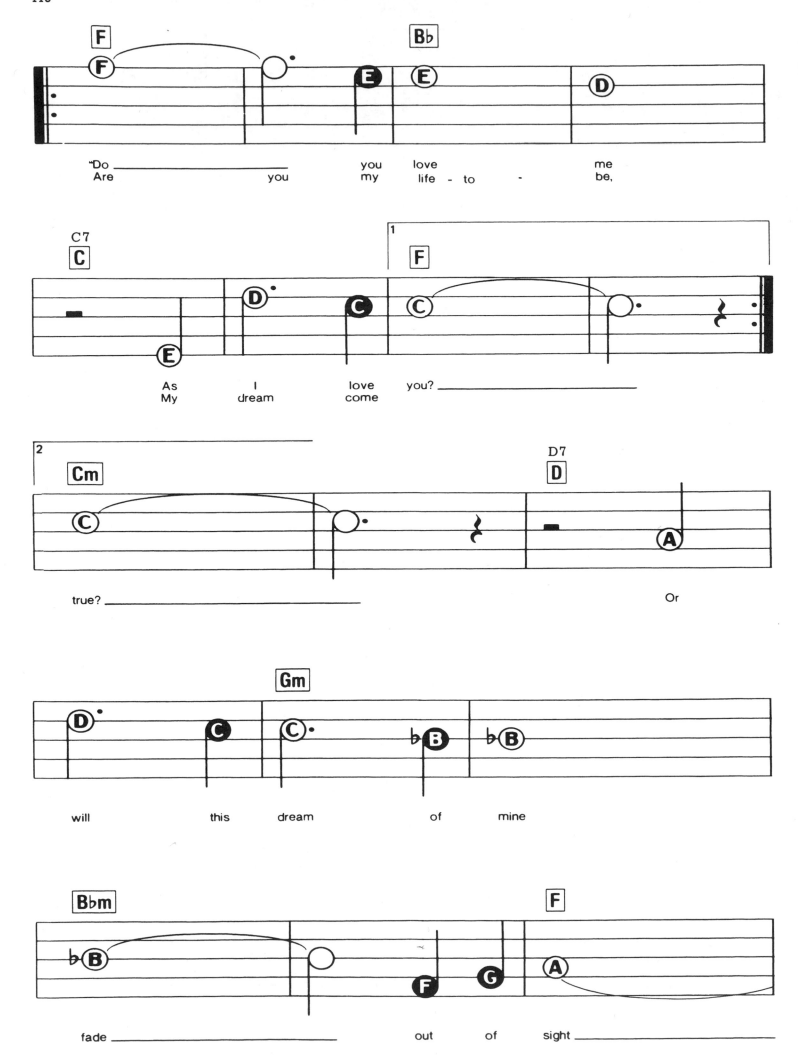

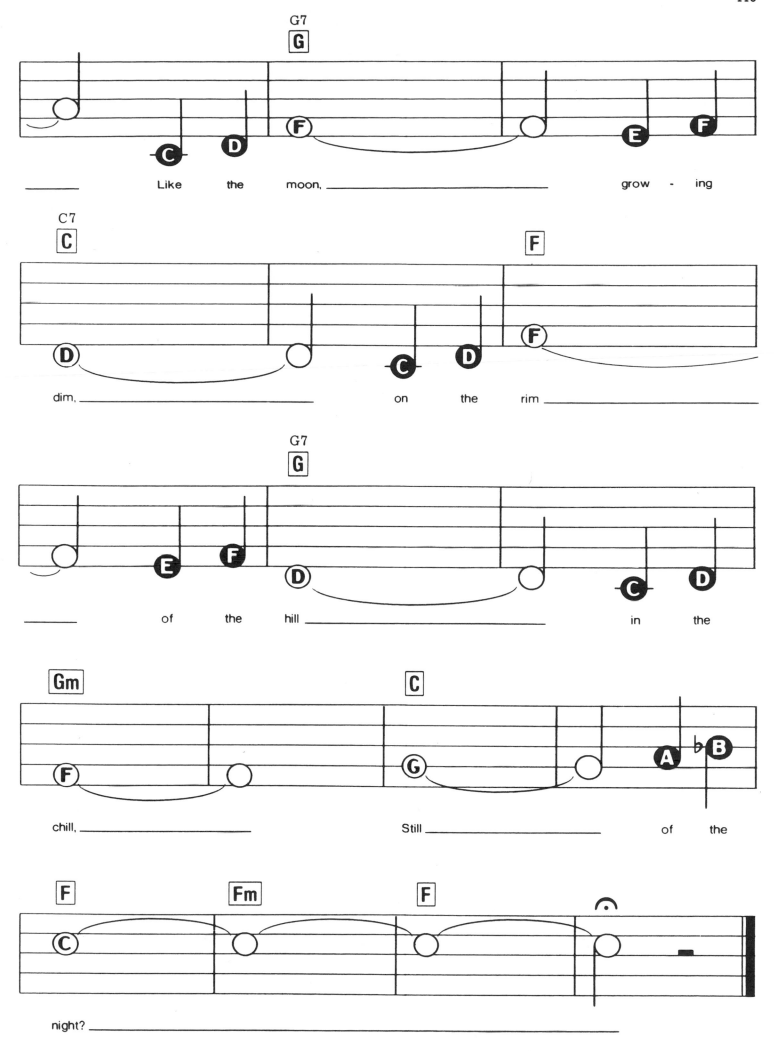

Isn't It Romantic?

from the Paramount Picture LOVE ME TONIGHT

Registration 2
Rhythm: Swing or Ballad

Words by Lorenz Hart
Music by Richard Rodgers

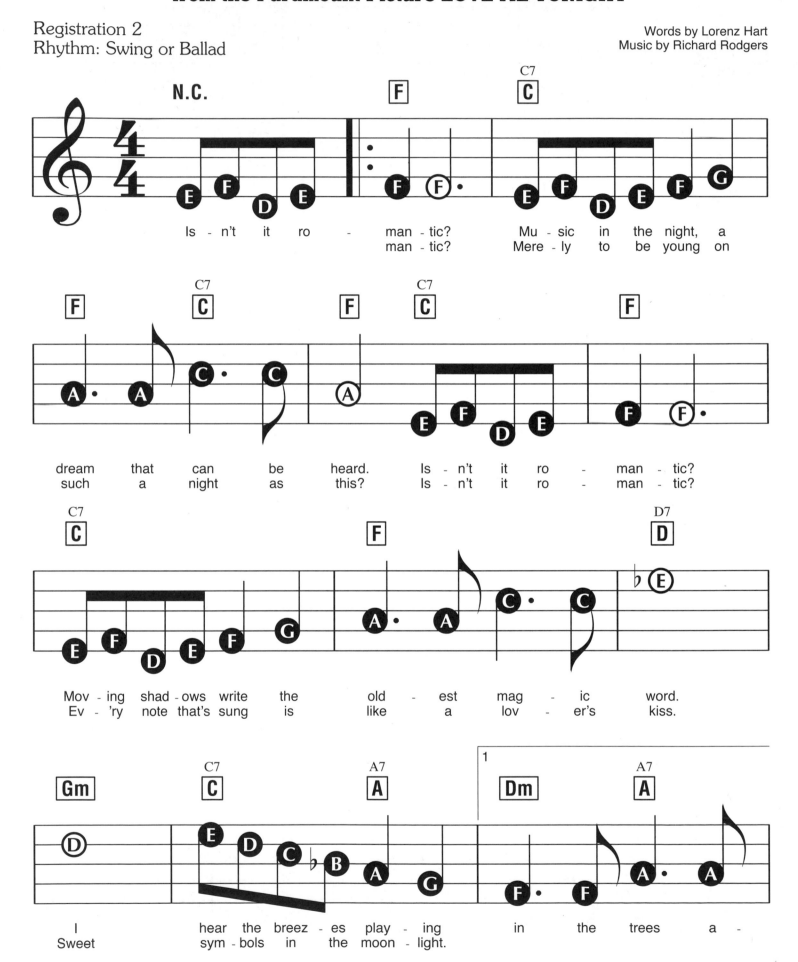

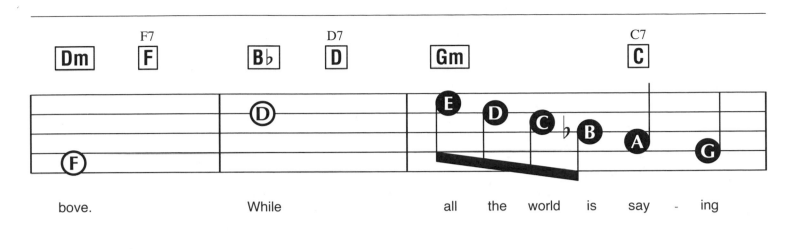

bove.   While   all   the   world   is   say - ing

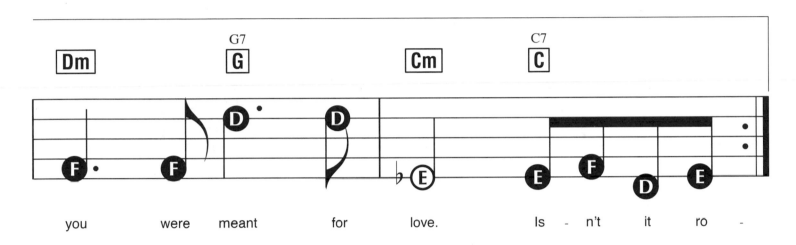

you   were   meant   for   love.   Is - n't   it   ro -

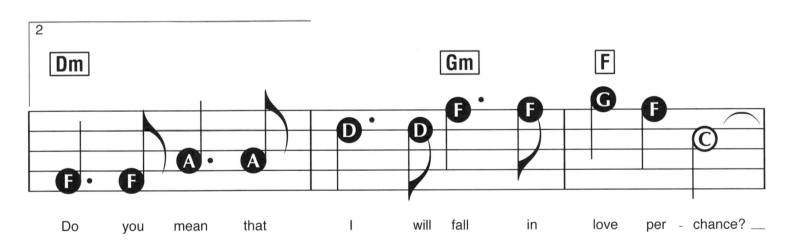

Do   you   mean   that   I   will   fall   in   love   per - chance? __

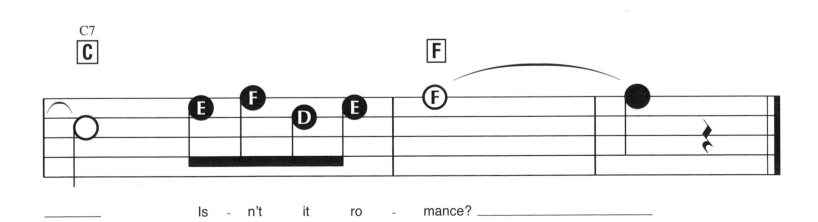

_____   Is - n't   it   ro - mance? _____

It Don't Mean a Thing
(If It Ain't Got That Swing)

Registration 7
Rhythm: Swing

Words and Music by Duke Ellington
and Irving Mills

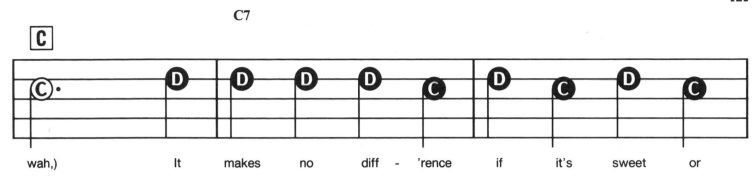

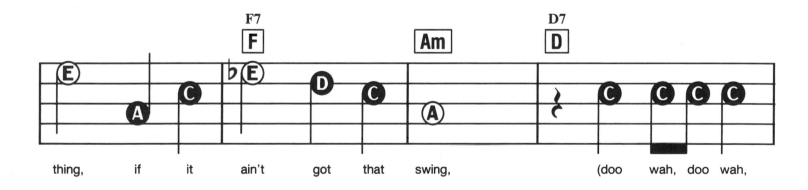

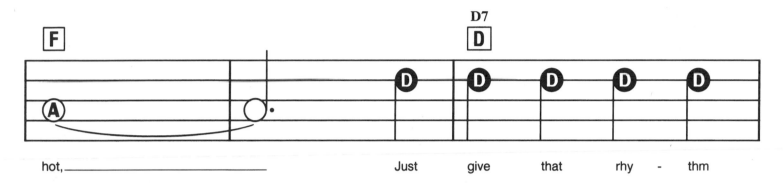

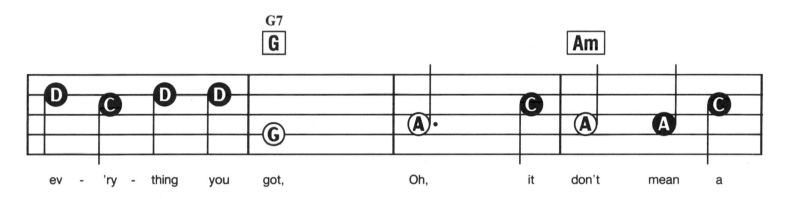

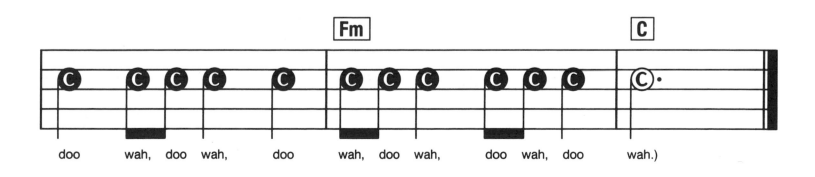

It's De-Lovely
from RED, HOT AND BLUE!

Registration 2
Rhythm: Swing

Words and Music by
Cole Porter

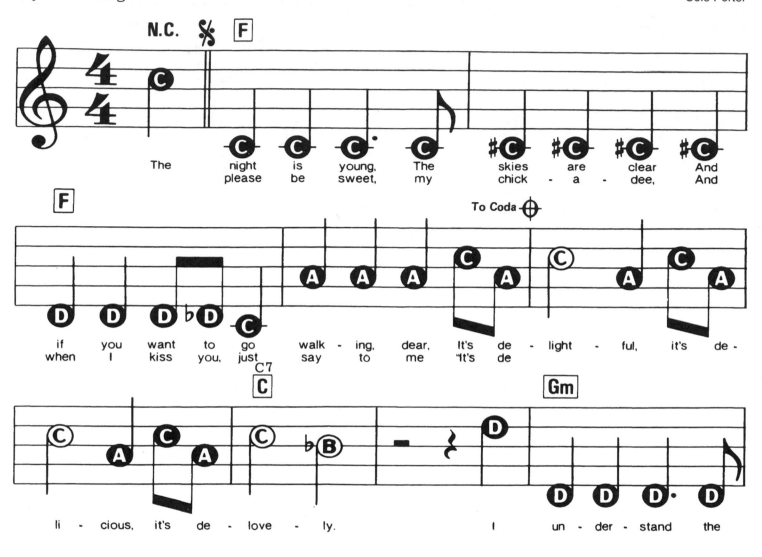

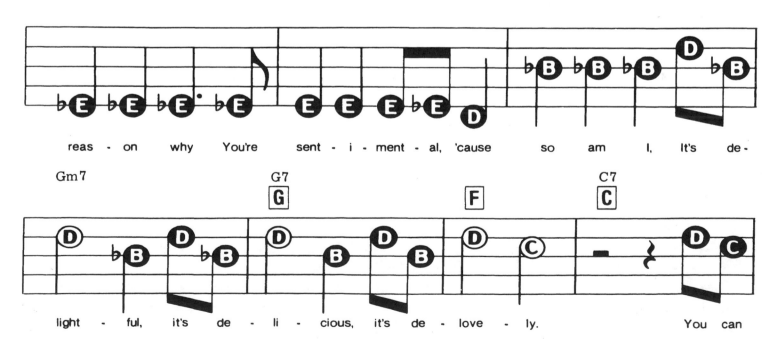

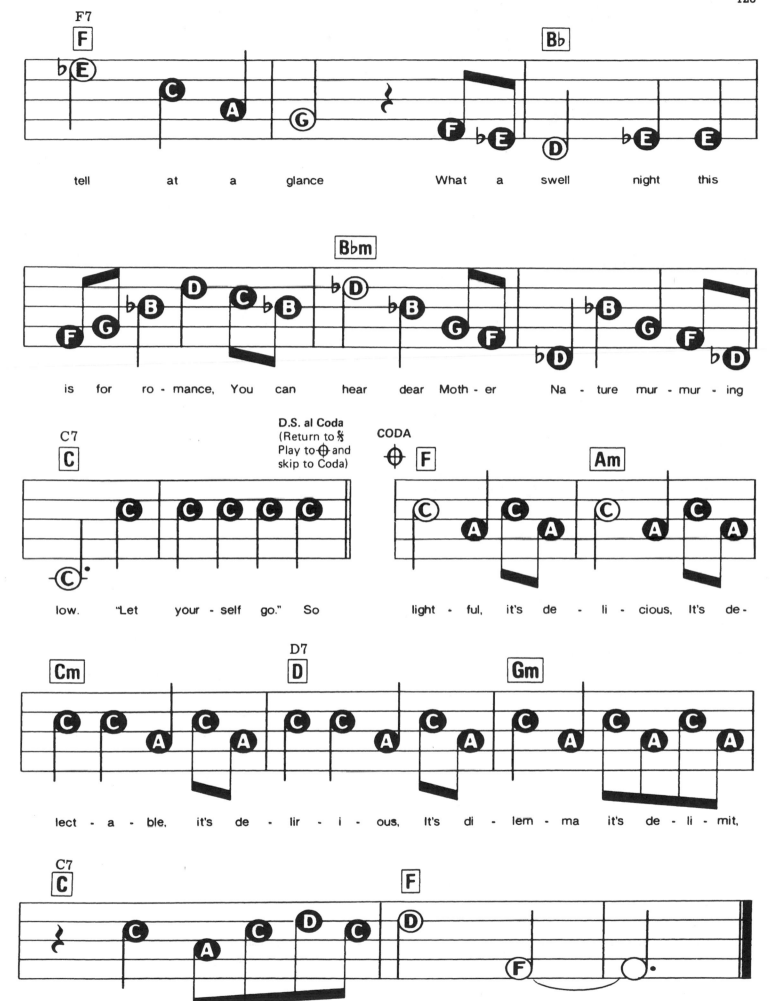

tell at a glance What a swell night this

is for ro - mance, You can hear dear Moth - er Na - ture mur - mur - ing

low. "Let your - self go." So

lift - ful, it's de - li - cious, It's de -

lect - a - ble, it's de - lir - i - ous, It's di - lem - ma it's de - limit,

It's de - luxe,* it's de - love - ly." _____

*Pronounced "delukes"

It's Easy to Remember
from the Paramount Picture MISSISSIPPI

Registration 1
Rhythm: Fox Trot or Ballad

Words by Lorenz Hart
Music by Richard Rodgers

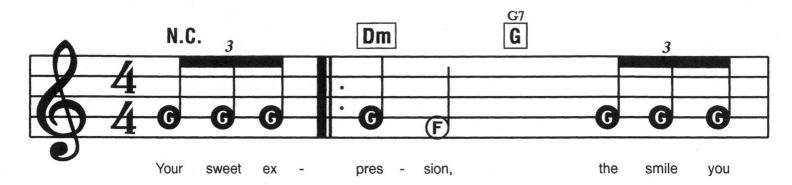

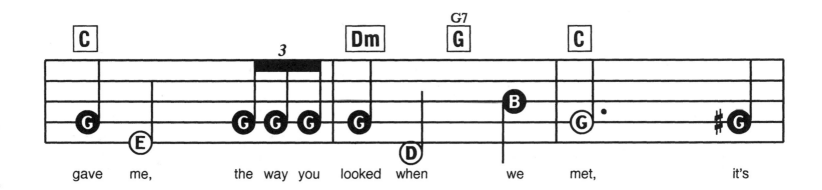

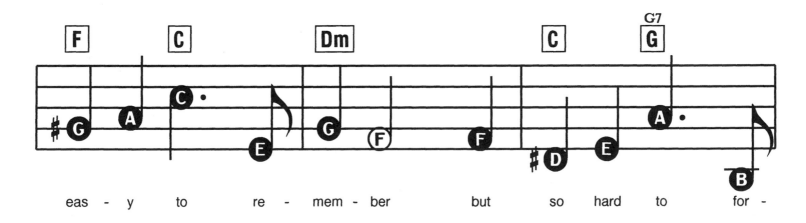

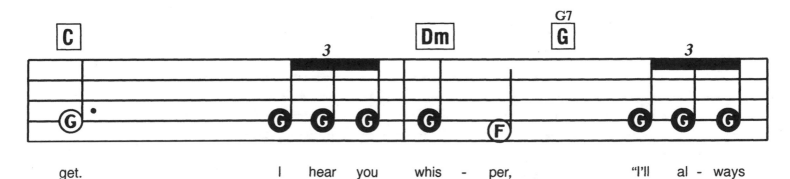

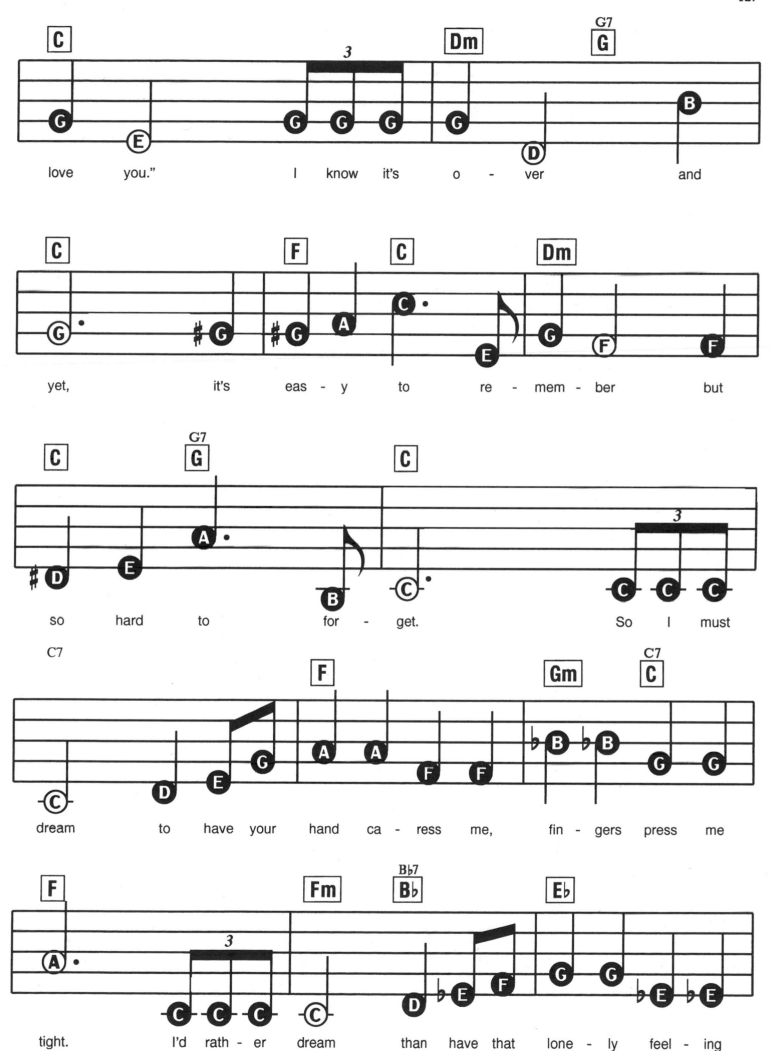

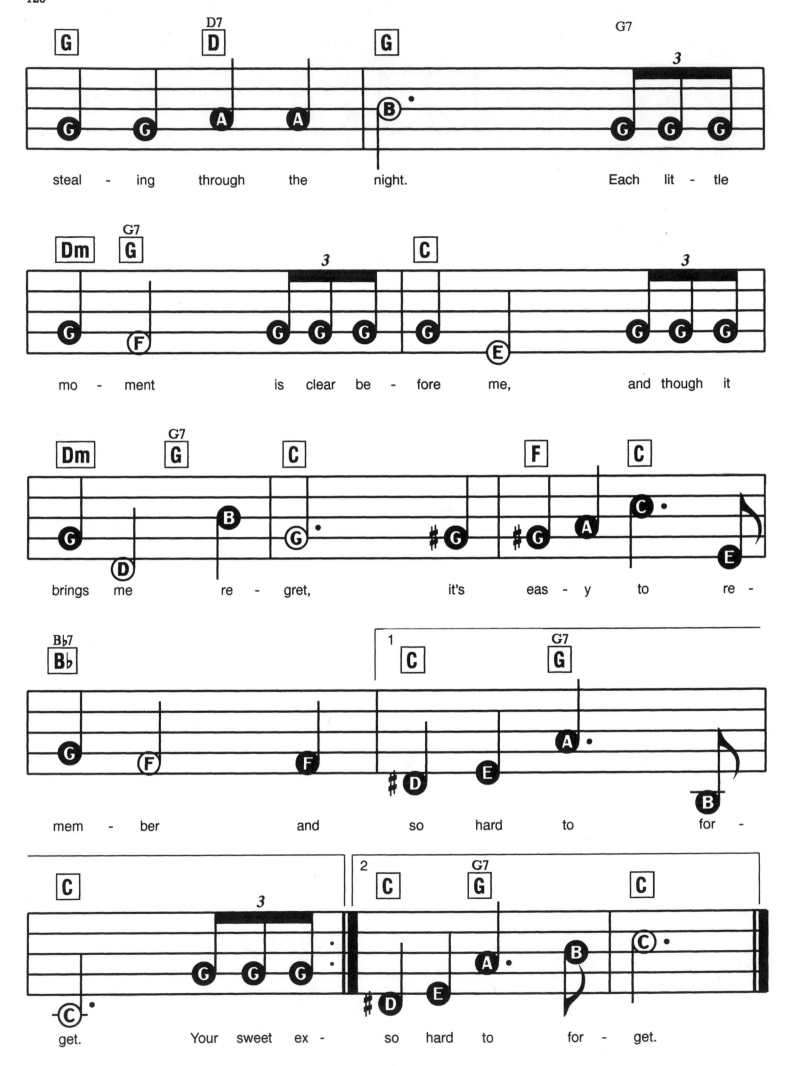

Let Yourself Go
from the Motion Picture FOLLOW THE FLEET

Registration 2
Rhythm: Swing

Words and Music by
Irving Berlin

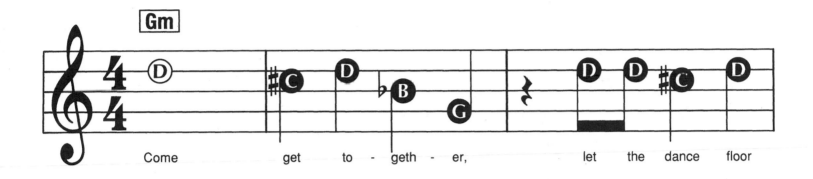

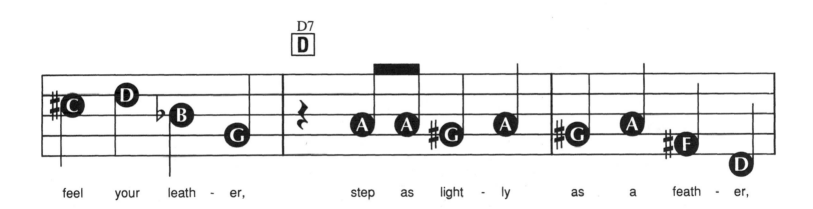

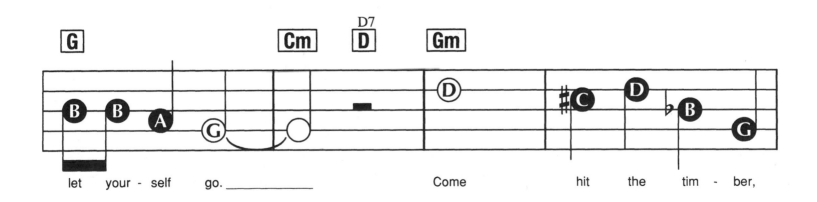

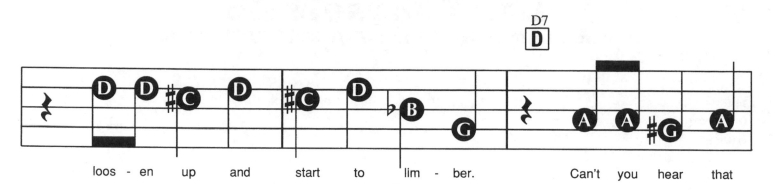

loos - en up and start to lim - ber. Can't you hear that

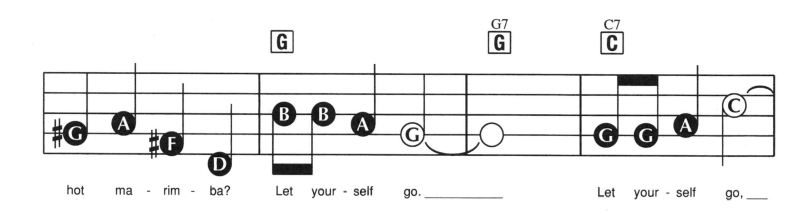

hot ma - rim - ba? Let your - self go. _____ Let your - self go, ___

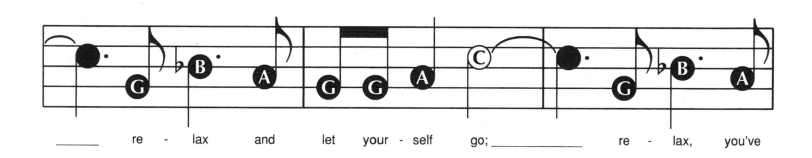

_____ re - lax and let your - self go; _____ re - lax, you've

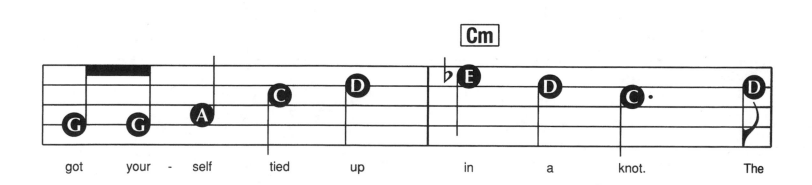

got your - self tied up in a knot. The

131

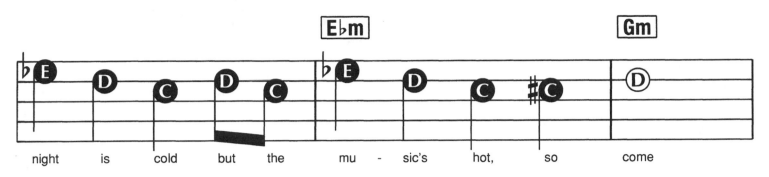

night is cold but the mu - sic's hot, so come

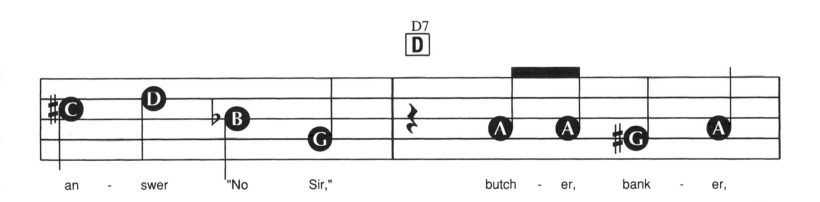

cud - dle clos - er, don't you dare to

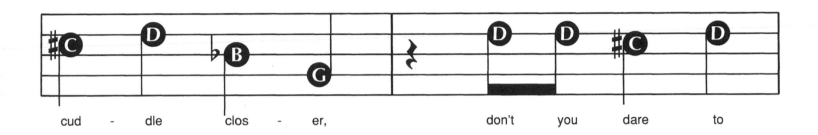

an - swer "No Sir," butch - er, bank - er,

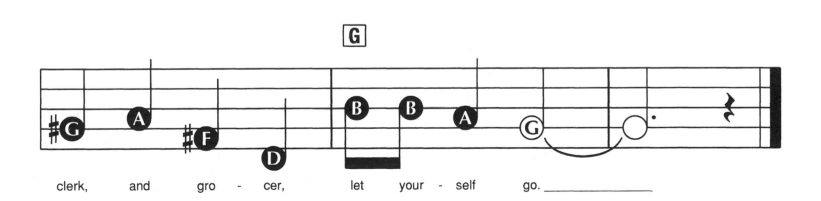

clerk, and gro - cer, let your - self go. _____

It's Only a Paper Moon
featured in the Motion Picture TAKE A CHANCE

Registration 4
Rhythm: Swing

Lyric by Billy Rose and E.Y. "Yip" Harburg
Music by Harold Arlen

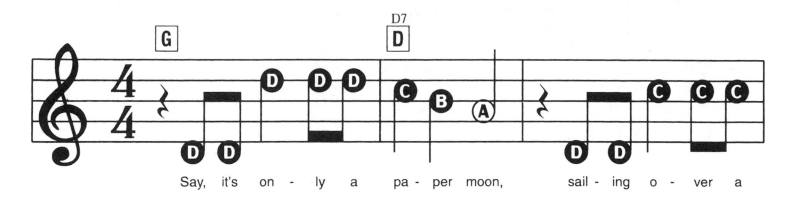

Say, it's on - ly a pa - per moon, sail - ing o - ver a

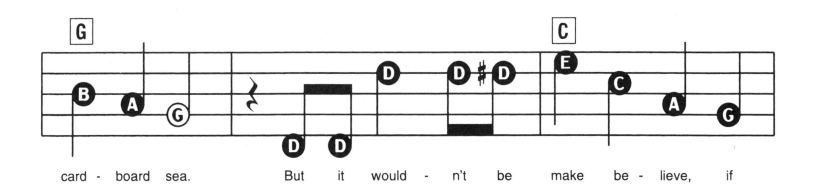

card - board sea. But it would - n't be make be - lieve, if

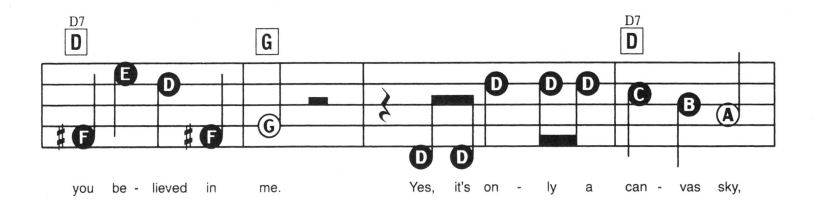

you be - lieved in me. Yes, it's on - ly a can - vas sky,

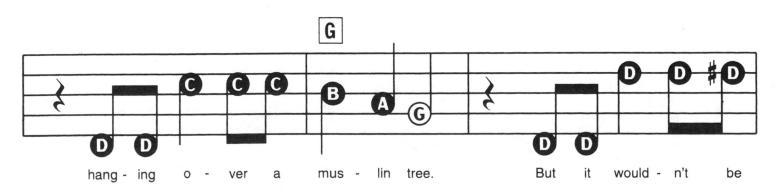

hang - ing o - ver a mus - lin tree. But it would - n't be

133

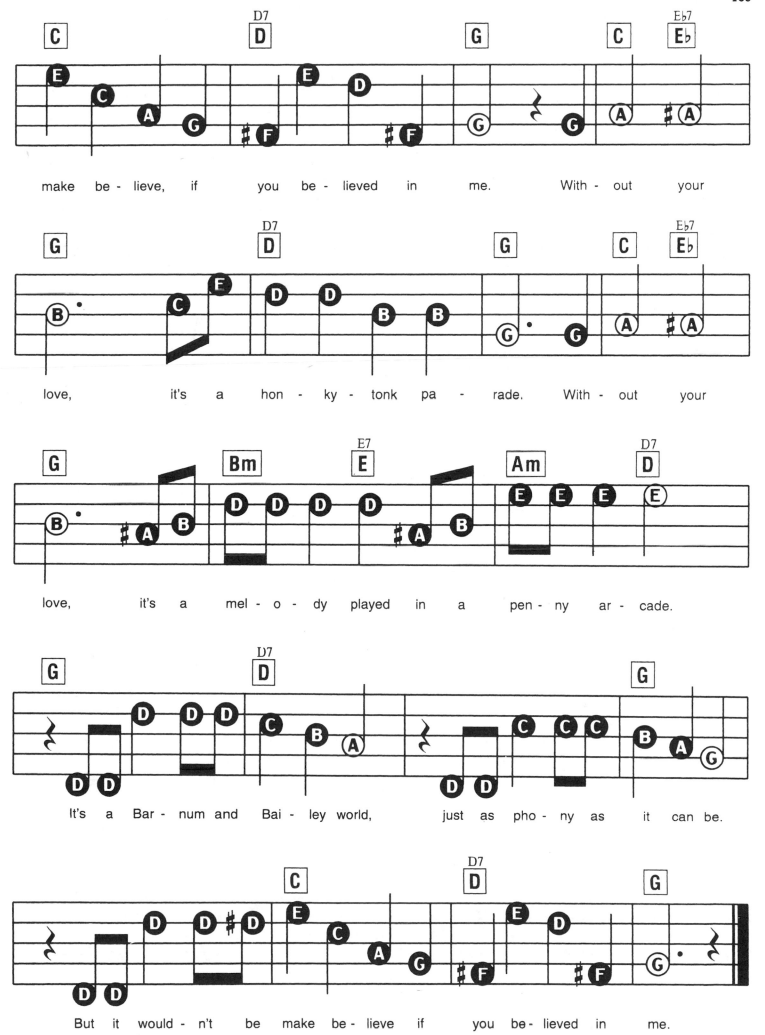

Just One More Chance

Registration 4
Rhythm: Swing

Words by Sam Coslow
Music by Arthur Johnston

Just one more chance to prove it's you a - lone I

care for. Each night I say a lit - tle prayer for

just one more chance. Just one more night,

to taste the kiss - es that en - chant me. I'd want no oth - ers if you'd

grant me just one more chance. I've learned the mean - ing of re -

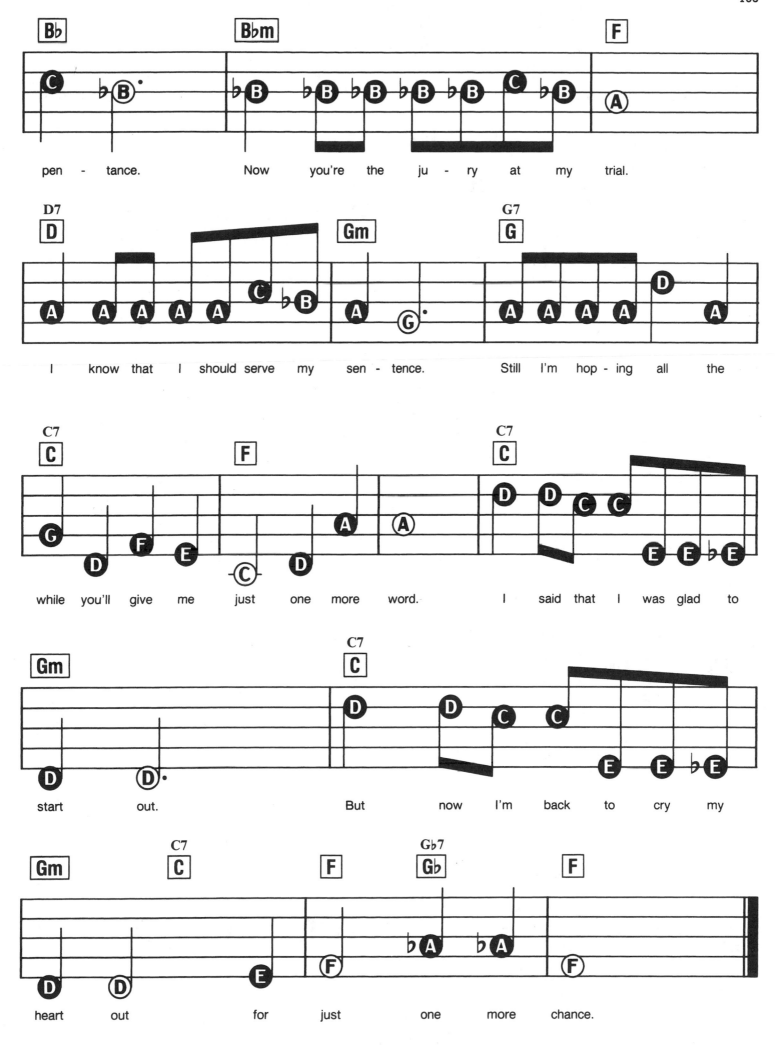

The Lady Is a Tramp
from BABES IN ARMS

Registration 7
Rhythm: Fox Trot or Swing

Words by Lorenz Hart
Music by Richard Rodgers

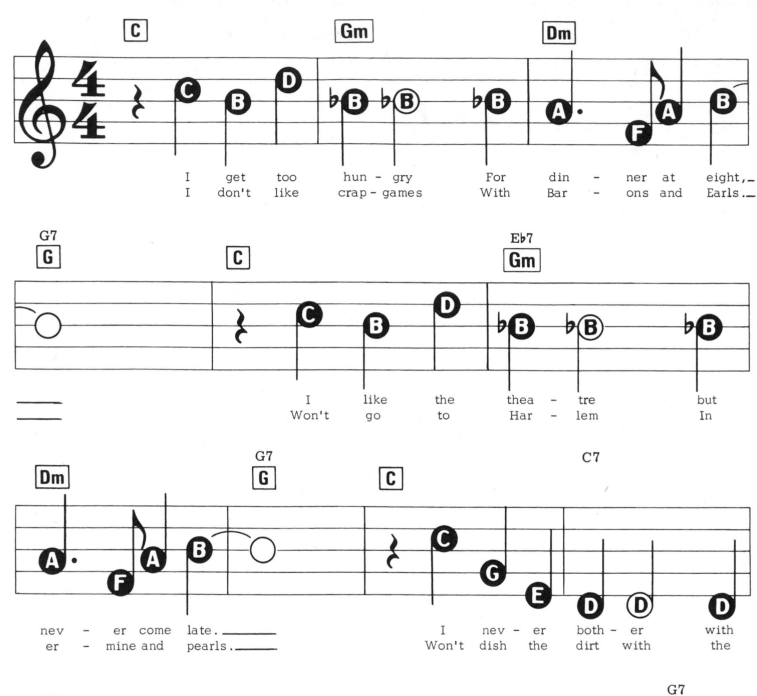

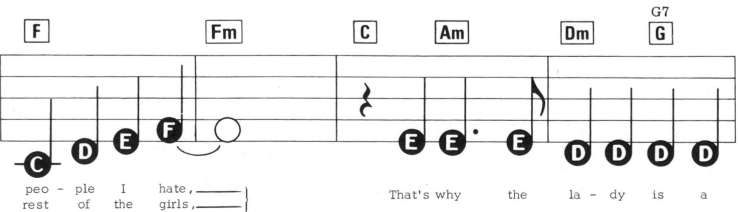

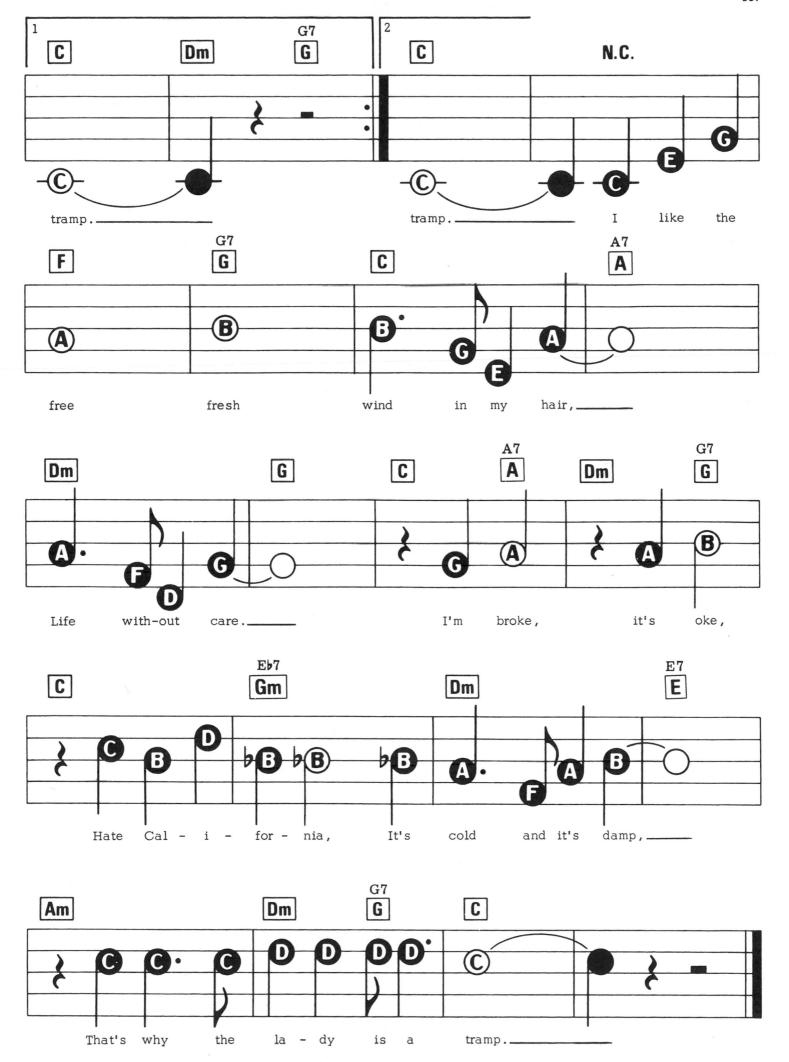

Lazy River
from THE BEST YEARS OF OUR LIVES

Registration 1
Rhythm: Fox Trot or Swing

Words and Music by Hoagy Carmichael
and Sidney Arodin

Up a la - zy riv - er by the old mill - run, That

la - zy, la - zy riv - er in the noon - day sun,

Lin - ger in the shade of a kind old tree;

Throw a - way your trou - bles, dream a dream with me

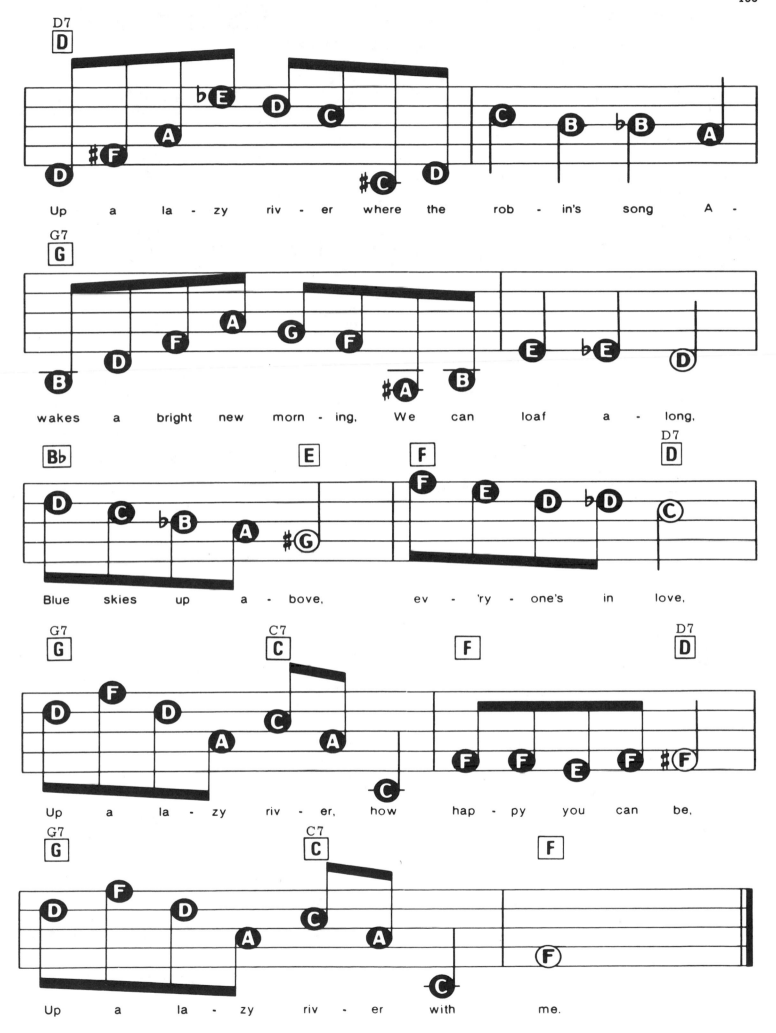

Let's Call the Whole Thing Off
from SHALL WE DANCE

Registration 1
Rhythm: Swing

Music and Lyrics by George Gershwin
and Ira Gershwin

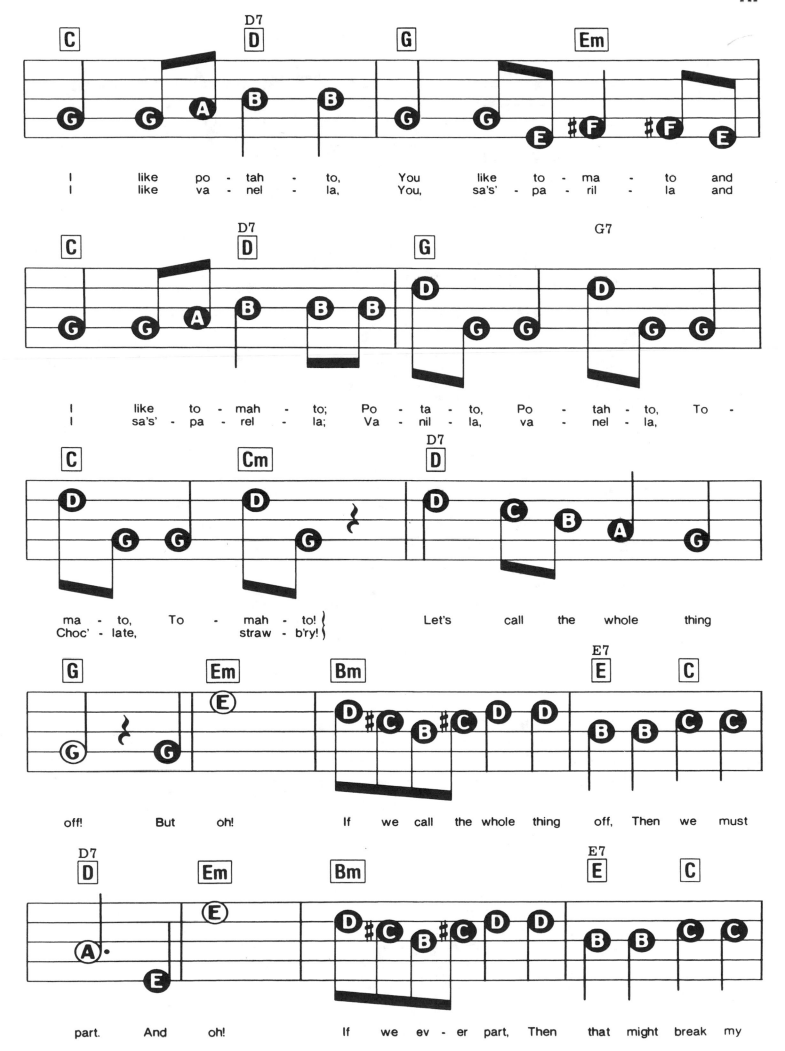

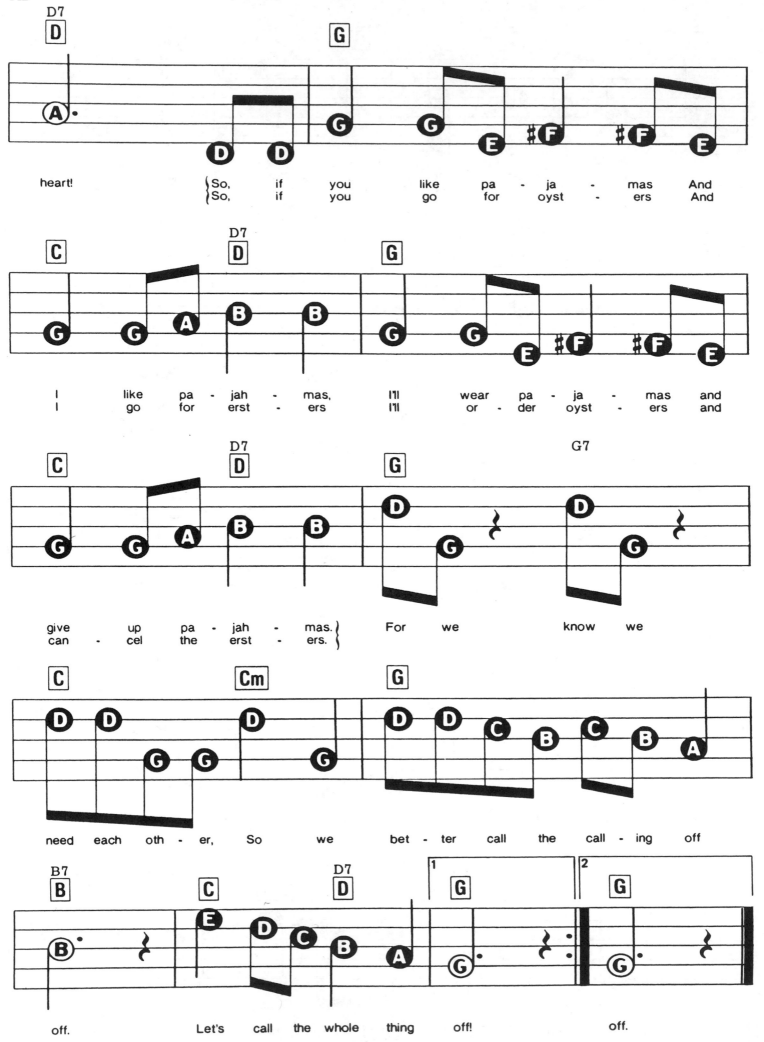

Lullaby of Broadway
from GOLD DIGGERS OF 1935

Registration 5
Rhythm: Swing or Jazz

Words by Al Dubin
Music by Harry Warren

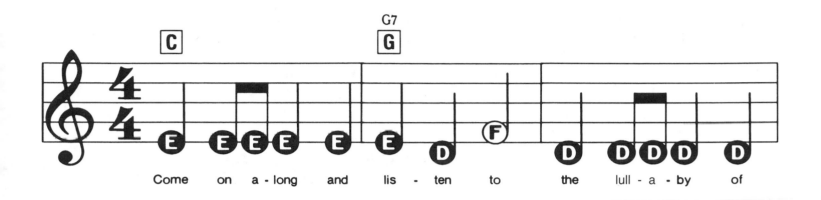

Come on a - long and lis - ten to the lull - a - by of

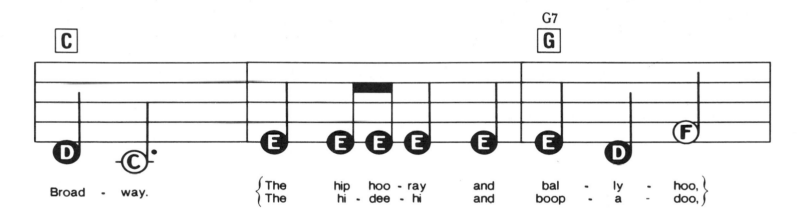

Broad - way.

{ The hip hoo - ray and bal - ly - hoo,
  The hi - dee - hi and boop - a - doo, }

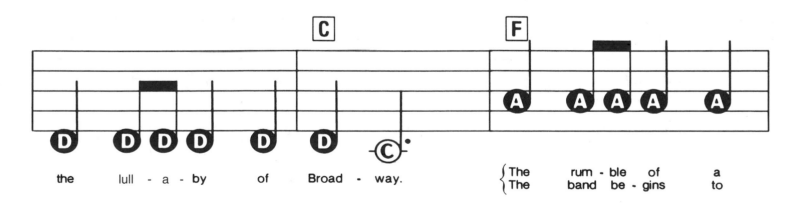

the lull - a - by of Broad - way.

{ The rum - ble of a
  The band be - gins to }

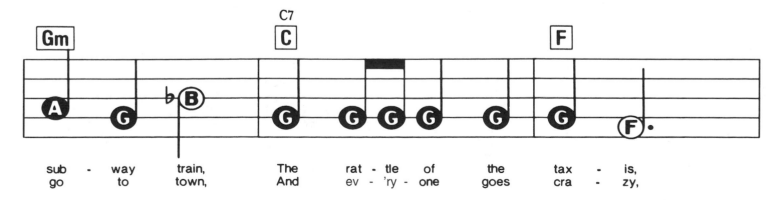

sub - way train, The rat - tle of the tax - is,
go to town, And ev - 'ry - one goes cra - zy,

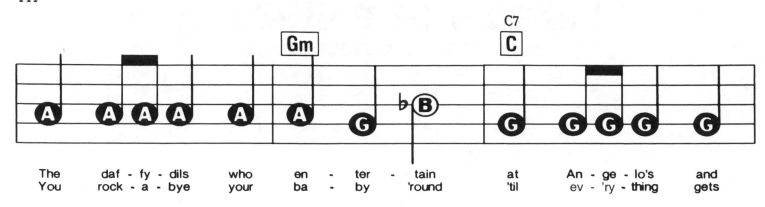

The daf - fy - dils who en - ter - tain at An - ge - lo's and
You rock - a - bye your ba - by 'round 'til ev - 'ry - thing gets

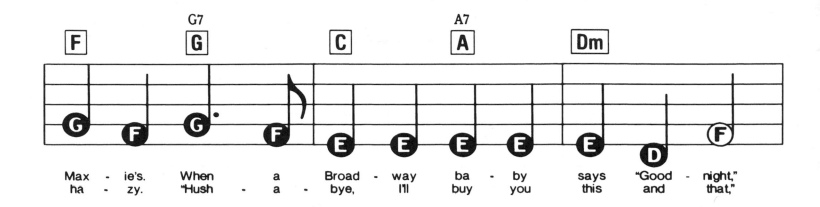

Max - ie's. When a Broad - way ba - by says "Good - night,"
ha - zy. "Hush - a - bye, I'll buy you this and that,"

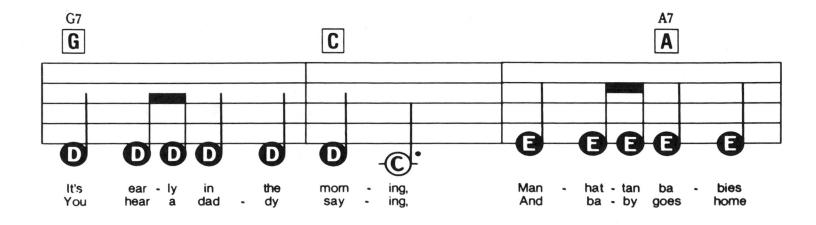

It's ear - ly in the morn - ing, Man - hat - tan ba - bies
You hear a dad - dy say - ing, And ba - by goes home

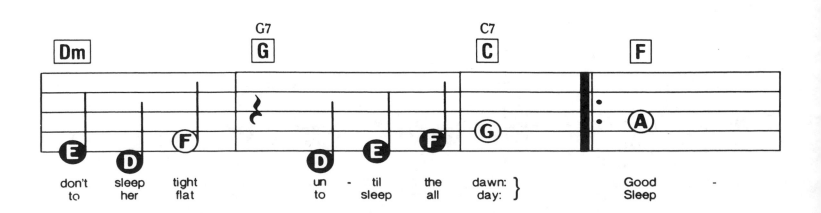

don't sleep tight un - til the dawn: Good -
to her flat to sleep all day: Sleep

145

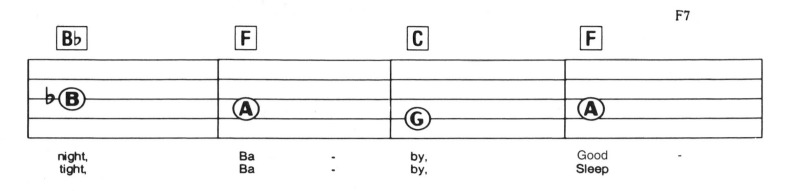

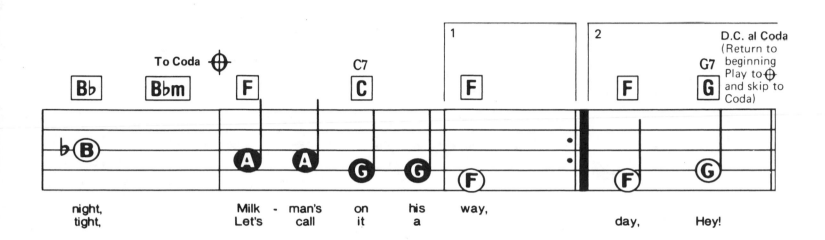

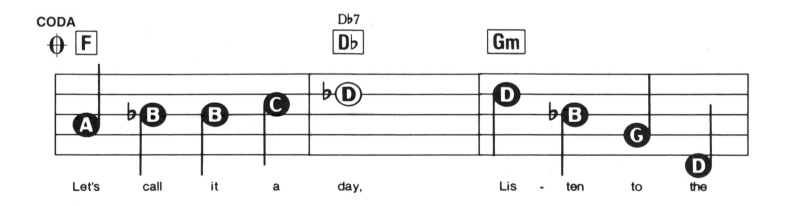

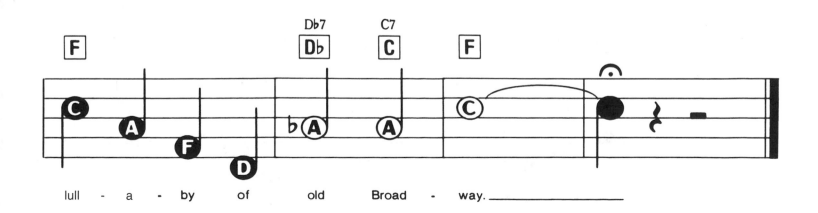

Let's Fall in Love

Registration 9
Rhythm: Fox Trot or Swing

Words by Ted Koehler
Music by Harold Arlen

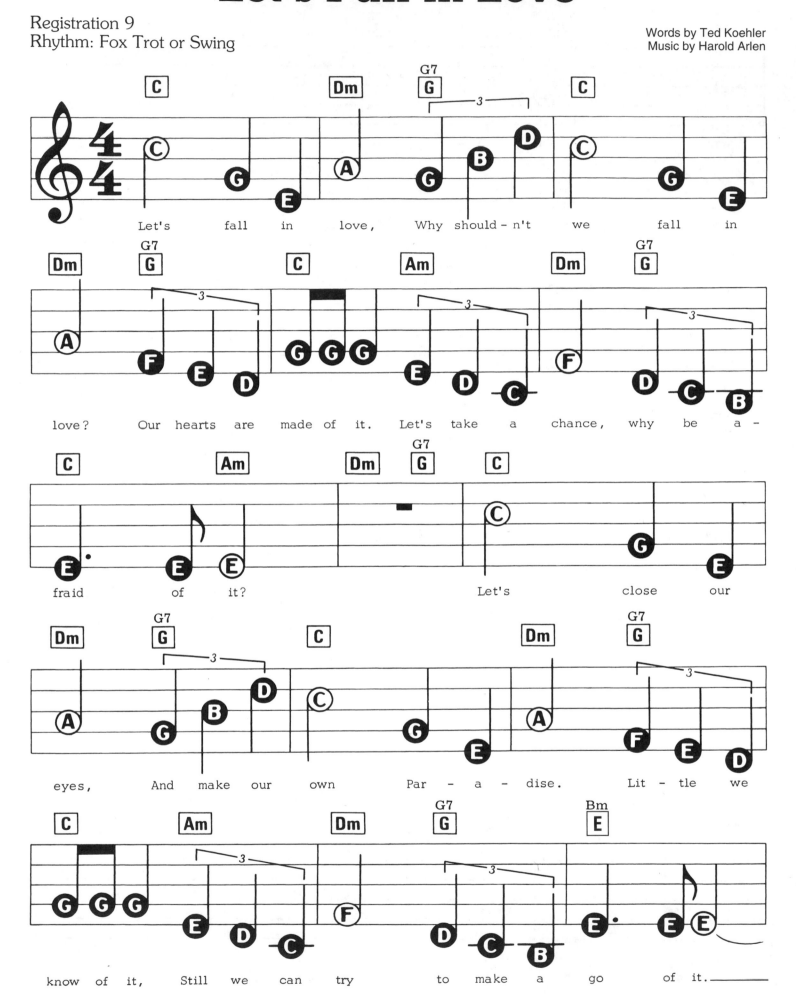

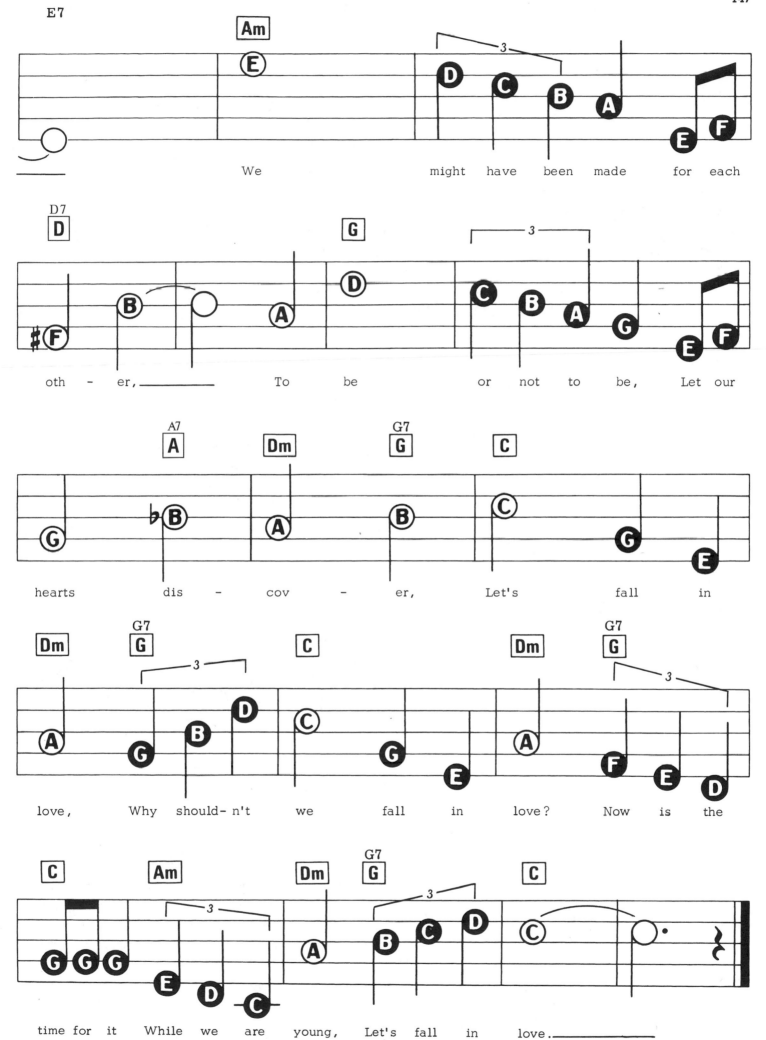

Little Girl Blue
from JUMBO

Registration 4
Rhythm: Fox Trot or Ballad

Words by Lorenz Hart
Music by Richard Rodgers

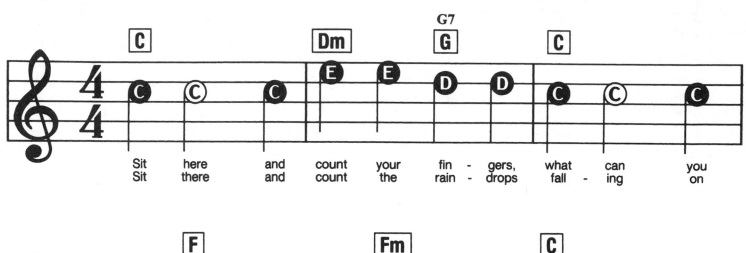

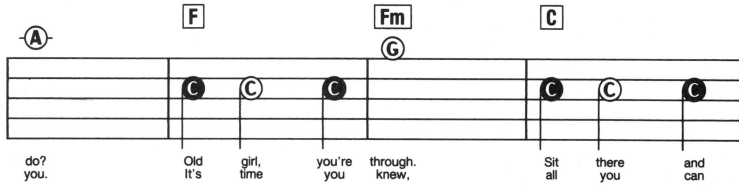

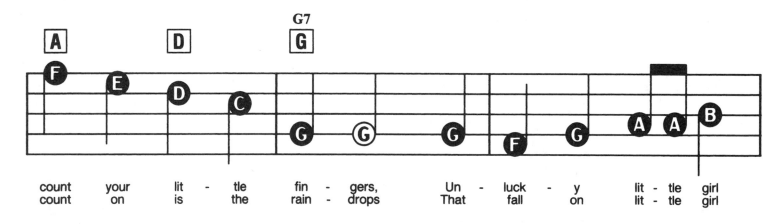

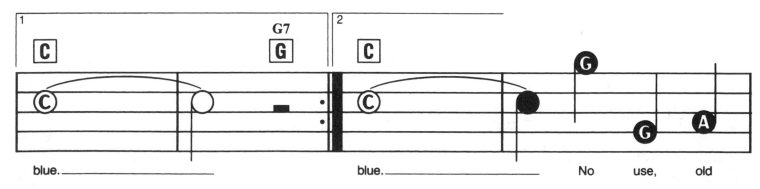

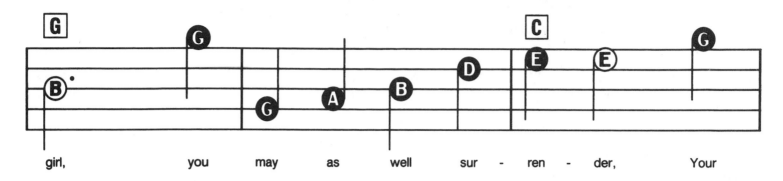

girl, you may as well sur - ren - der, Your

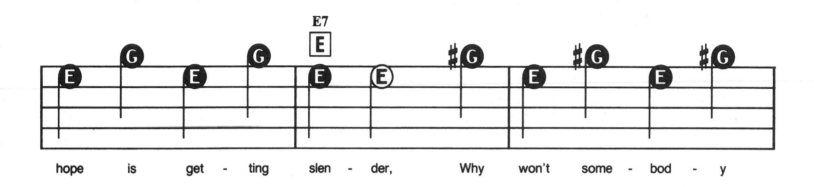

hope is get - ting slen - der, Why won't some - bod - y

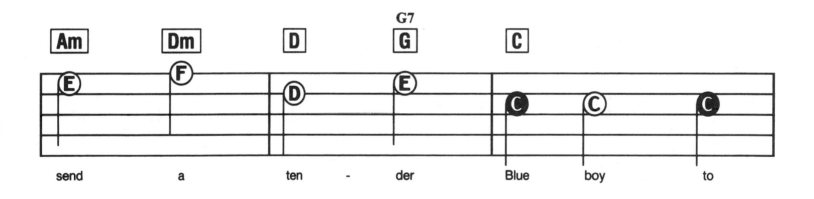

send a ten - der Blue boy to

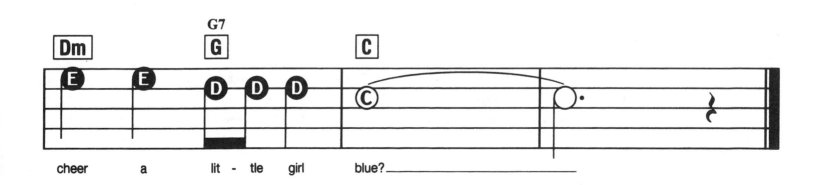

cheer a lit - tle girl blue?_____

Love Is Here to Stay
from AN AMERICAN IN PARIS

Registration 4
Rhythm: Fox Trot or Ballad

Music and Lyrics by George Gershwin
and Ira Gershwin

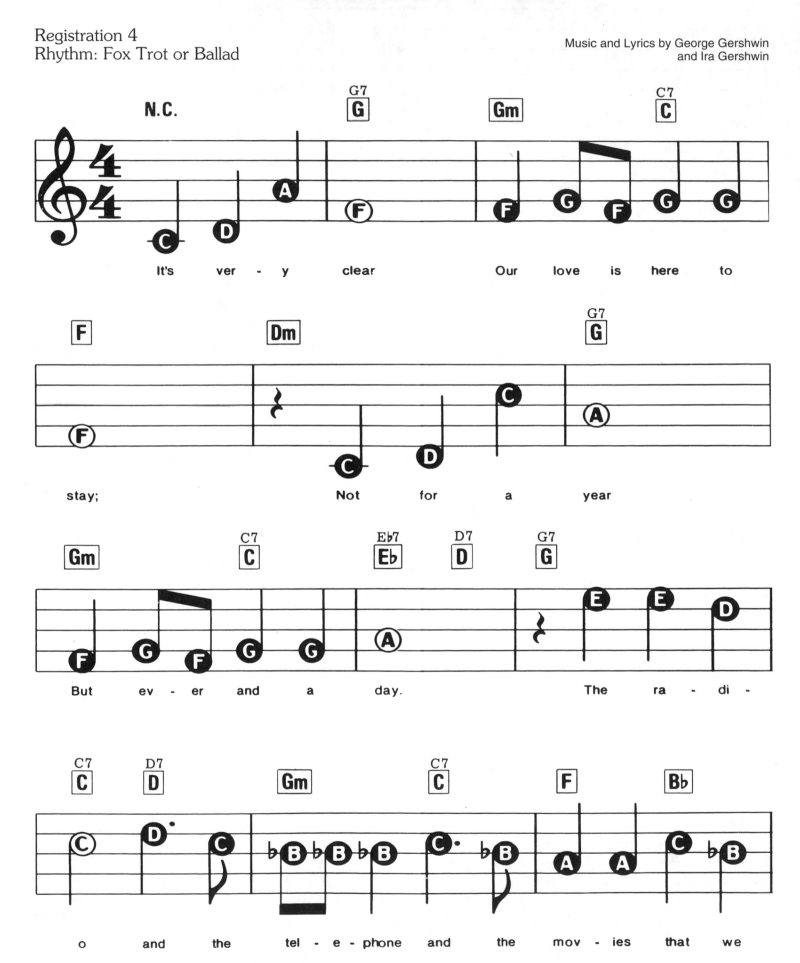

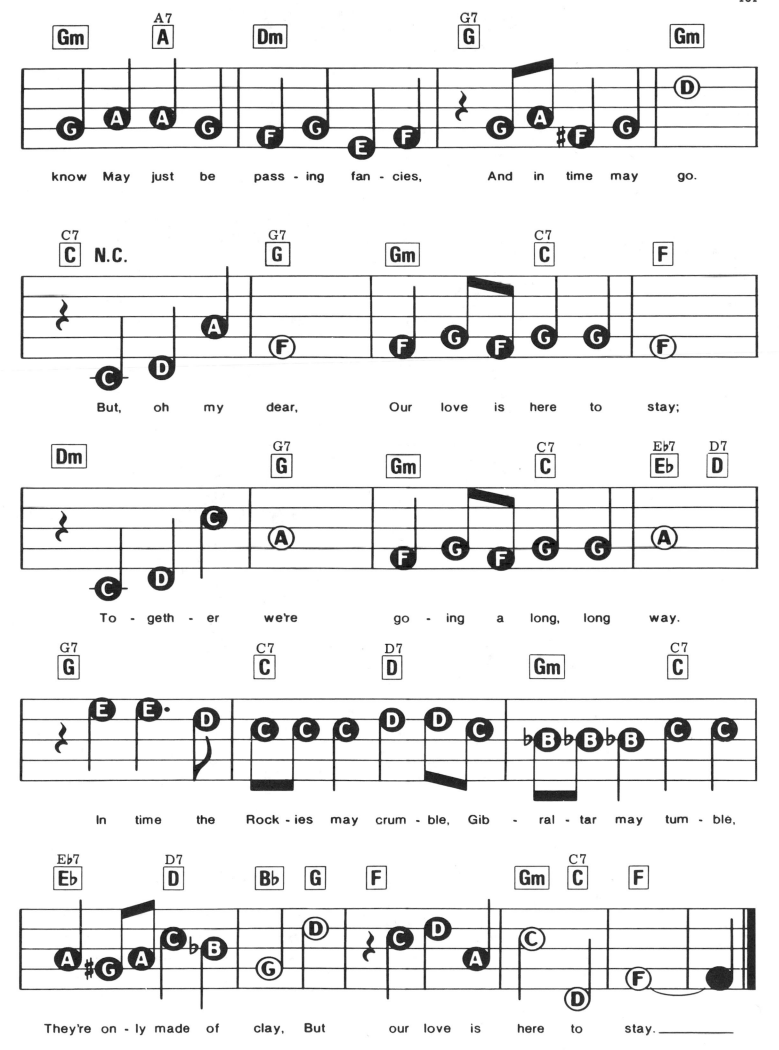

Love Walked In
from GOLDWYN FOLLIES

Registration 9
Rhythm: Swing or Jazz

Music and Lyrics by George Gershwin
and Ira Gershwin

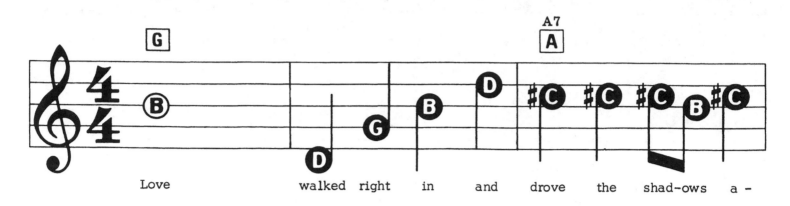

Love walked right in and drove the shad-ows a-

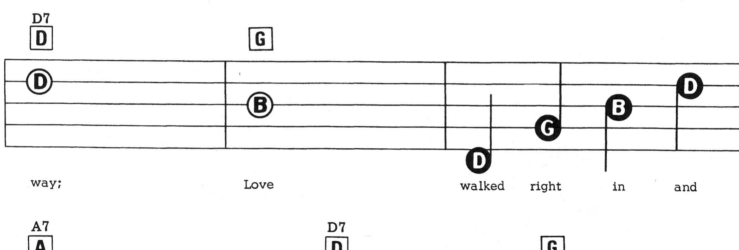

way; Love walked right in and

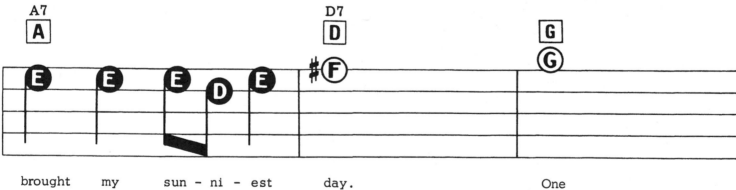

brought my sun - ni - est day. One

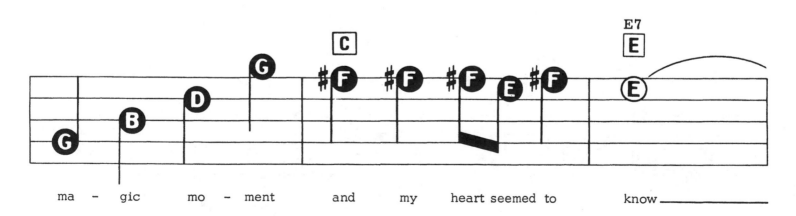

ma - gic mo - ment and my heart seemed to know

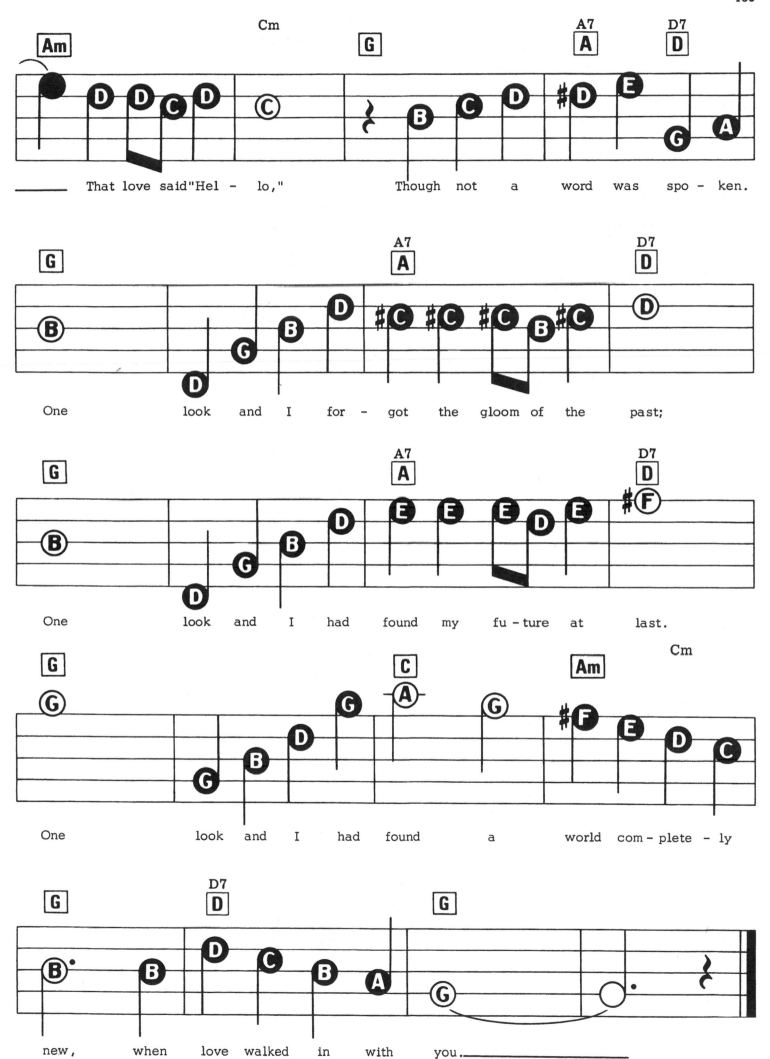

Lover
from the Paramount Picture LOVE ME TONIGHT

Registration 6
Rhythm: Waltz

Words by Lorenz Hart
Music by Richard Rodgers

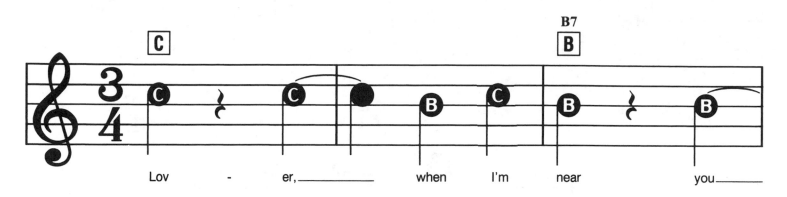

Lov - er,_____ when I'm near you_____

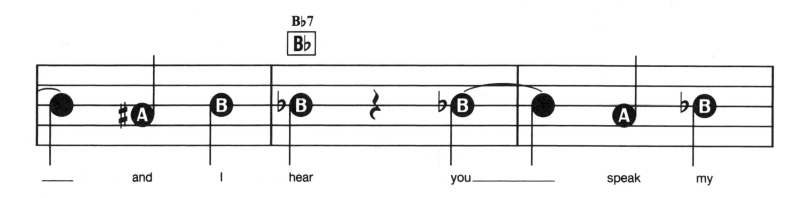

____ and I hear you_____ speak my

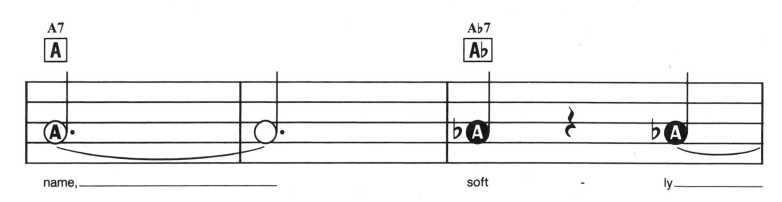

name,_____ soft - ly

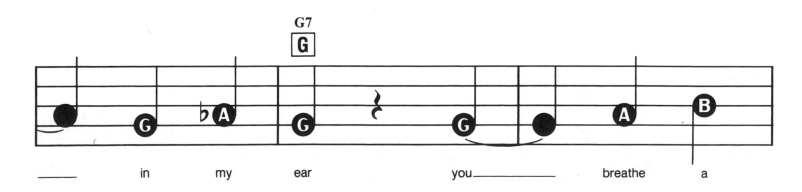

____ in my ear you_____ breathe a

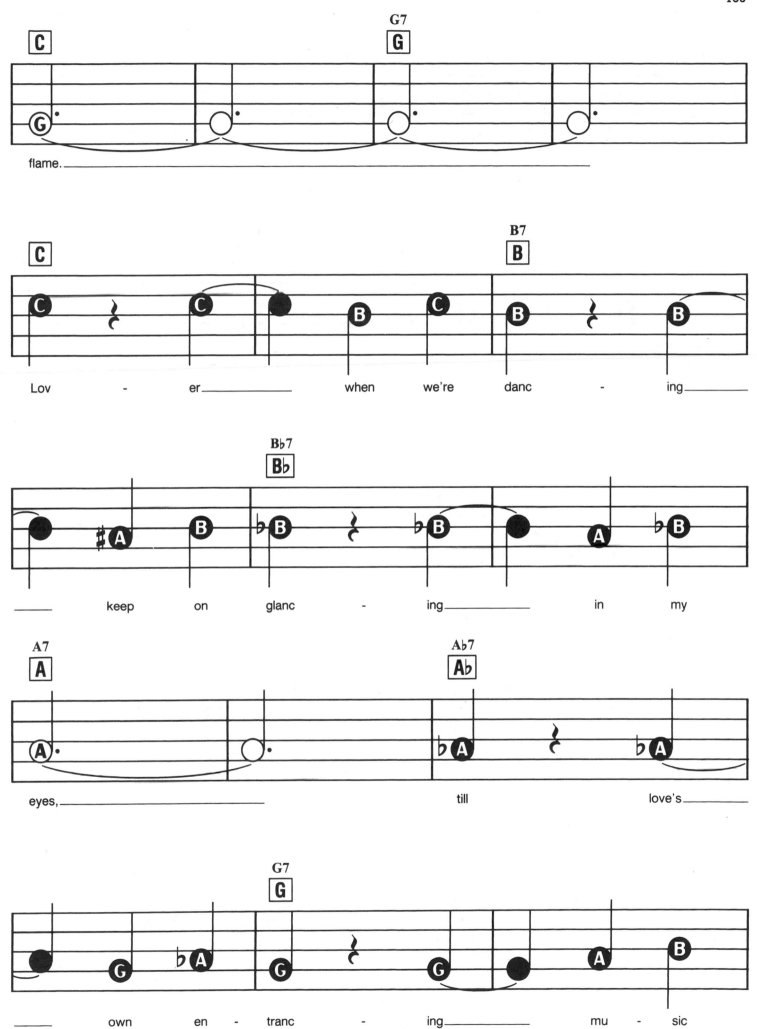

flame.

Lov - er_____ when we're danc - ing_____

_____ keep on glanc - ing_____ in my

eyes,_____ till love's_____

_____ own en - tranc - ing_____ mu - sic

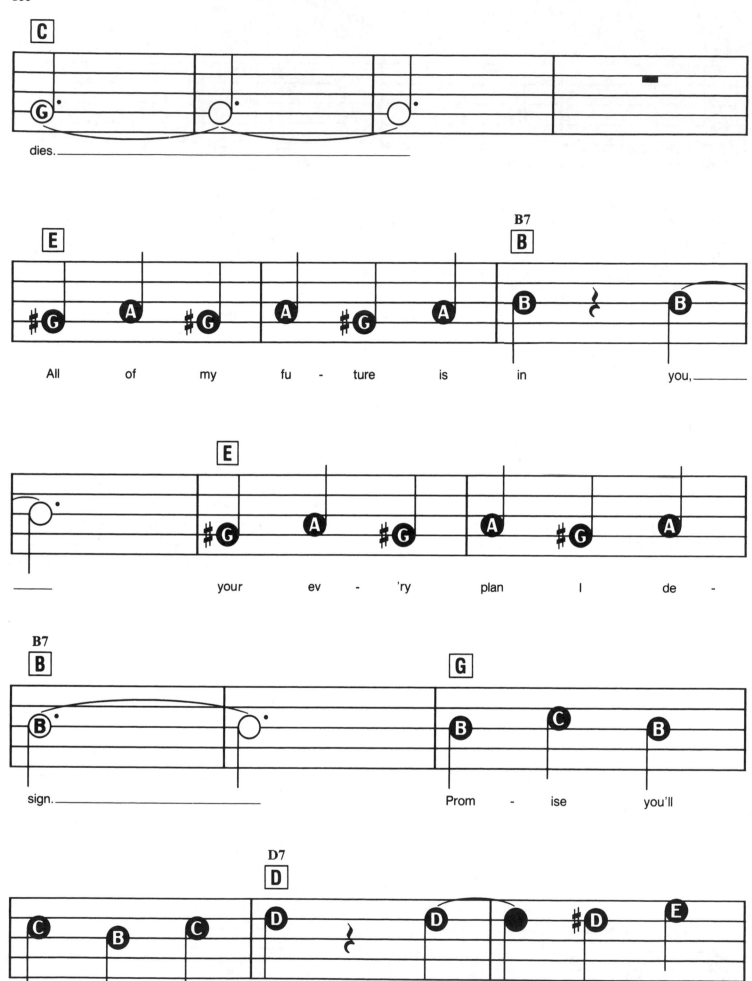

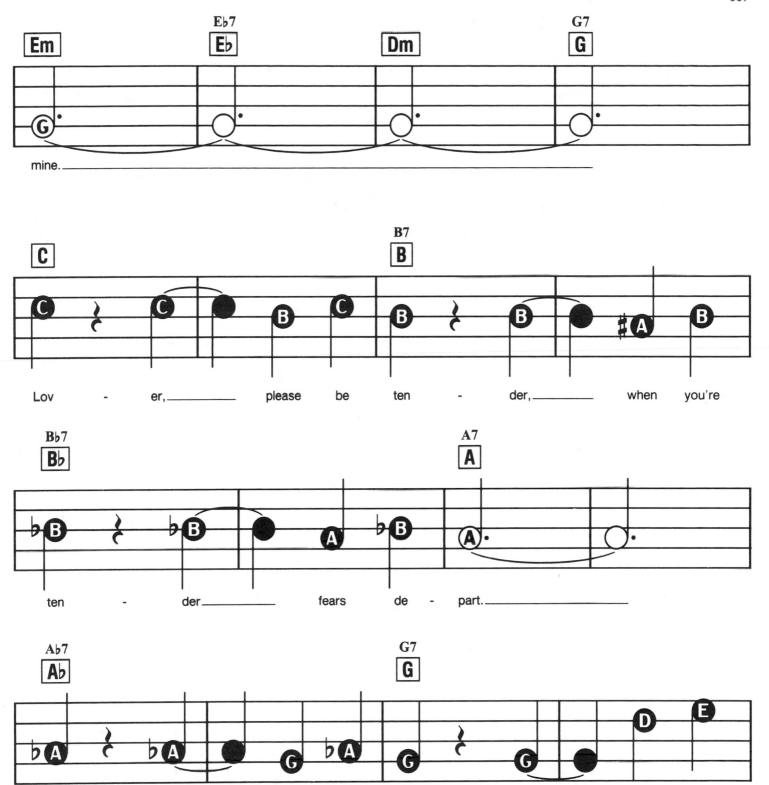

mine.

Lov - er,_____ please be ten - der,_____ when you're

ten - der_____ fears de - part._____

Lov - er,_____ I sur - ren - der_____ to my

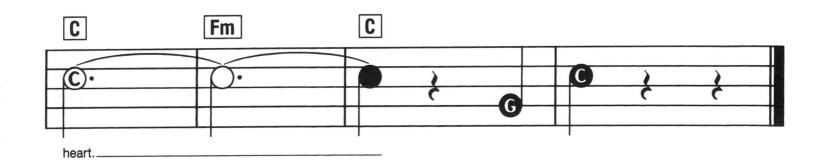

heart._____

Lullaby of the Leaves

Registration 10
Rhythm: Fox Trot or Swing

Words by Al Dubin
Music by Harry Warren

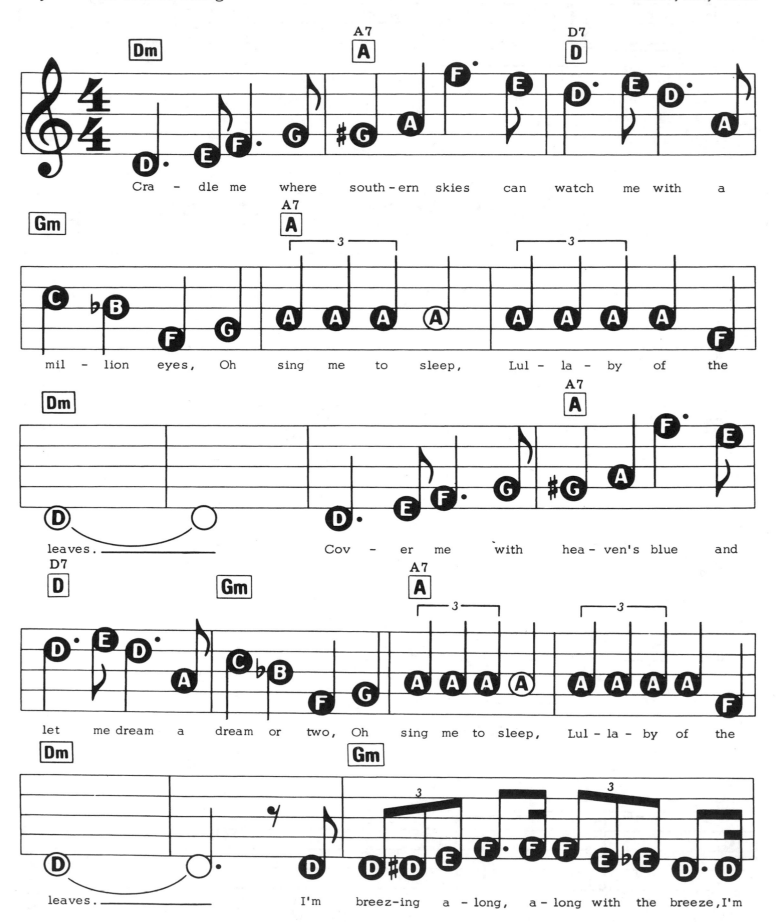

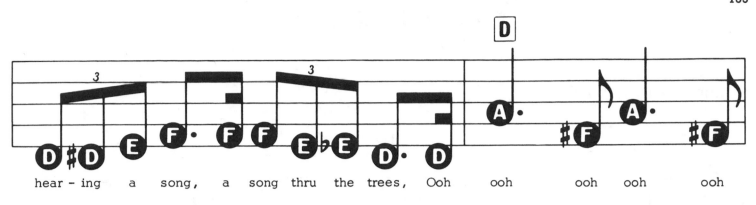

hear - ing a song, a song thru the trees, Ooh ooh ooh ooh ooh

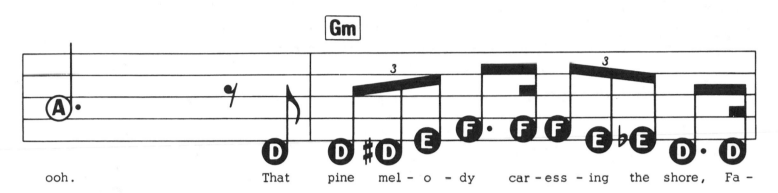

ooh. That pine mel - o - dy car - ess - ing the shore, Fa -

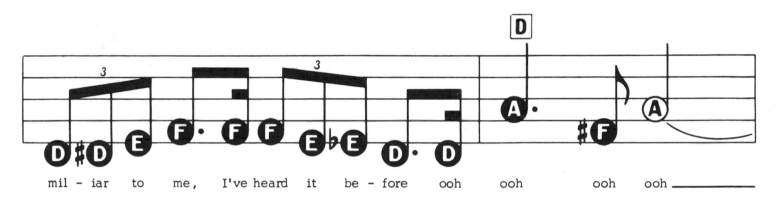

mil - iar to me, I've heard it be - fore ooh ooh ooh ooh _____

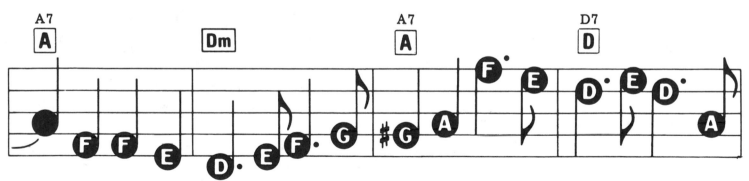

_____ That's south - land, don't I feel it in my soul, and don't I know I've

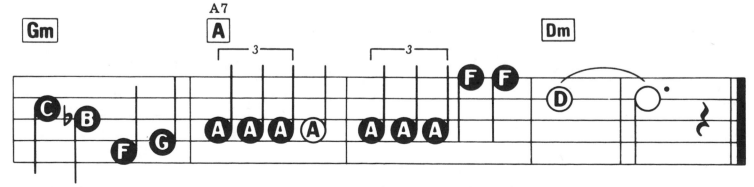

reached my goal, Oh sing me to sleep, Lul - la - by of the leaves. _____

Mood Indigo

Registration 4
Rhythm: Swing or Ballad

Words and Music by Duke Ellington,
Irving Mills and Albany Bigard

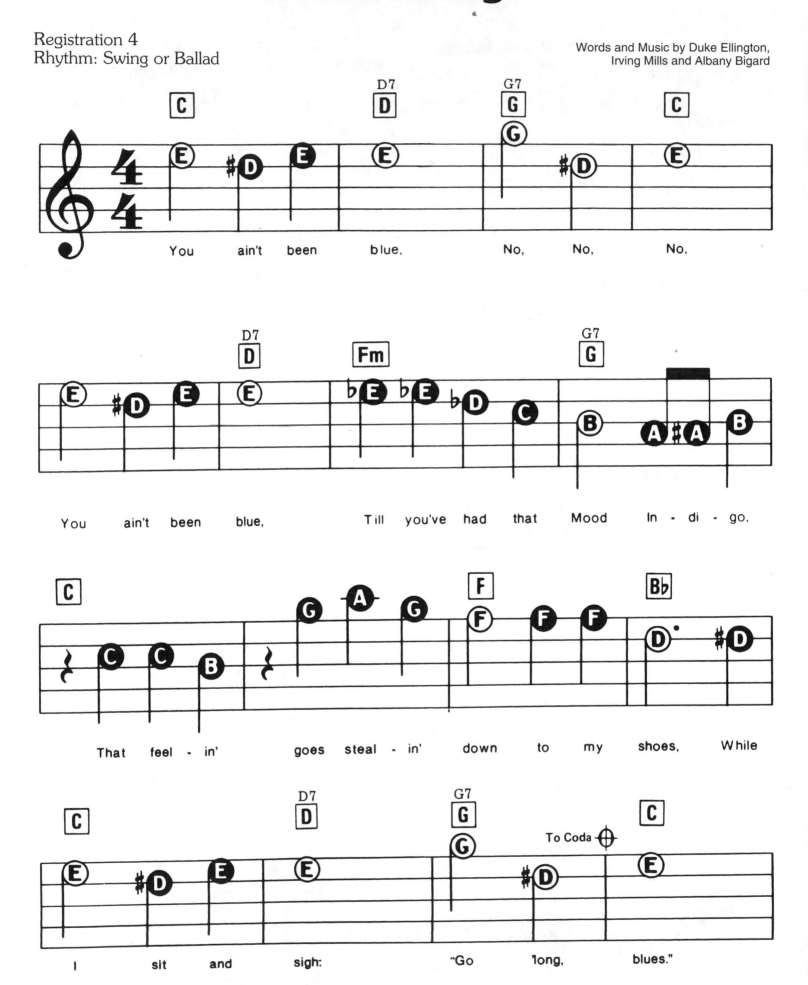

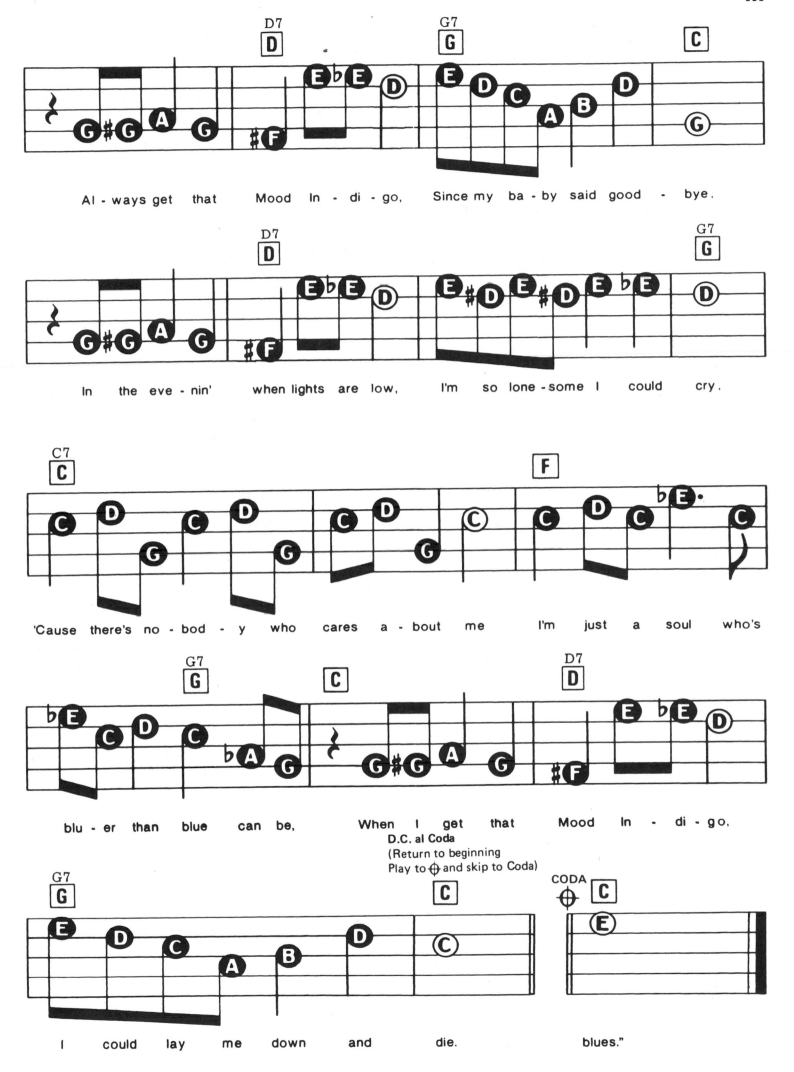

Moonglow

Registration 2
Rhythm: Fox Trot

Words and Music by Will Hudson,
Eddie De Lange and Irving Mills

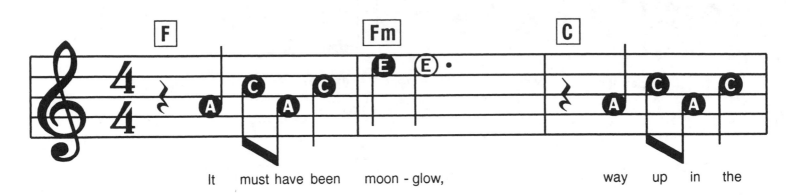

It must have been moon - glow, way up in the

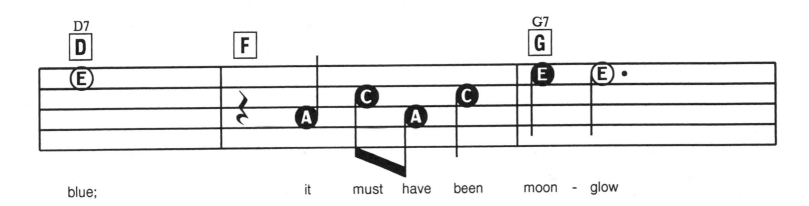

blue; it must have been moon - glow

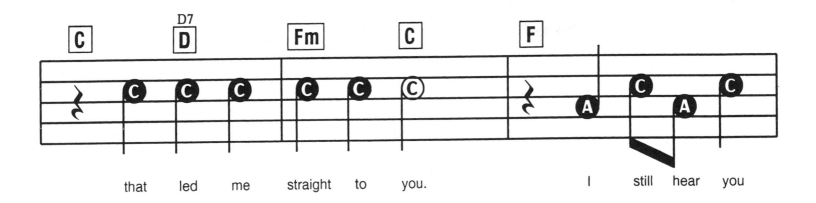

that led me straight to you. I still hear you

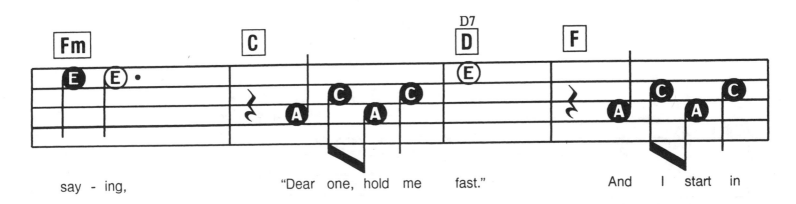

say - ing, "Dear one, hold me fast." And I start in

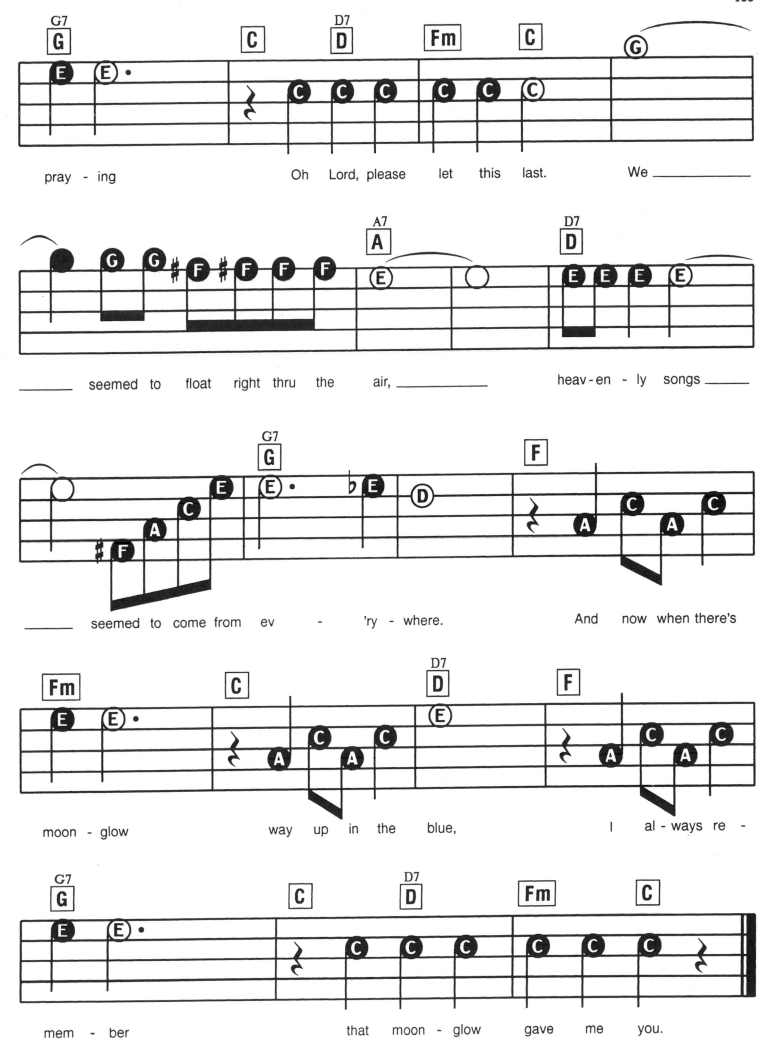

163

My Funny Valentine
from BABES IN ARMS

Registration 1
Rhythm: Ballad

Words by Lorenz Hart
Music by Richard Rodgers

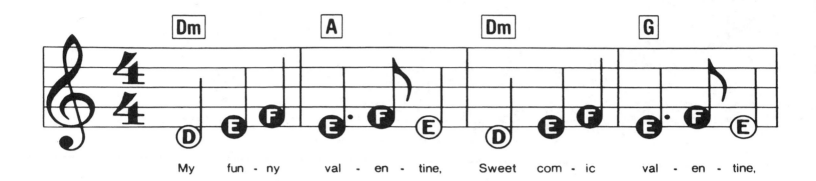

My fun-ny val-en-tine, Sweet com-ic val-en-tine,

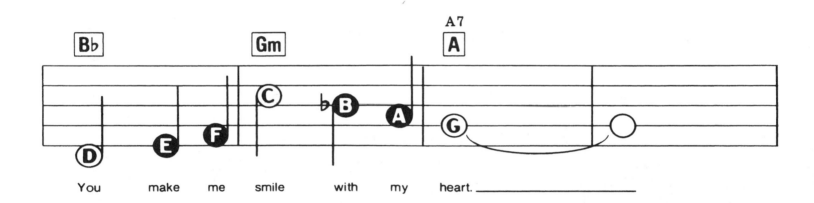

You make me smile with my heart. _____

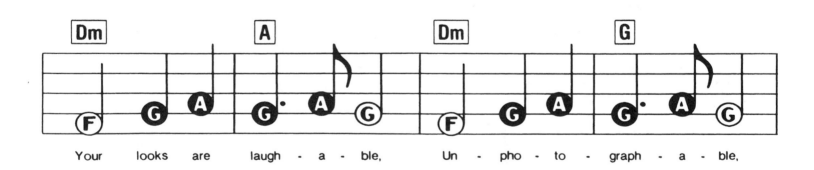

Your looks are laugh-a-ble, Un-pho-to-graph-a-ble,

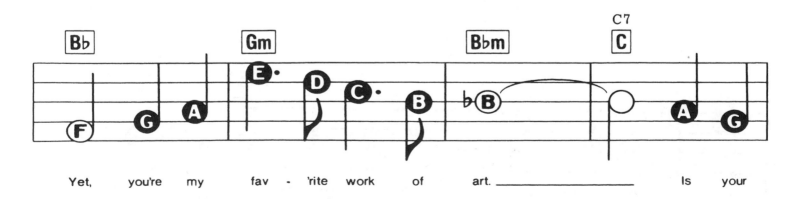

Yet, you're my fav-'rite work of art. _____ Is your

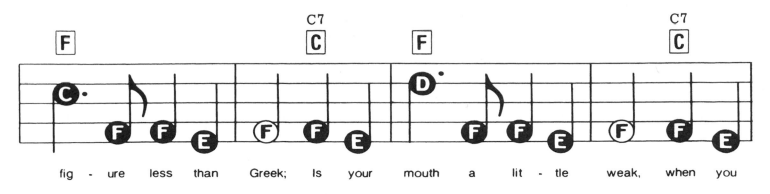

fig - ure less than Greek; Is your mouth a lit - tle weak, when you

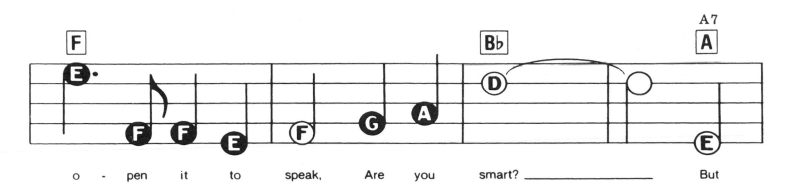

o - pen it to speak, Are you smart? _____ But

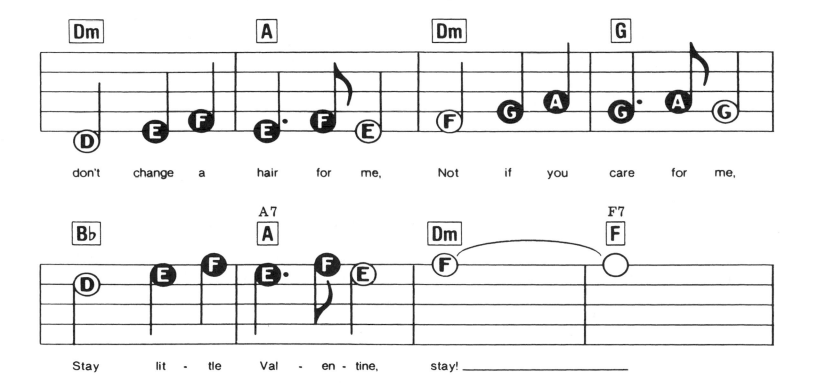

don't change a hair for me, Not if you care for me,

Stay lit - tle Val - en - tine, stay! _____

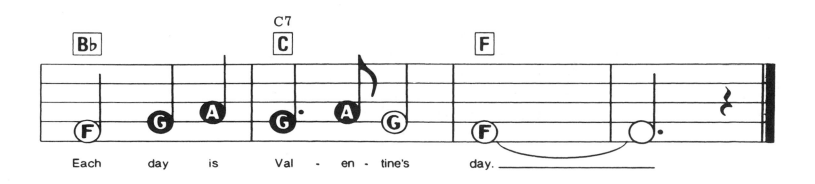

Each day is Val - en - tine's day. _____

My Romance
from JUMBO

Registration 5
Rhythm: Fox Trot or Ballad

Words by Lorenz Hart
Music by Richard Rodgers

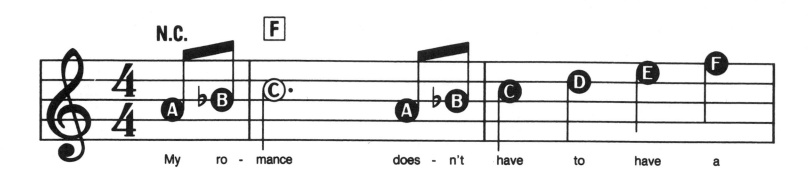

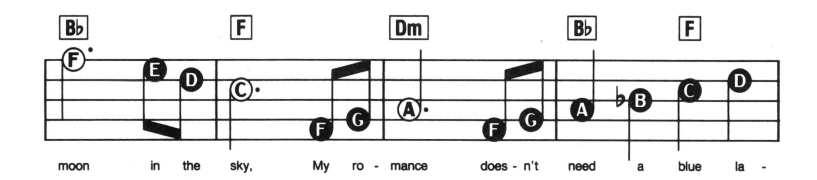

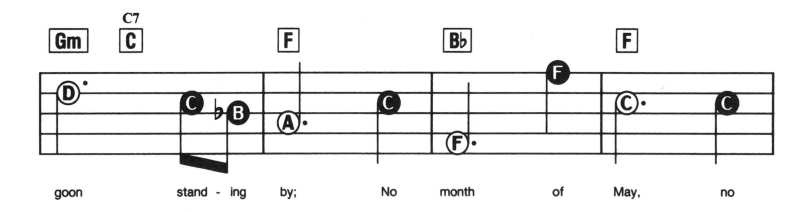

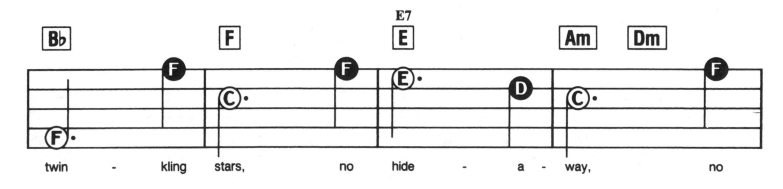

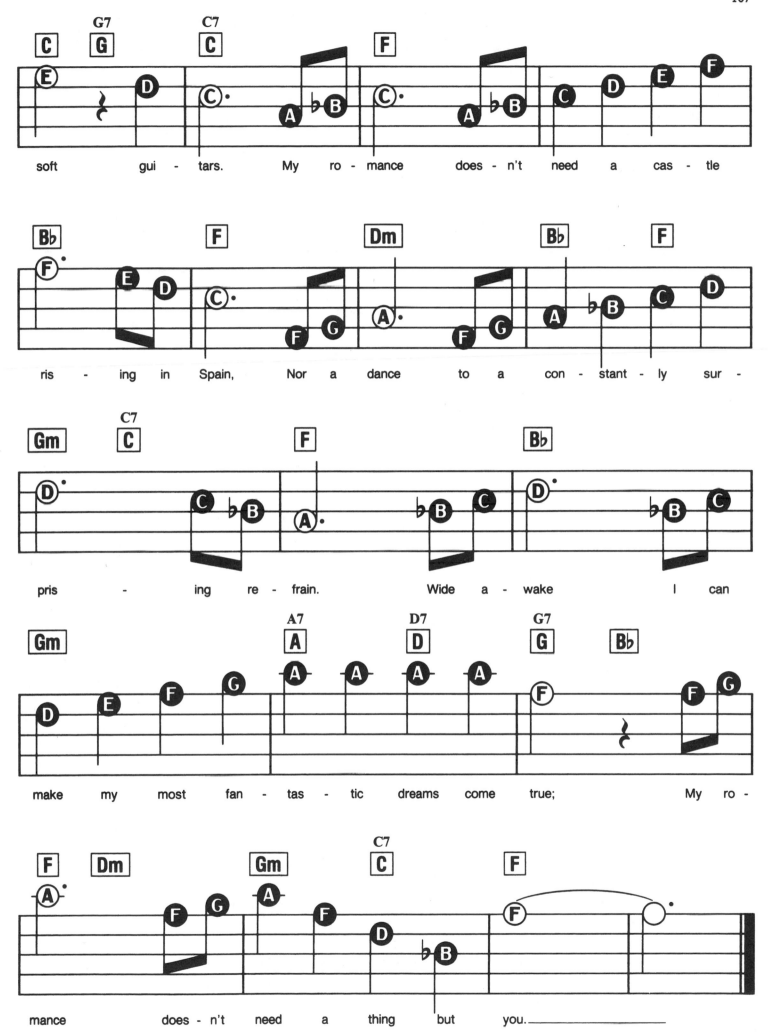

The Nearness of You
from the Paramount Picture ROMANCE IN THE DARK

Registration 9
Rhythm: Ballad or Fox Trot

Words by Ned Washington
Music by Hoagy Carmichael

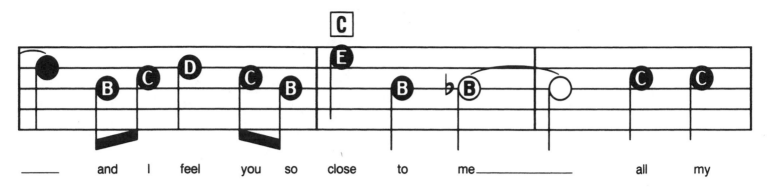

and I feel you so close to me_____ all my

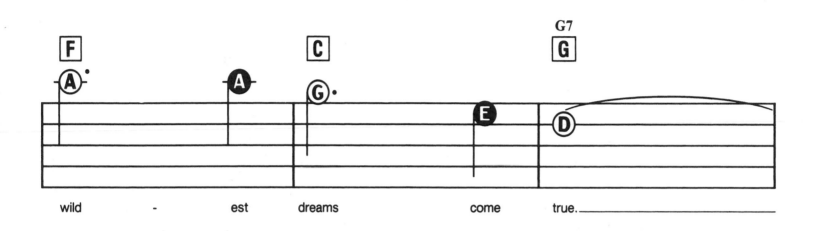

wild - est dreams come true._____

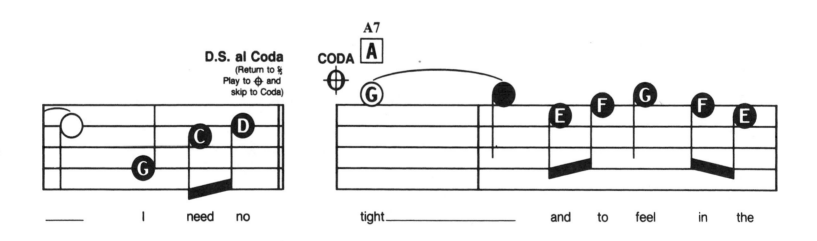

_____ I need no   tight_____ and to feel in the

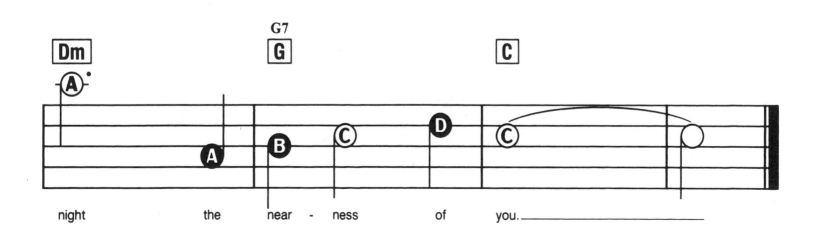

night   the near - ness of you._____

Nevertheless
(I'm in Love with You)

Registration 4
Rhythm: Fox Trot or Ballad

Words and Music by Bert Kalmar
and Harry Ruby

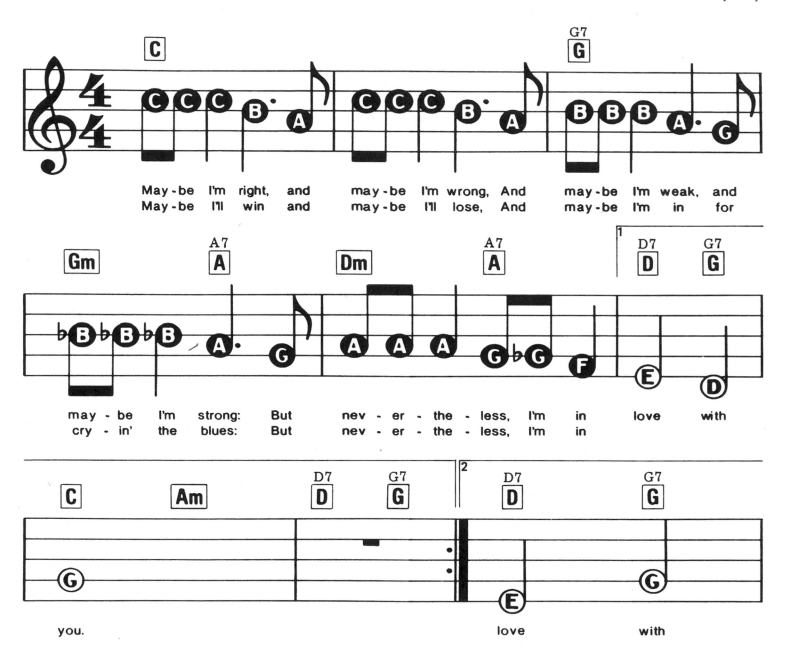

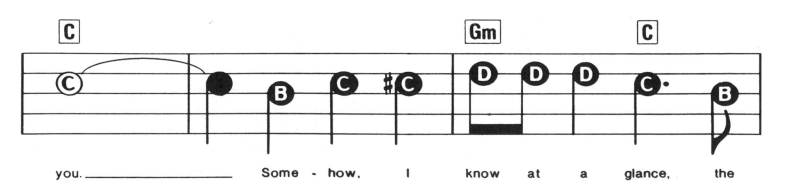

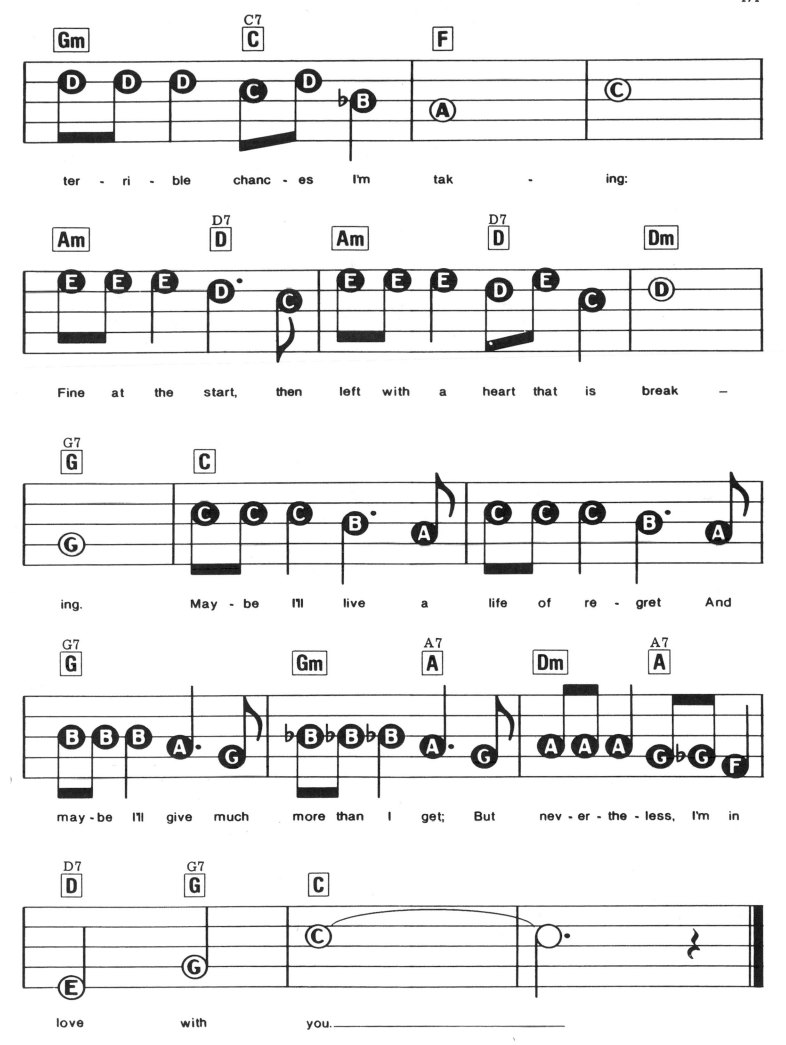

Nice Work If You Can Get It
from A DAMSEL IN DISTRESS

Registration 7
Rhythm: Swing

Music and Lyrics by George Gershwin
and Ira Gershwin

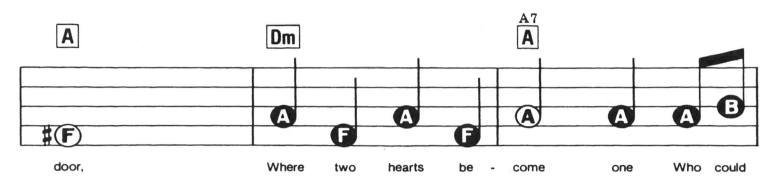

door,   Where two hearts be - come   one   Who could

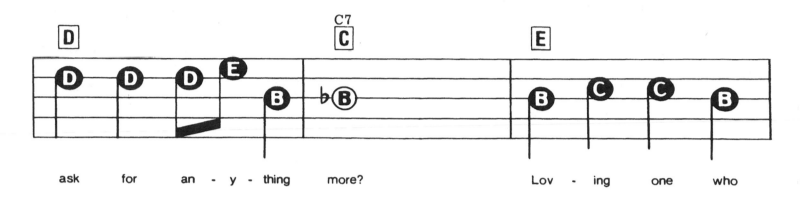

ask   for   an - y - thing   more?   Lov - ing   one   who

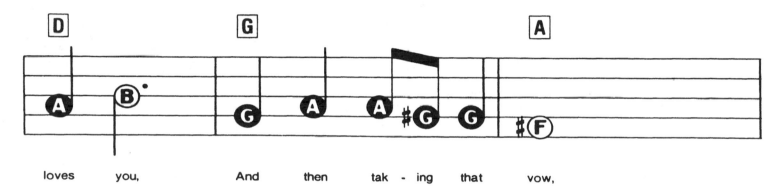

loves   you,   And   then   tak - ing   that   vow,

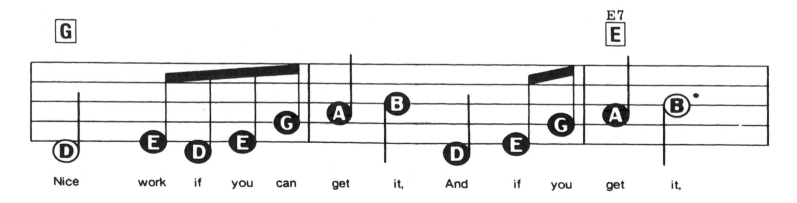

Nice   work   if   you   can   get   it,   And   if   you   get   it,

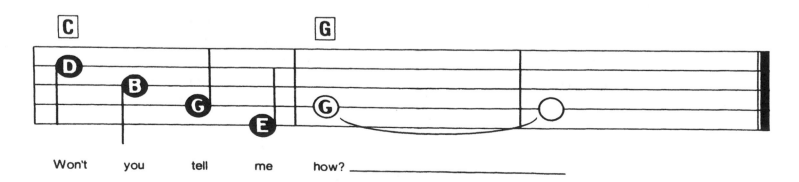

Won't   you   tell   me   how? _____

Night and Day
from THE GAY DIVORCEE

Registration 7
Rhythm: Fox Trot or Swing

Words and Music by
Cole Porter

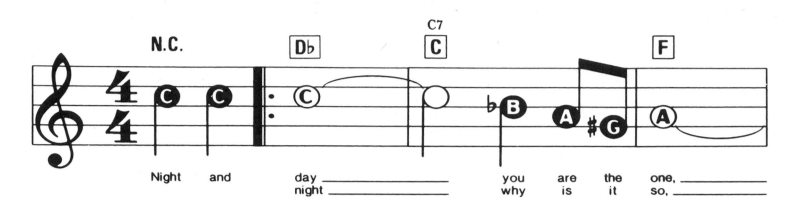

Night and day _____ you are the one, _____
night _____ why is it so, _____

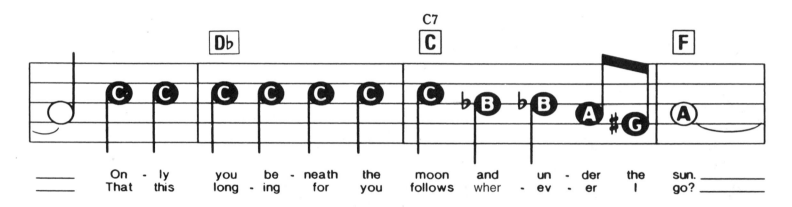

_____ On - ly you be - neath the moon and un - der the sun. _____
_____ That this long - ing for you follows wher - ev - er I go? _____

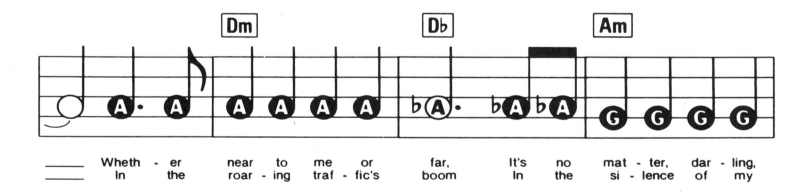

_____ Wheth - er near to me or far, It's no mat - ter, dar - ling,
_____ In the roar - ing traf - fic's boom In the si - lence of my

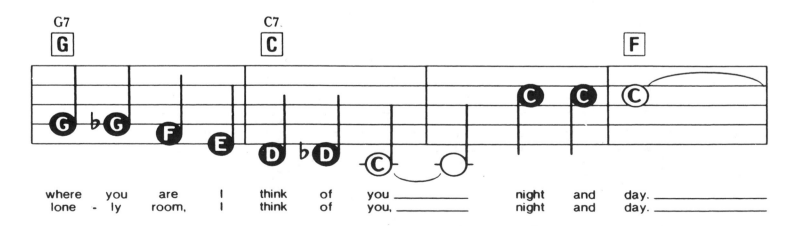

where you are I think of you _____ night and day. _____
lone - ly room, I think of you, _____ night and day. _____

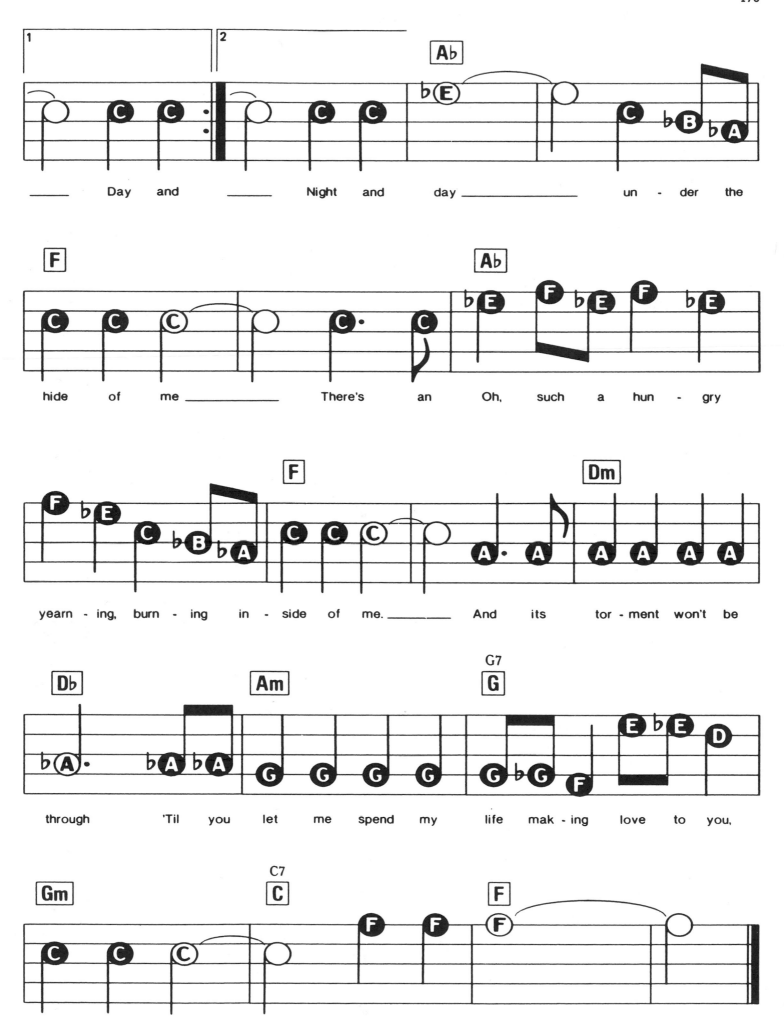

On the Sunny Side of the Street

Registration 7
Rhythm: Fox Trot or Swing

Lyric by Dorothy Fields
Music by Jimmy McHugh

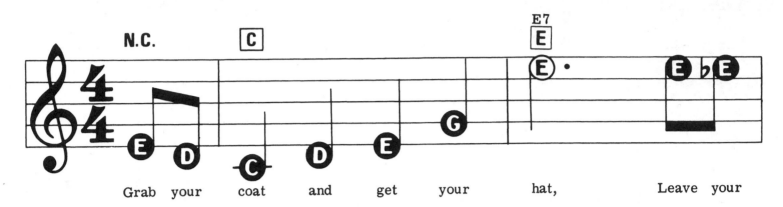

Grab your coat and get your hat, Leave your

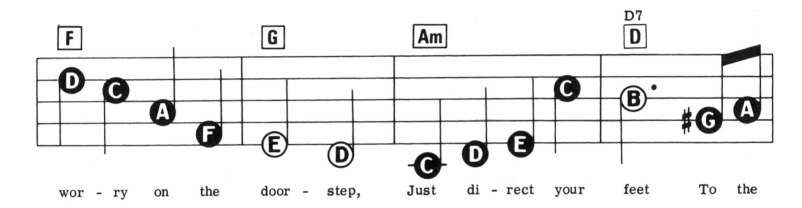

wor - ry on the door - step, Just di - rect your feet To the

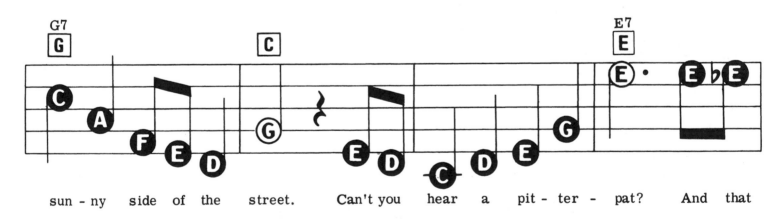

sun - ny side of the street. Can't you hear a pit - ter - pat? And that

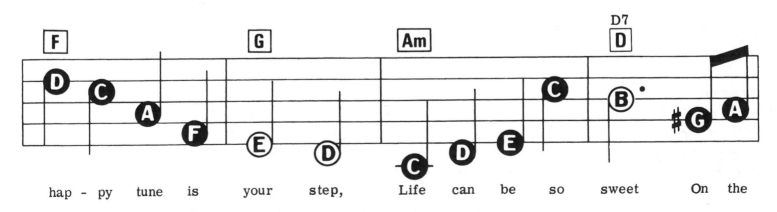

hap - py tune is your step, Life can be so sweet On the

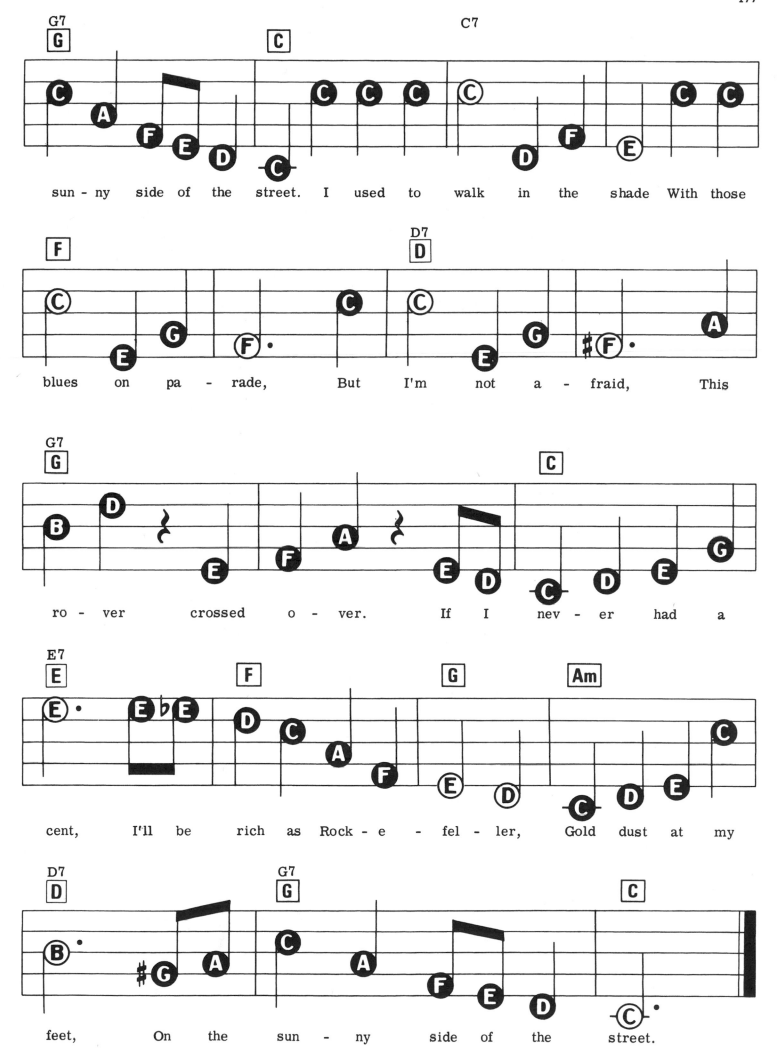

Once in a While

Registration 9
Rhythm: Fox Trot or Pops

Words by Bud Green
Music by Michael Edwards

Over the Rainbow
from THE WIZARD OF OZ

Registration 5
Rhythm: Fox Trot or Ballad

Music by Harold Arlen
Lyric by E.Y. "Yip" Harburg

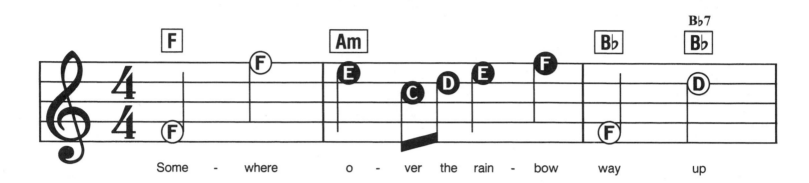

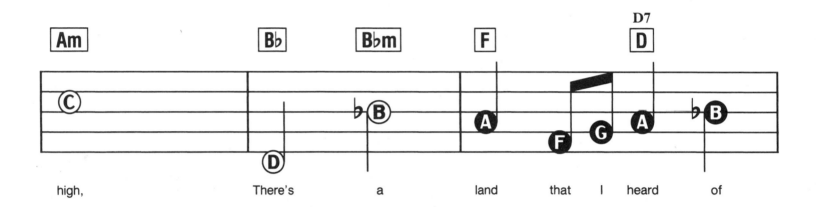

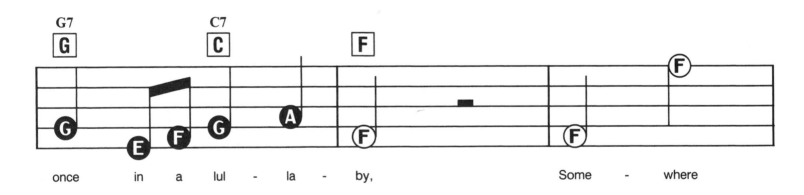

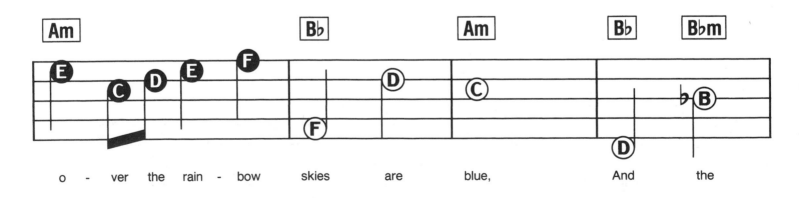

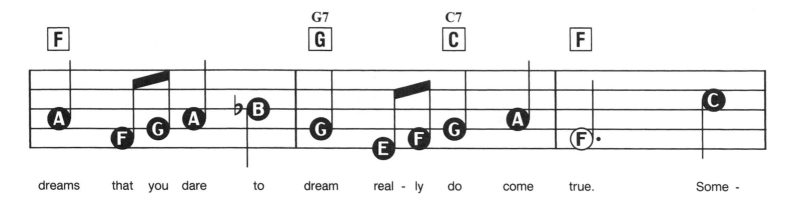

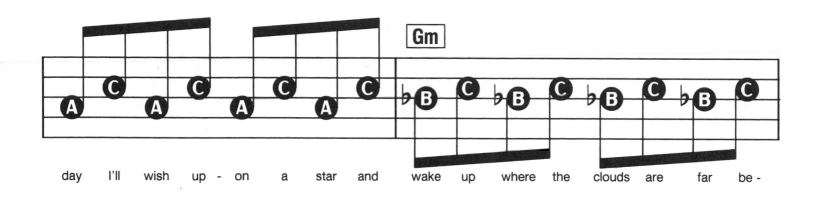

dreams that you dare to dream real - ly do come true. Some -

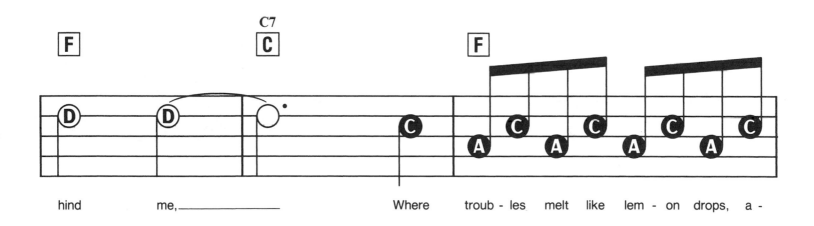

day I'll wish up - on a star and wake up where the clouds are far be -

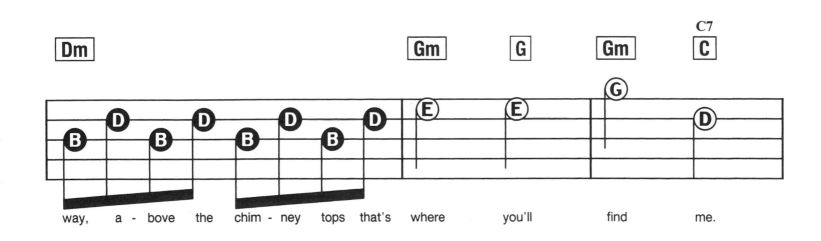

hind me,_____ Where troub - les melt like lem - on drops, a -

way, a - bove the chim - ney tops that's where you'll find me.

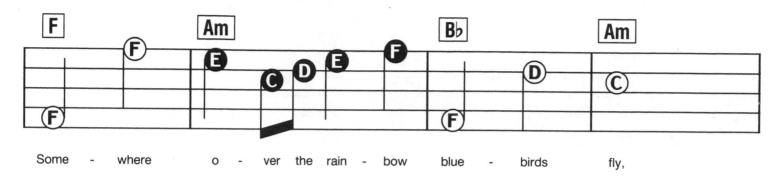

Some - where o - ver the rain - bow blue - birds fly,

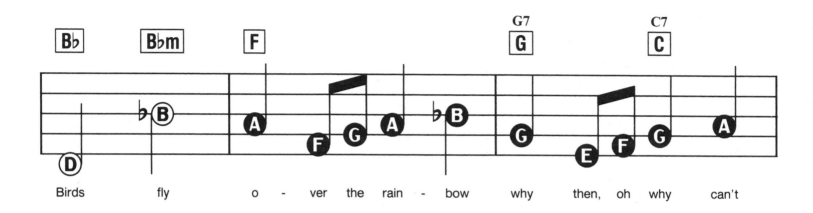

Birds fly o - ver the rain - bow why then, oh why can't

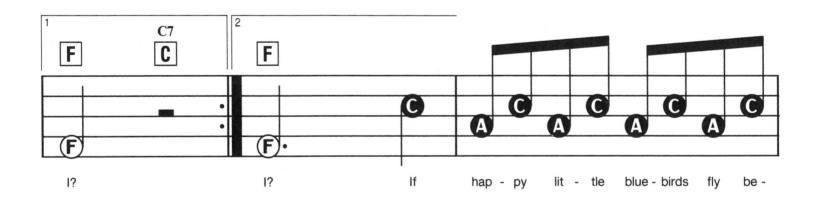

I? I? If hap - py lit - tle blue - birds fly be -

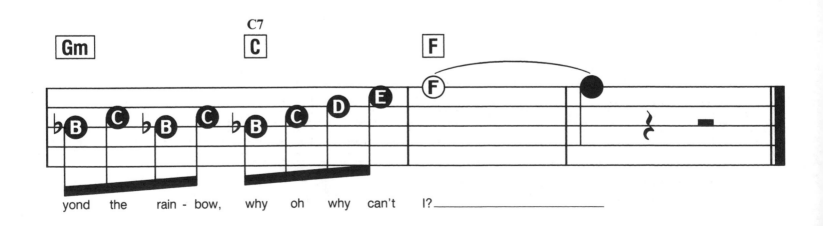

yond the rain - bow, why oh why can't I?

Solitude

Registration 7
Rhythm: Ballad

Words and Music by Duke Ellington,
Eddie De Lange and Irving Mills

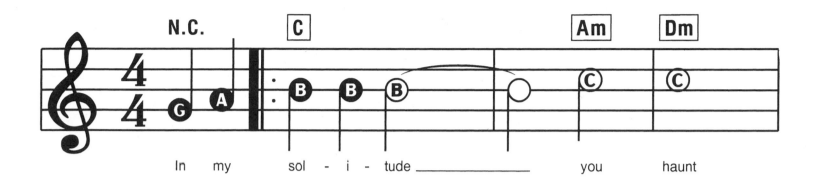

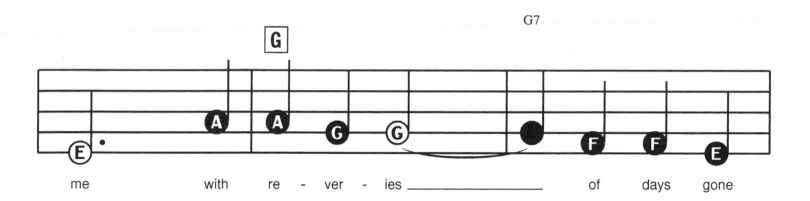

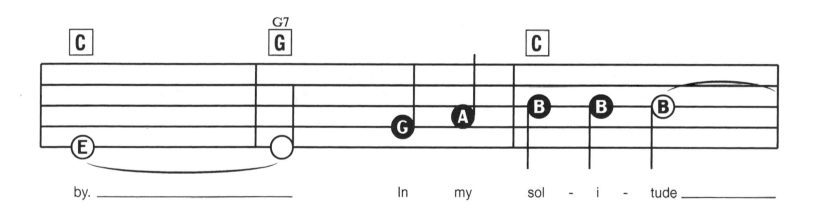

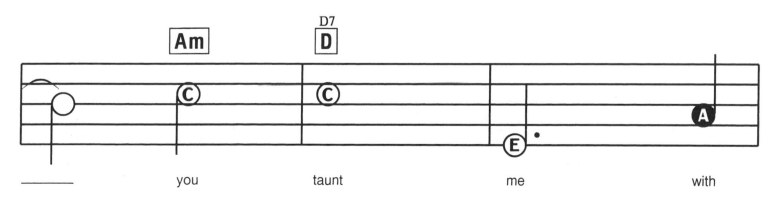

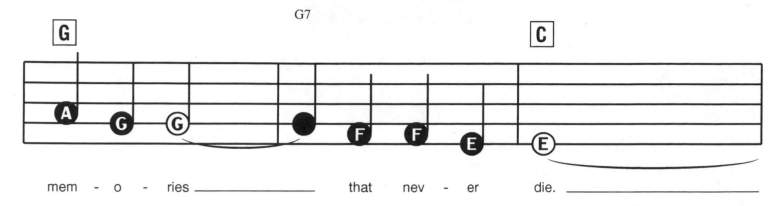

mem - o - ries _____ that nev - er die. _____

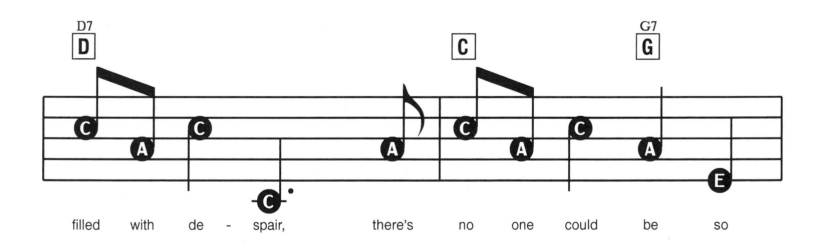

_____ I sit in my chair, I'm

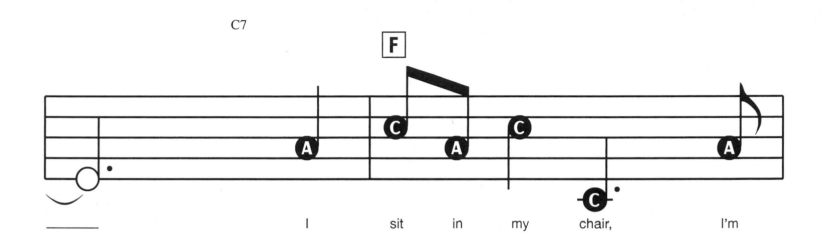

filled with de - spair, there's no one could be so

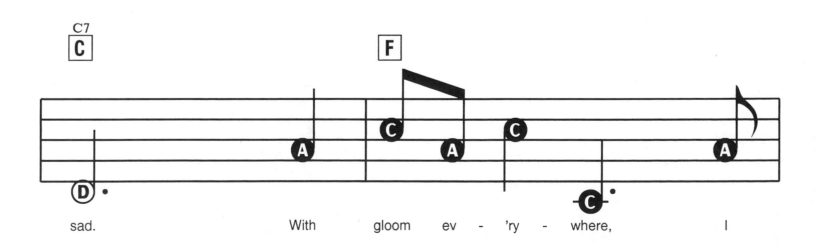

sad. With gloom ev - 'ry - where, I

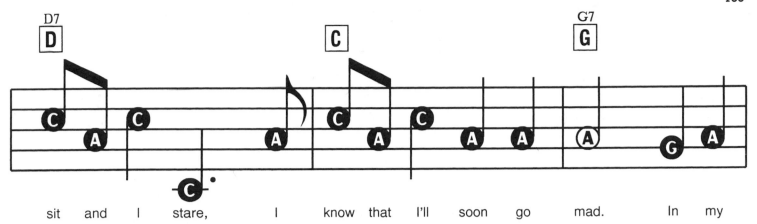

sit and I stare, I know that I'll soon go mad. In my

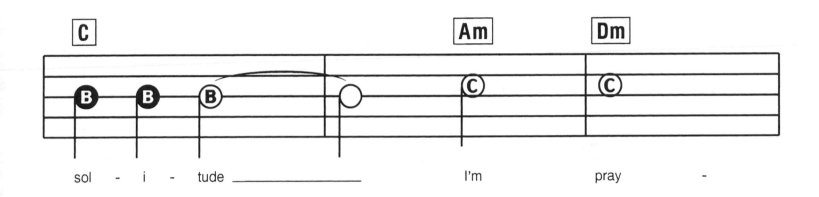

sol - i - tude _____ I'm pray -

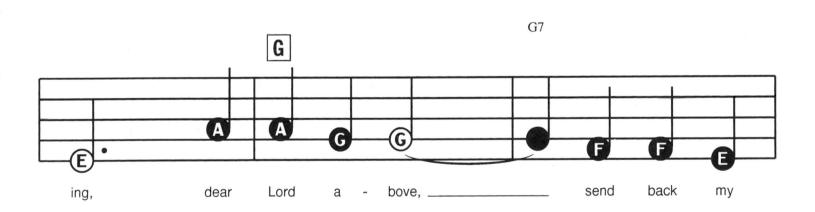

ing, dear Lord a - bove, _____ send back my

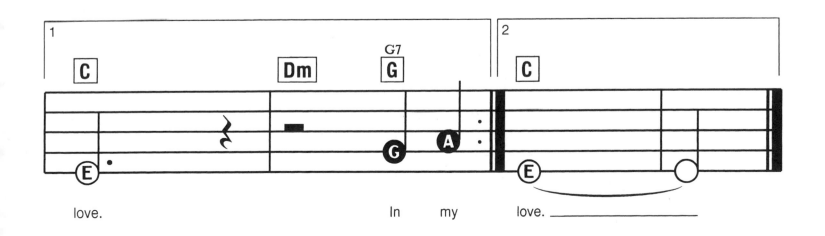

love. In my love. _____

Pennies from Heaven
from PENNIES FROM HEAVEN

Registration 2
Rhythm: Fox Trot or Swing

Words by John Burke
Music by Arthur Johnston

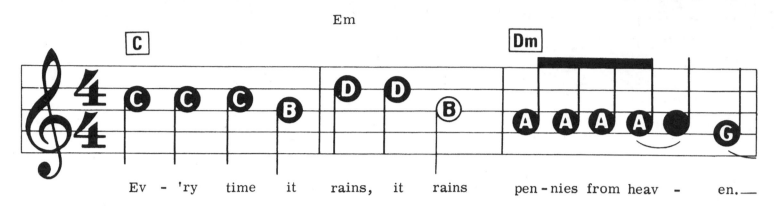

Ev - 'ry time it rains, it rains pen - nies from heav - en.—

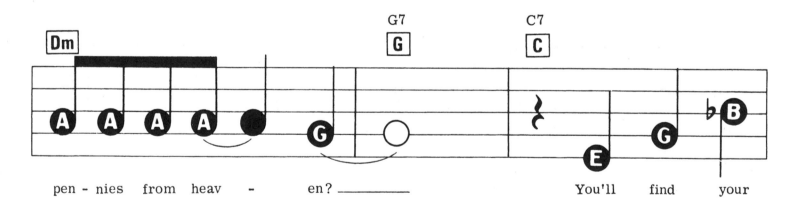

Don't you know each cloud con - tains

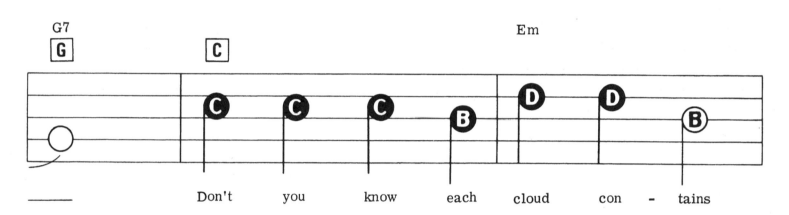

pen - nies from heav - en? ——— You'll find your

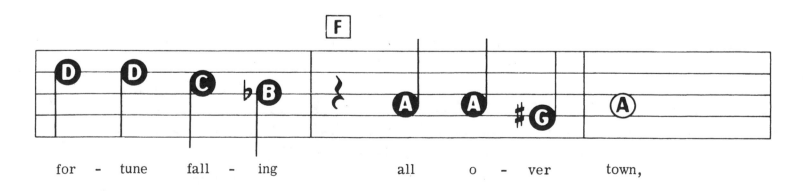

for - tune fall - ing all o - ver town,

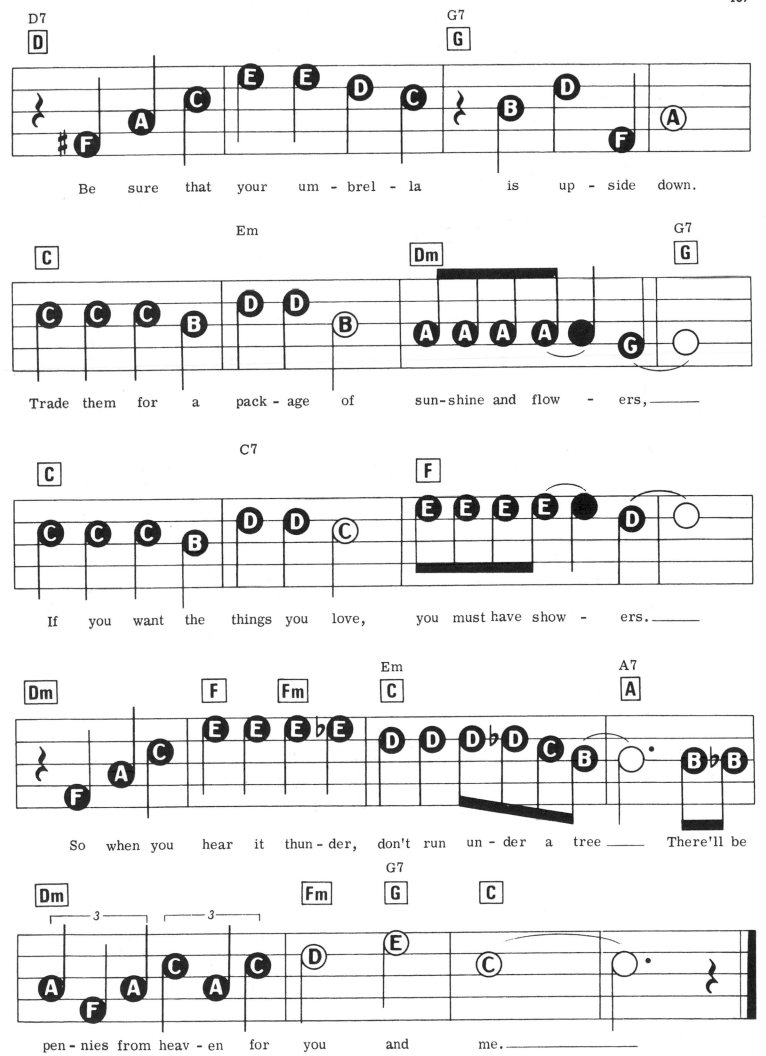

Pick Yourself Up
from SWING TIME

Registration 4
Rhythm: Fox Trot or Swing

Words by Dorothy Fields
Music by Jerome Kern

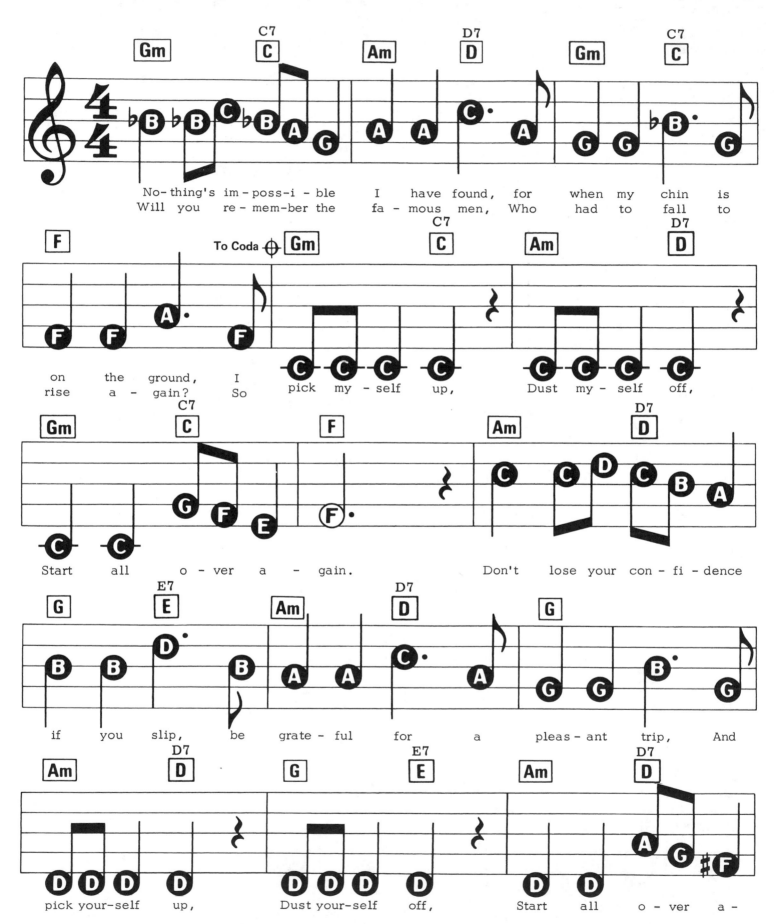

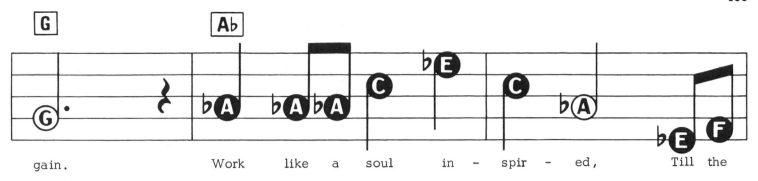

gain.   Work   like   a   soul   in - spir - ed,   Till   the

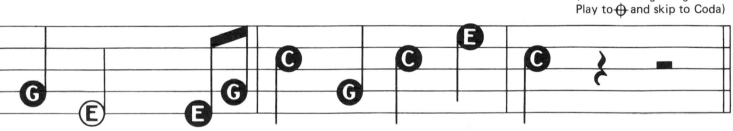

bat - tle   of   the   day   is   won.   You   may   be   sick   and

D.C. al Coda
(Return to beginning
Play to ⊕ and skip to Coda)

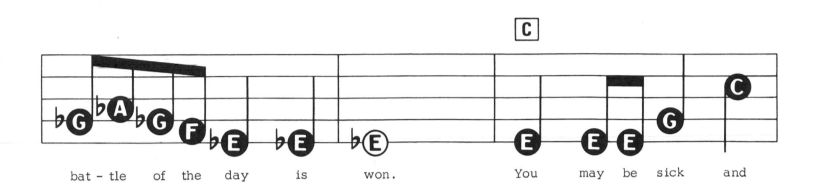

tir - ed,   But   you'll   be   a   man,   my   son!

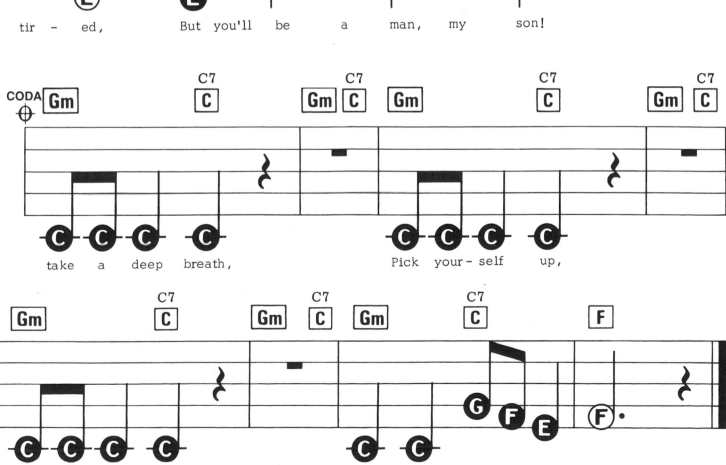

take   a   deep   breath,   Pick   your - self   up,

Dust   your - self   off,   Start   all   o - ver   a - gain.

September Song
from the Musical KNICKERBOCKER HOLIDAY

Registration 2
Rhythm: Fox Trot or Ballad

Words by Maxwell Anderson
Music by Kurt Weill

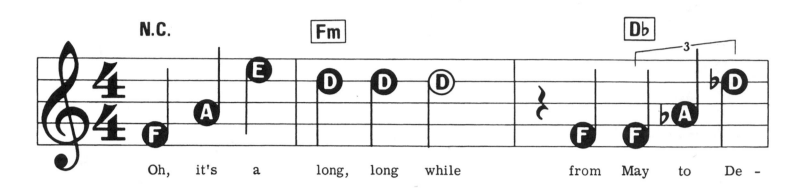

Oh, it's a long, long while from May to De -

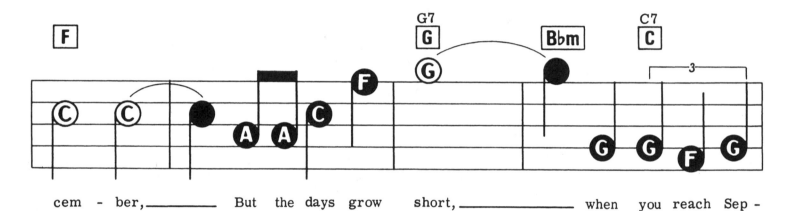

cem - ber,_____ But the days grow short,_____ when you reach Sep -

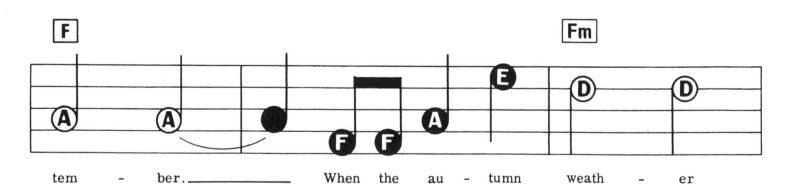

tem - ber._____ When the au - tumn weath - er

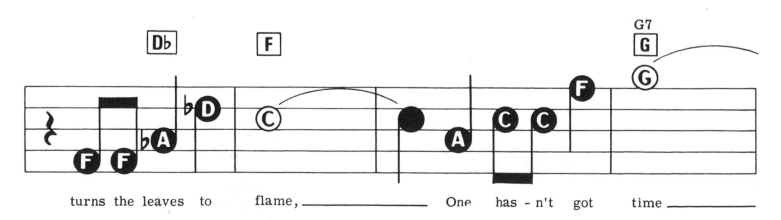

turns the leaves to flame,_____ One has - n't got time _____

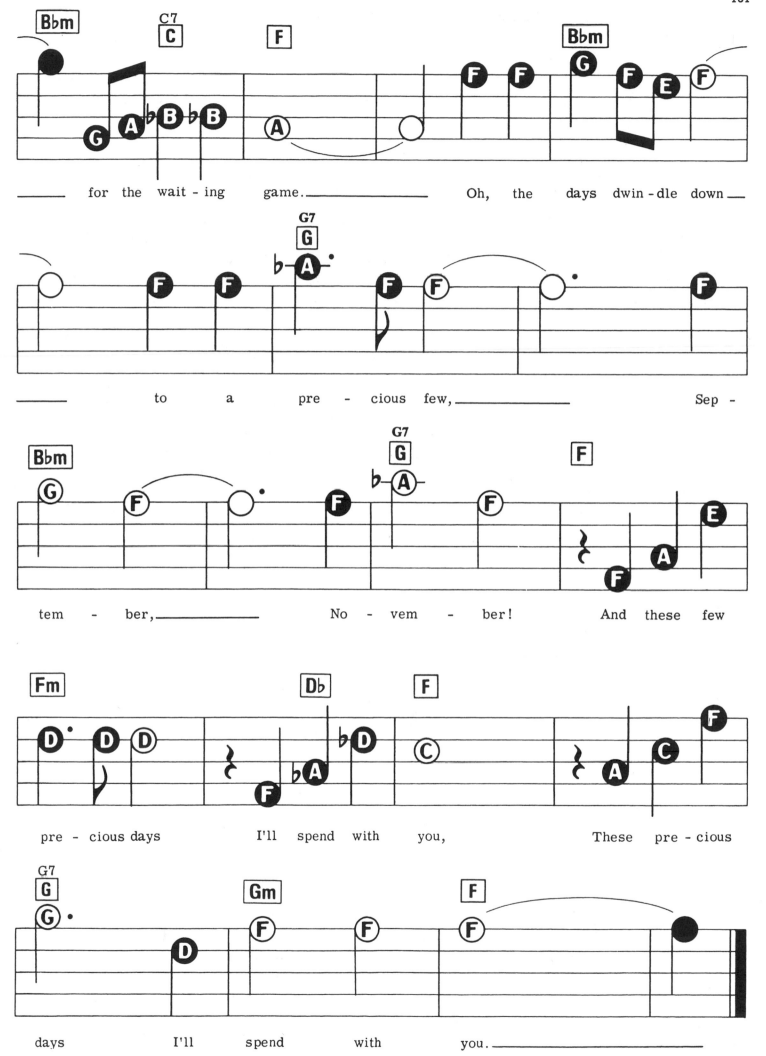

for the wait - ing game.＿＿＿ Oh, the days dwin - dle down ＿

＿ to a pre - cious few,＿＿＿ Sep -

tem - ber,＿＿＿ No - vem - ber! And these few

pre - cious days I'll spend with you, These pre - cious

days I'll spend with you.＿＿＿

Sing, Sing, Sing

Registration 4
Rhythm: Swing

Words and Music by
Louis Prima

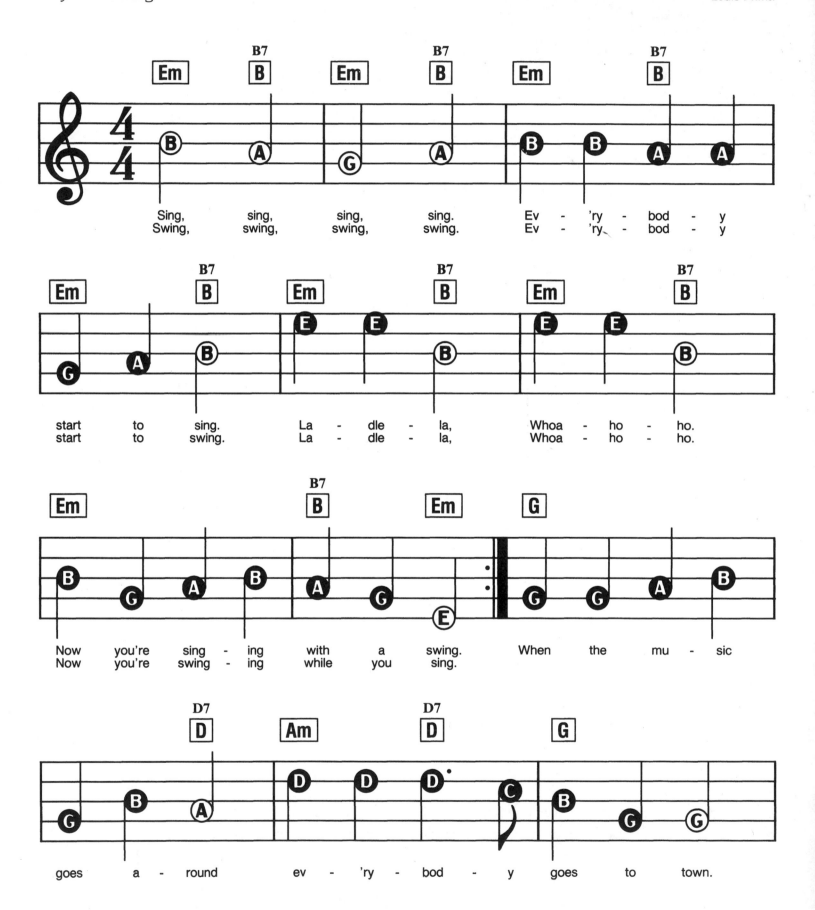

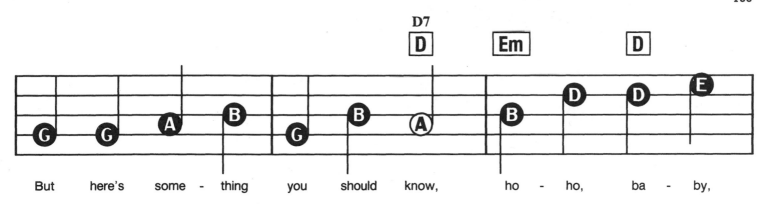

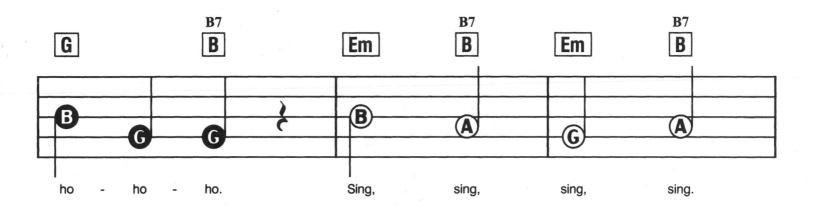

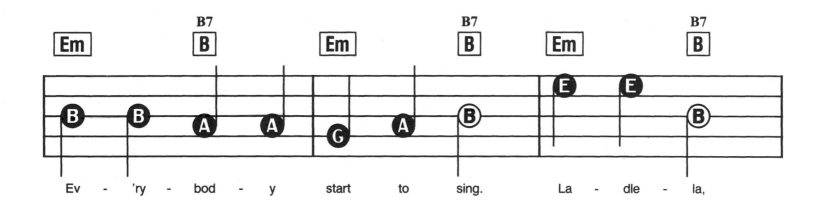

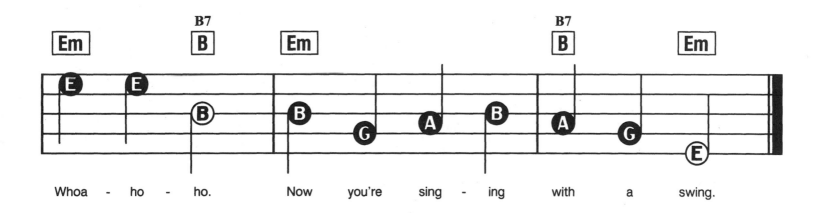

Smoke Gets in Your Eyes
from ROBERTA

Registration 10
Rhythm: Ballad or Swing

Words by Otto Harbach
Music by Jerome Kern

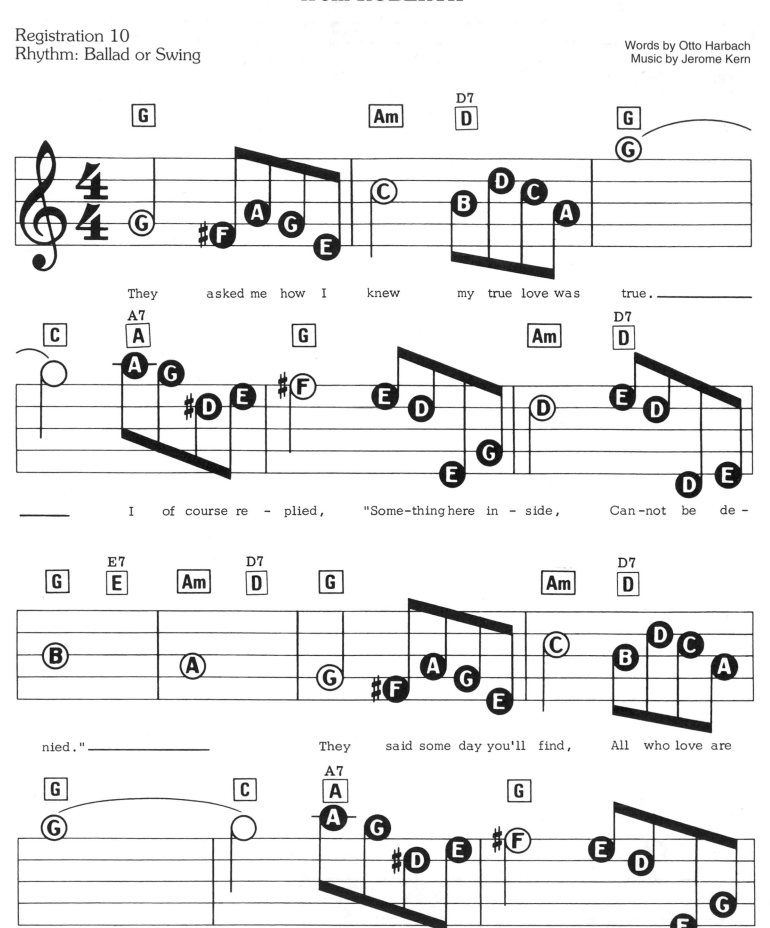

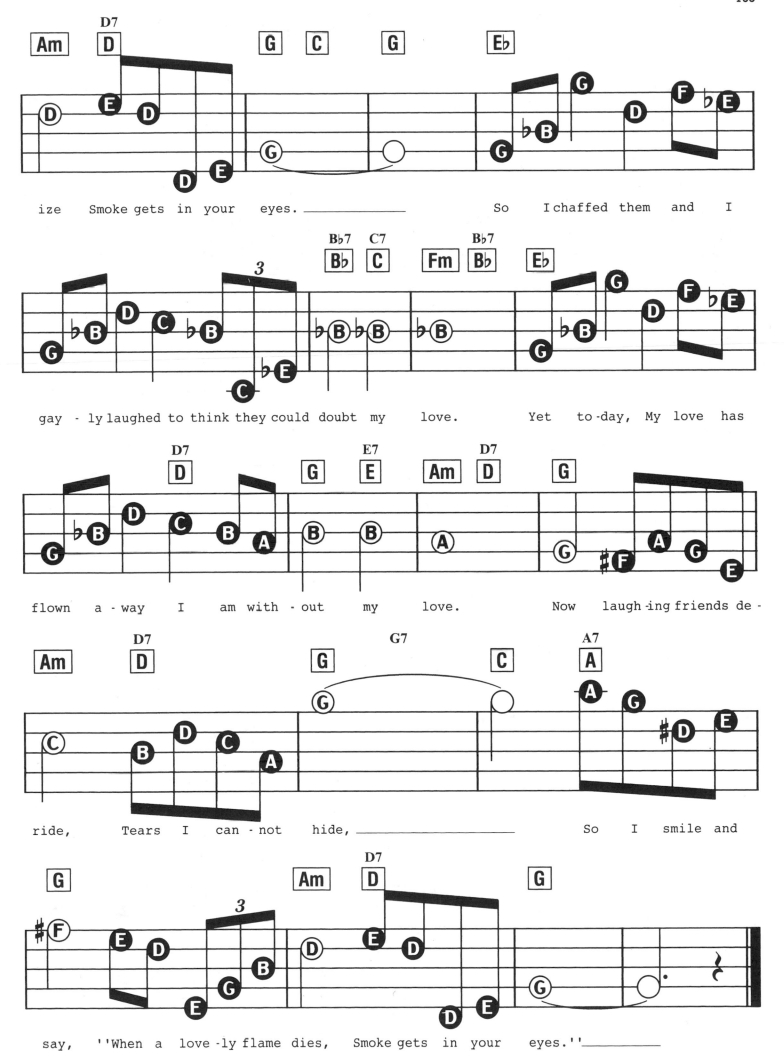

ize   Smoke gets in your   eyes. _____   So   I chaffed them   and   I

gay - ly laughed to think they could doubt my   love.   Yet   to-day, My love has

flown a - way   I   am with - out   my   love.   Now   laugh-ing friends de -

ride,   Tears   I   can-not   hide, _____   So   I   smile and

say,   ''When a love-ly flame dies,   Smoke gets in your   eyes.''_____

Stars Fell on Alabama

Registration 1
Rhythm: Swing or Ballad

Words by Mitchell Parish
Music by Frank Perkins

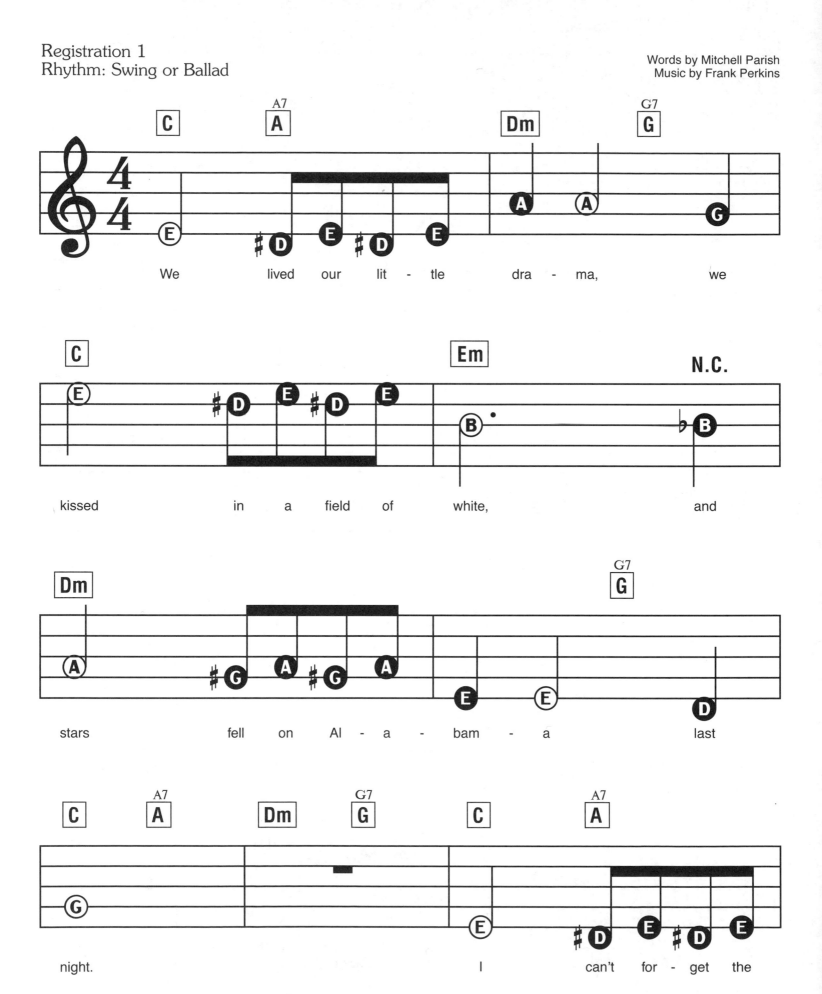

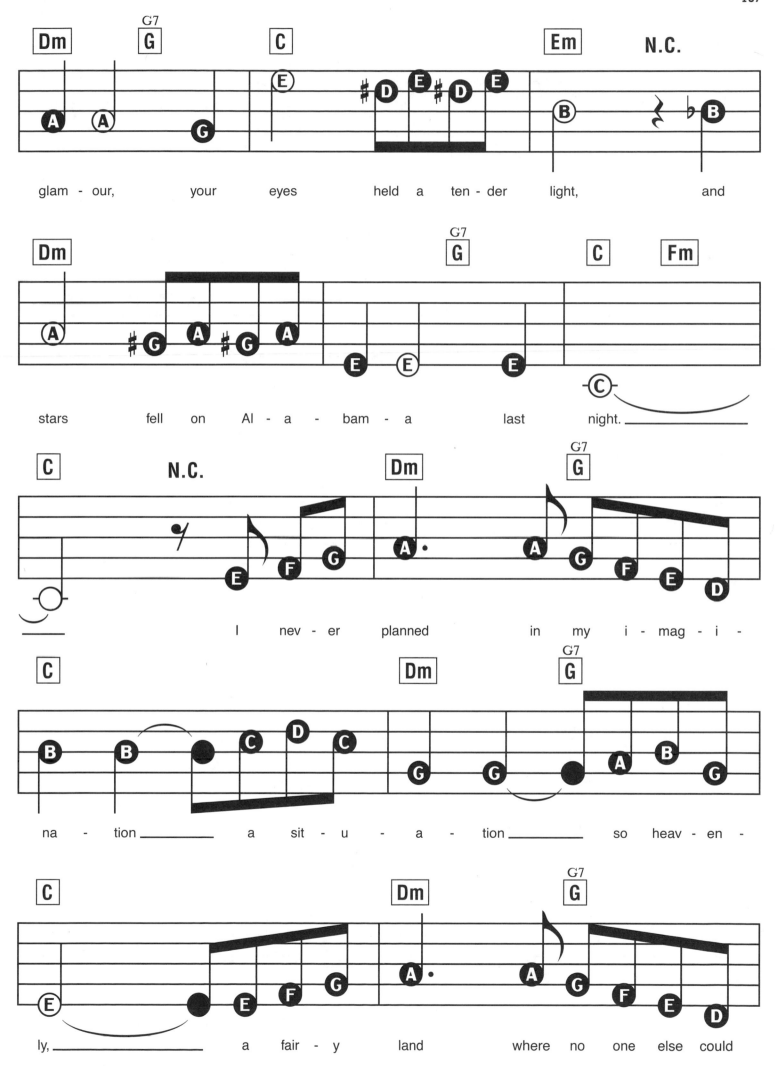

198

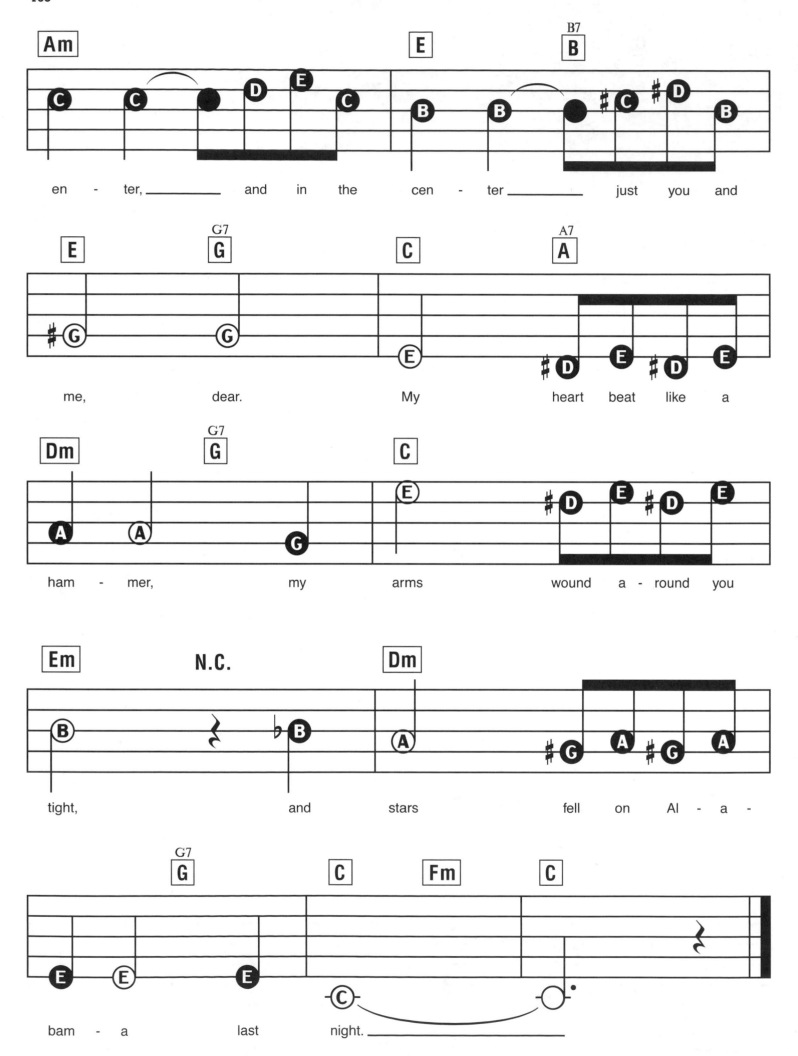

Thanks for the Memory
from the Paramount Picture BIG BROADCAST OF 1938

Registration 3
Rhythm: Swing or Ballad

Words and Music by Leo Robin
and Ralph Rainger

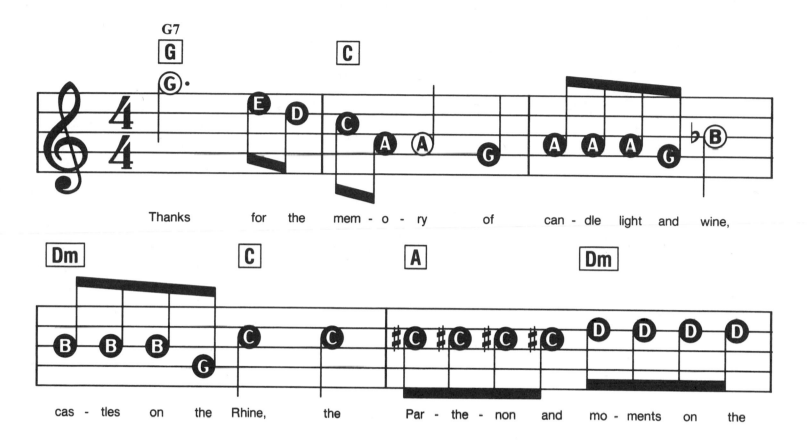

Thanks for the mem-o-ry of can-dle light and wine,

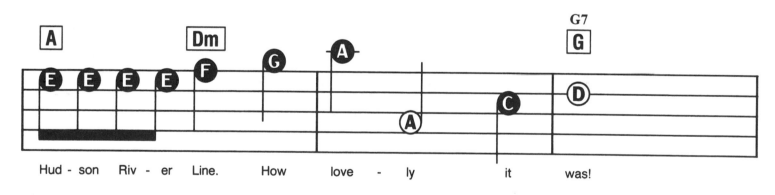

cas-tles on the Rhine, the Par-the-non and mo-ments on the

Hud-son Riv-er Line. How love-ly it was!

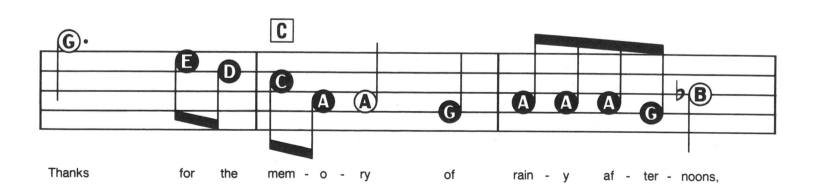

Thanks for the mem-o-ry of rain-y af-ter-noons,

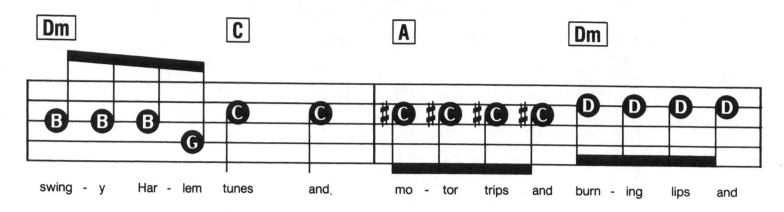

swing - y Har - lem tunes and, mo - tor trips and burn - ing lips and

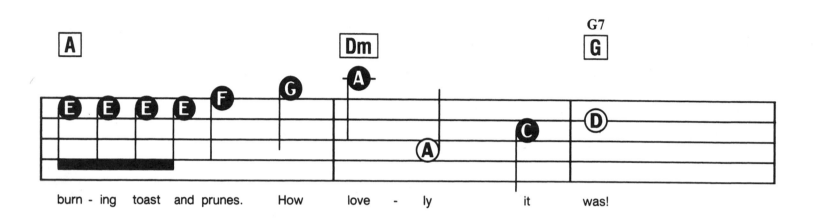

burn - ing toast and prunes. How love - ly it was!

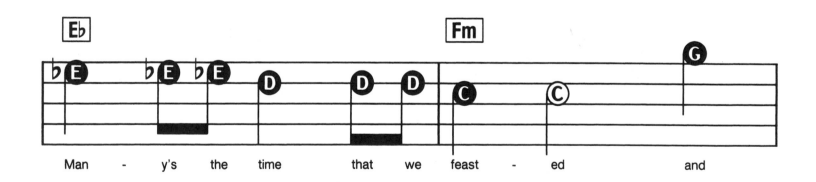

Man - y's the time that we feast - ed and

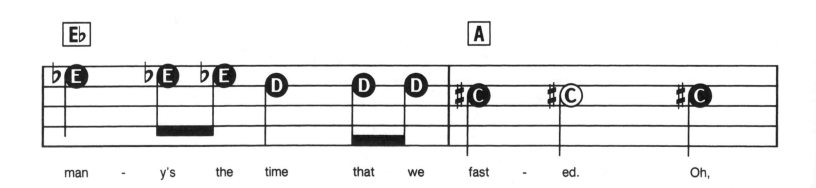

man - y's the time that we fast - ed. Oh,

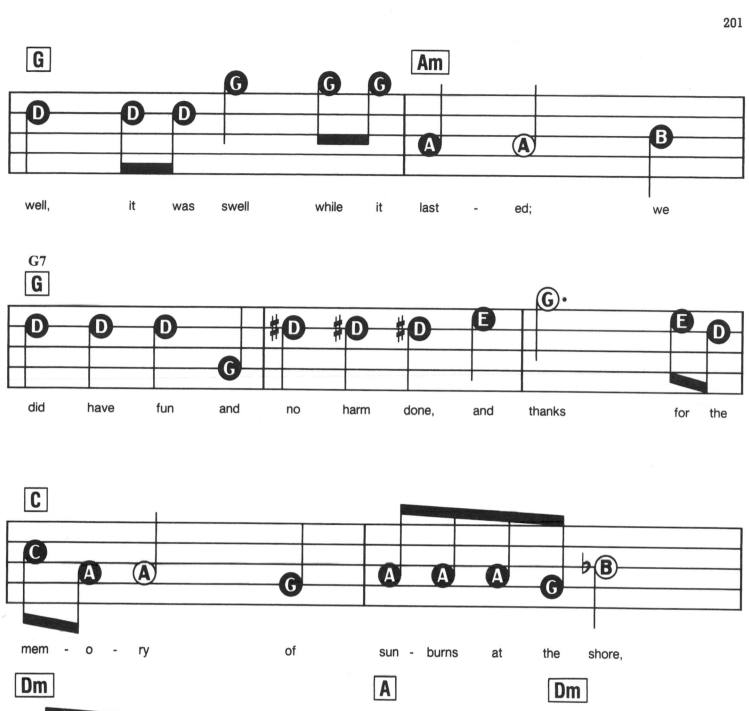

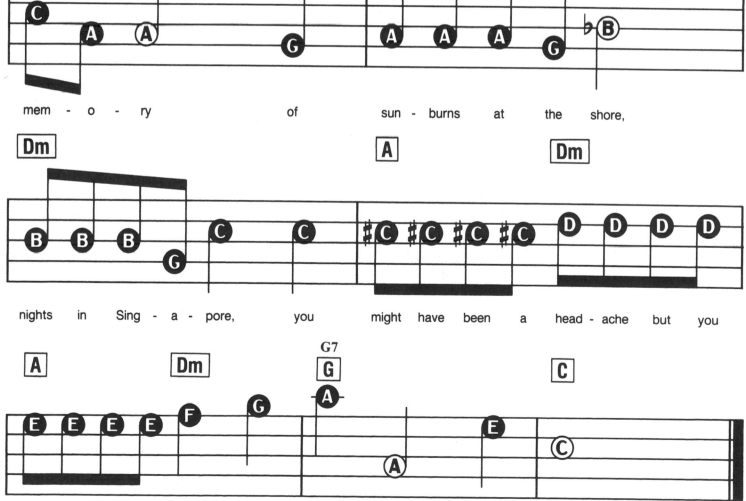

Stompin' at the Savoy

Registration 2
Rhythm: Swing

Words by Andy Razaf
Music by Benny Goodman, Edgar Sampson
and Chick Webb

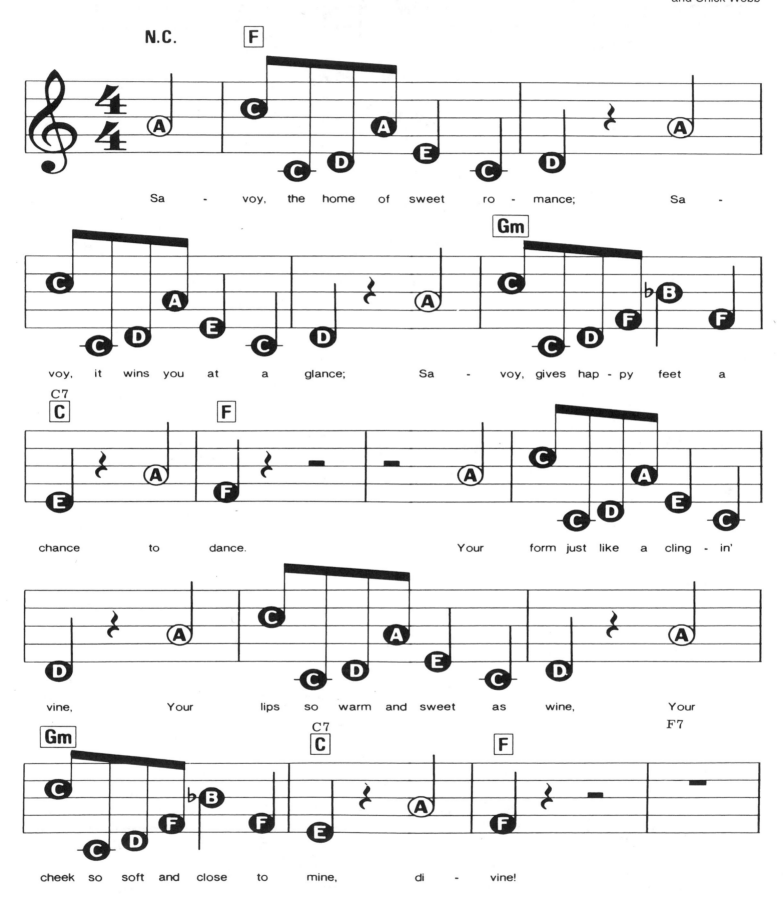

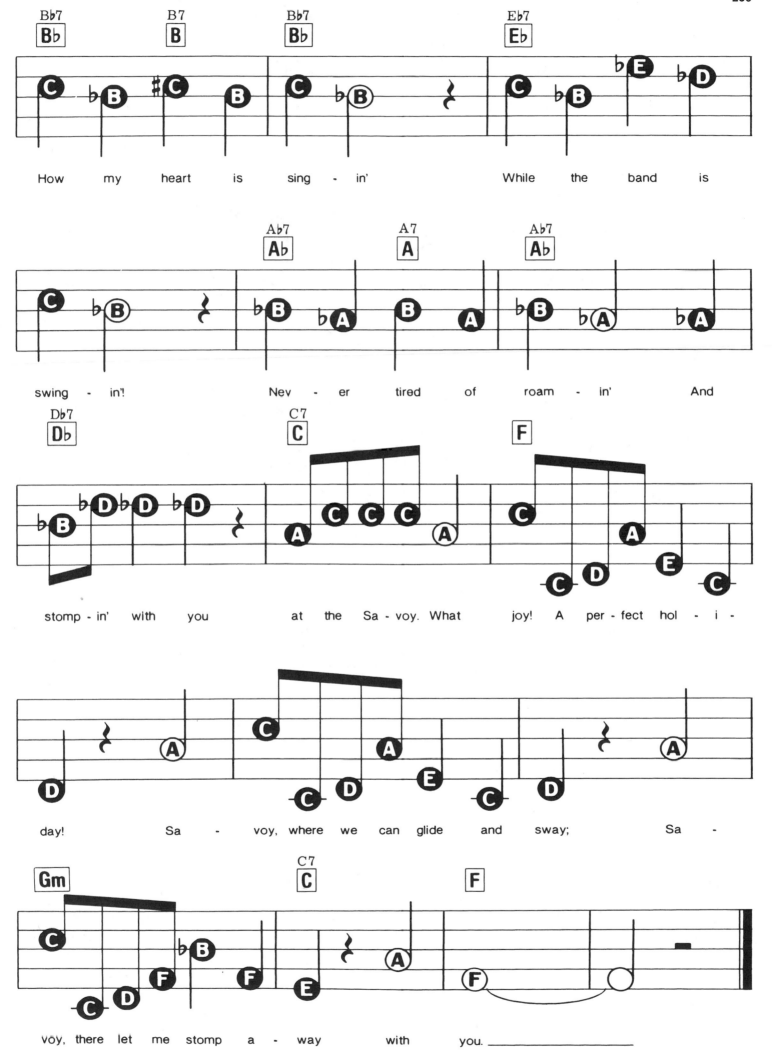

Stormy Weather
(Keeps Rainin' All the Time)
from COTTON CLUB PARADE OF 1933

Registration 2
Rhythm: Ballad

Lyric by Ted Koehler
Music by Harold Arlen

Don't know why, there's no sun up in the sky, storm-y
bare, gloom and mis-'ry ev-'ry-where, storm-y

weath - er, Since my man and I ain't to - geth - er,
weath - er, Just can't get my poor self to - geth - er,

keeps rain - in' all the time.____ Life is
I'm wea - ry all the

time,_____ the time,_____ So wea - ry all the time.____

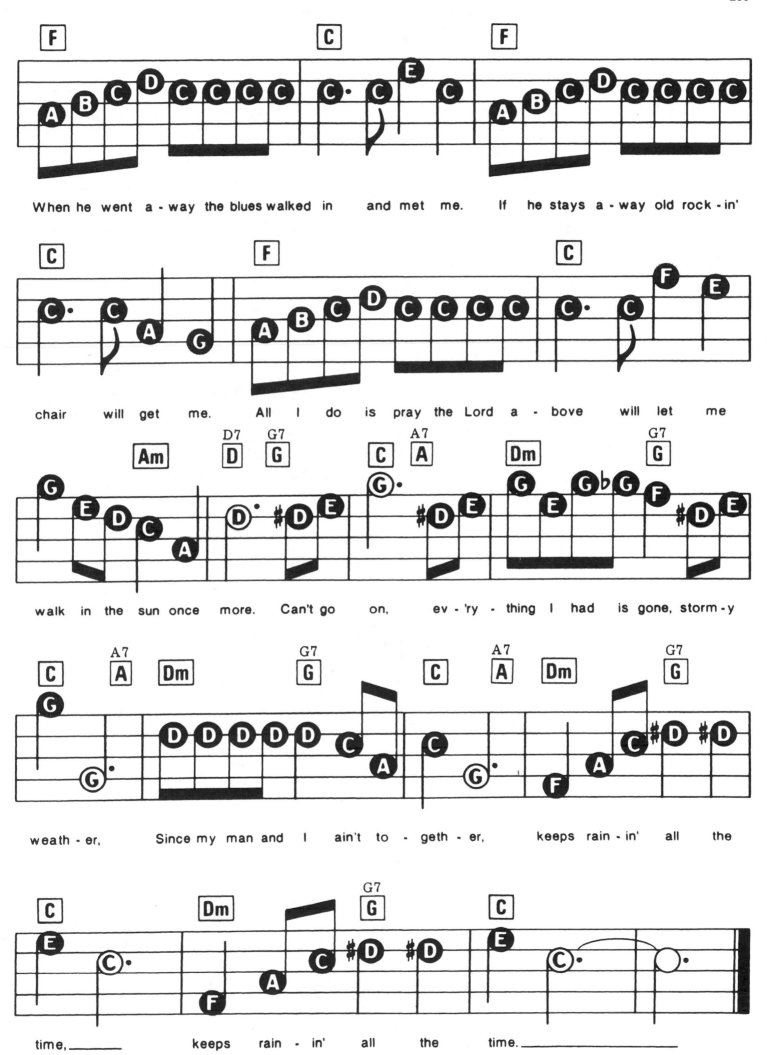

Summertime
from PORGY AND BESS®

Registration 10
Rhythm: Ballad or Blues

Music and Lyrics by George Gershwin,
DuBose and Dorothy Heyward
and Ira Gershwin

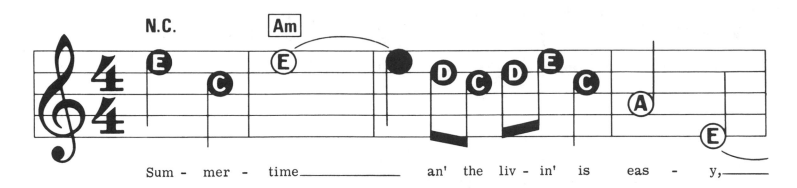

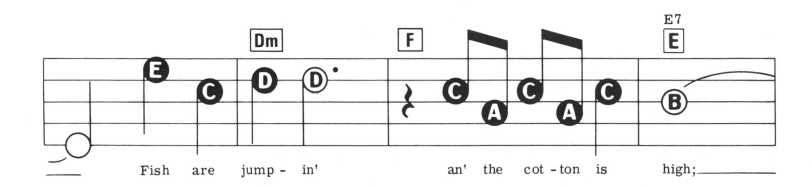

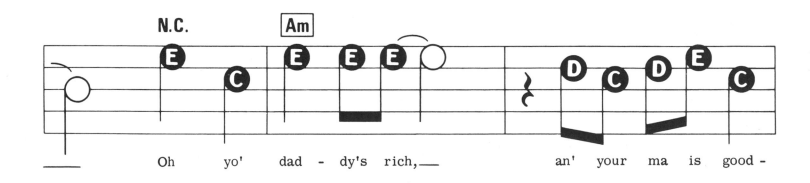

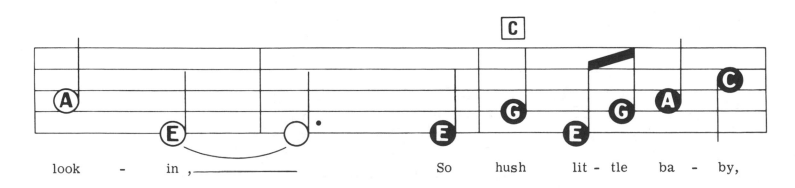

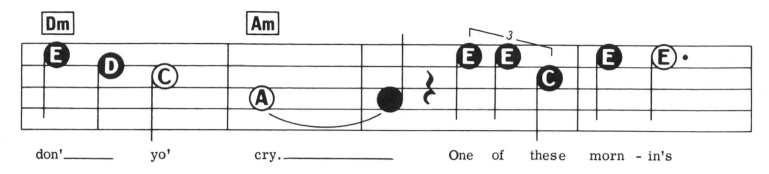

don'_____ yo' cry._____ One of these morn - in's

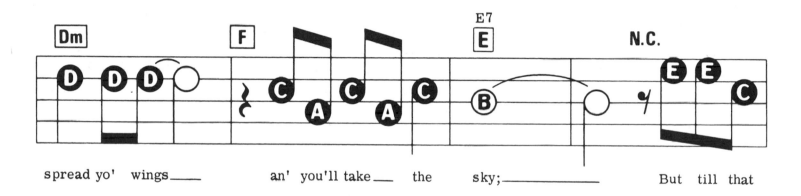

you goin' to rise____ up sing - in',_____ Then you'll

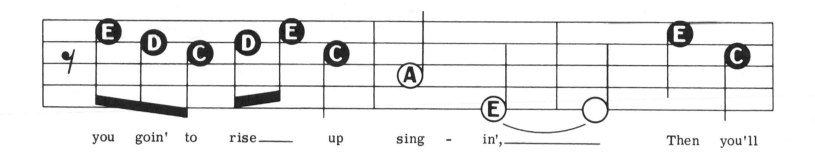

spread yo' wings____ an' you'll take____ the sky;_____ But till that

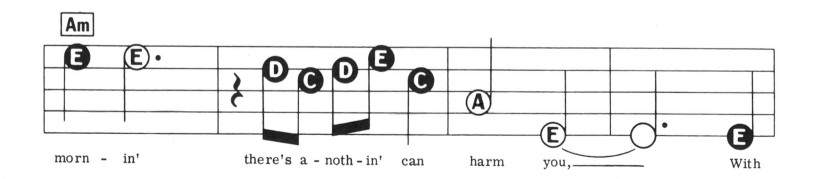

morn - in' there's a - noth - in' can harm you,_____ With

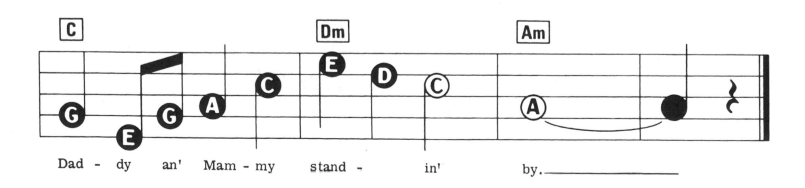

Dad - dy an' Mam - my stand - in' by._____

Ten Cents a Dance
from SIMPLE SIMON

Registration 1
Rhythm: Swing or Fox Trot

Music by Jerome Kern
Words by P.G. Wodehouse and Oscar Hammerstein II

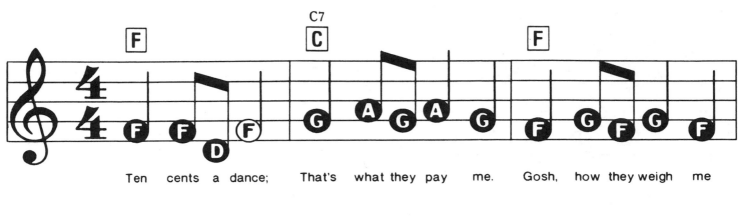

Ten cents a dance; That's what they pay me. Gosh, how they weigh me down!

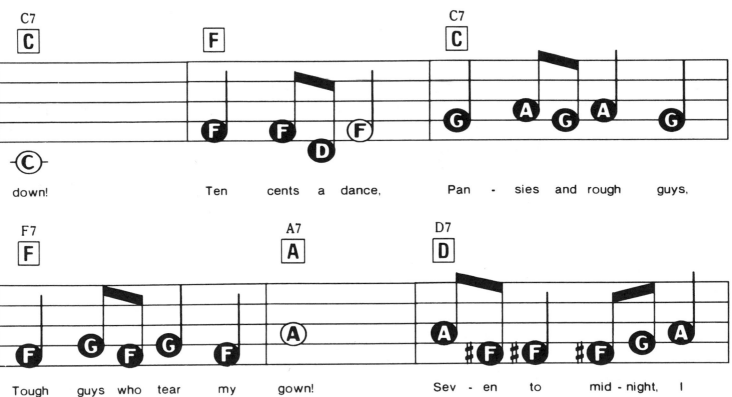

Ten cents a dance, Pan - sies and rough guys, Tough guys who tear my gown! Sev - en to mid - night, I

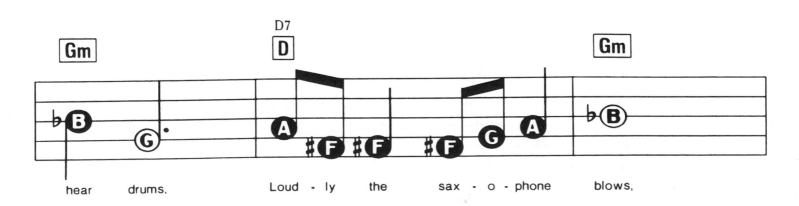

hear drums. Loud - ly the sax - o - phone blows,

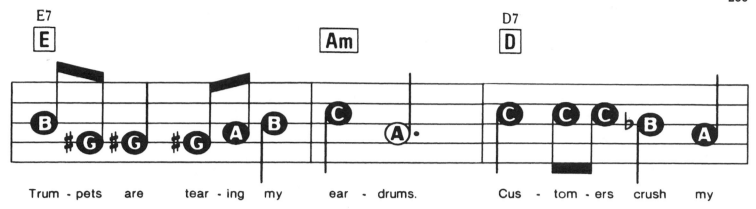

Trum - pets are tear - ing my ear - drums. Cus - tom - ers crush my

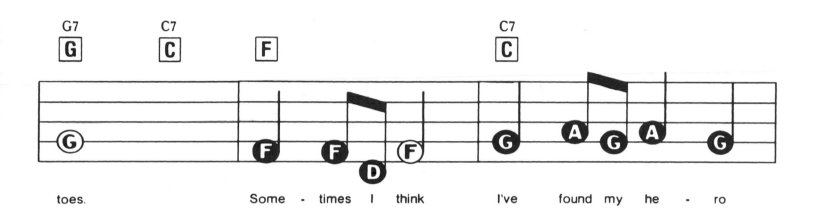

toes. Some - times I think I've found my he - ro

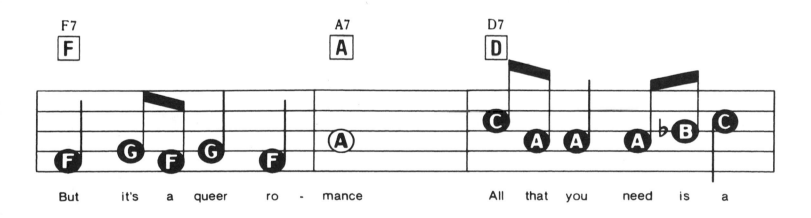

But it's a queer ro - mance All that you need is a

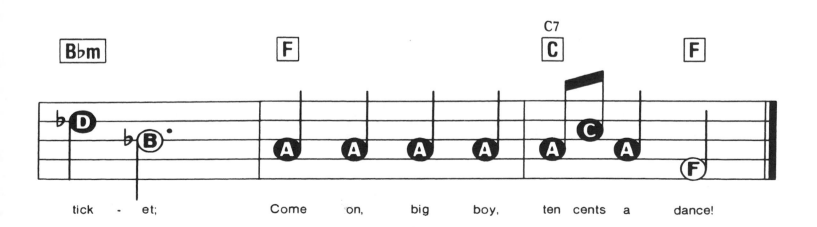

tick - et; Come on, big boy, ten cents a dance!

There Is No Greater Love

Registration 2
Rhythm: Swing

Words by Marty Symes
Music by Isham Jones

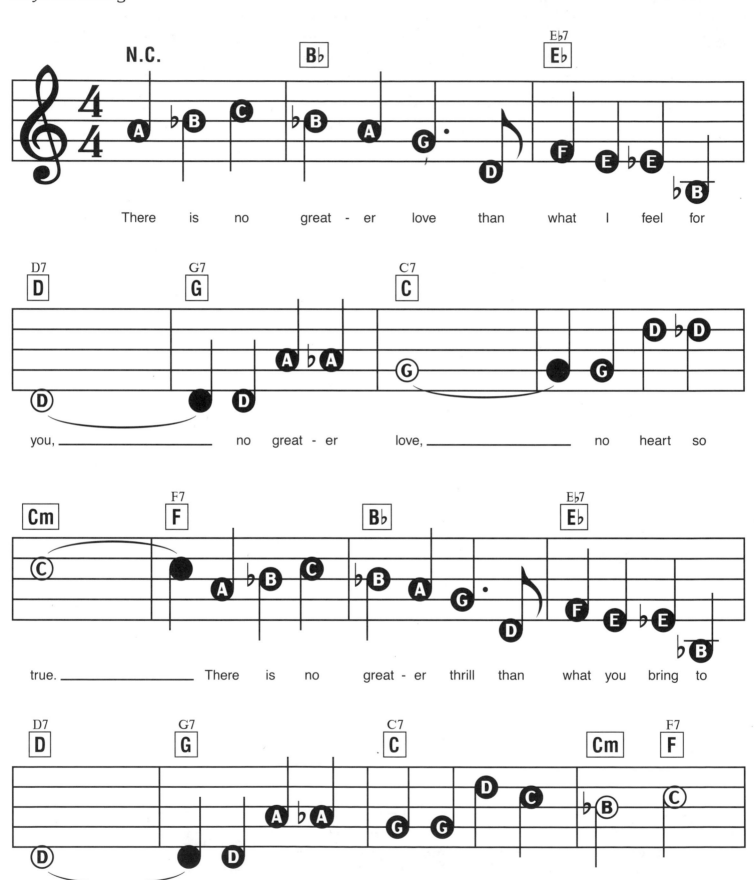

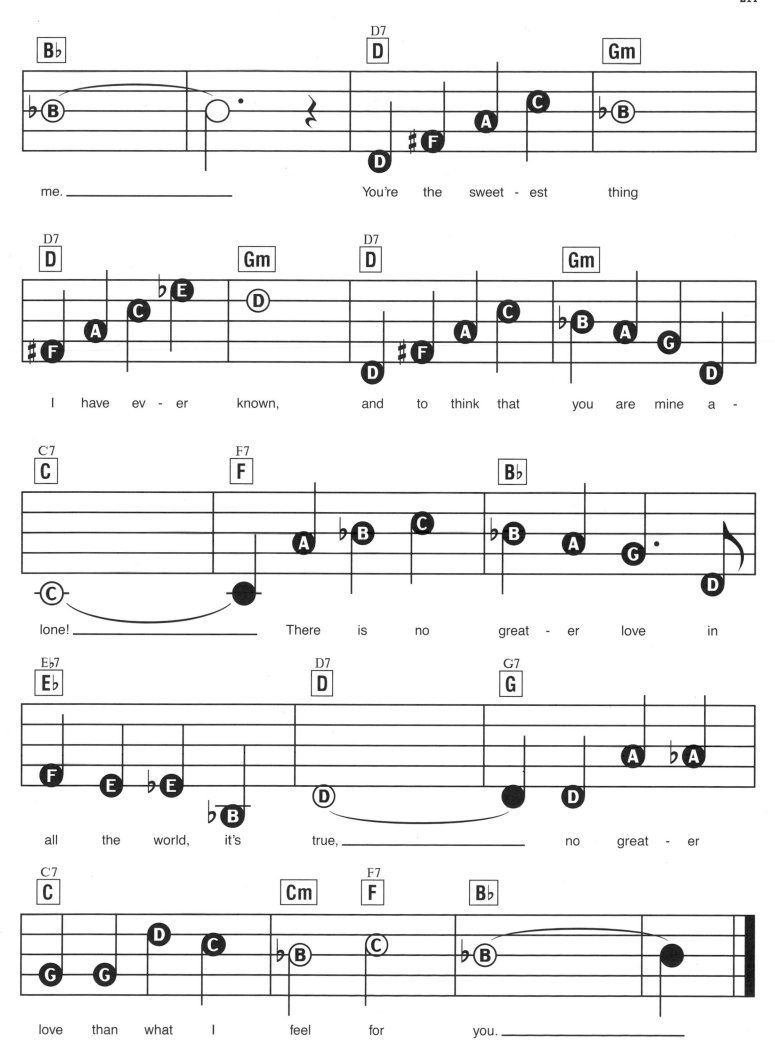

These Foolish Things
(Remind Me of You)

Registration 9
Rhythm: Fox Trot or Swing

Words by Holt Marvell
Music by Jack Strachey

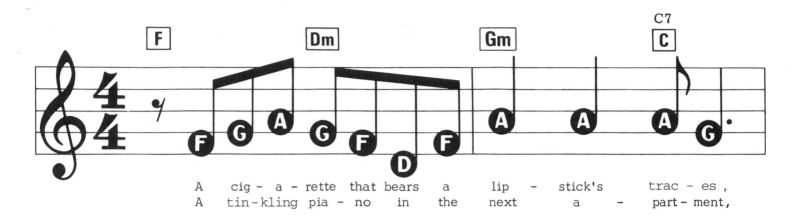

A cig-a-rette that bears a lip-stick's trac-es,
A tin-kling pia-no in the next a-part-ment,

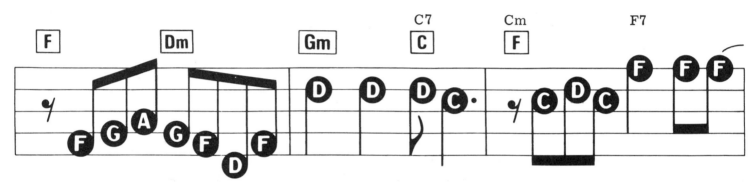

An air-line tick-et to ro-man-tic plac-es,
Those stum-bling words that told you what my heart meant,
And still my heart has wings._
A fair-ground's paint-ed swings,_

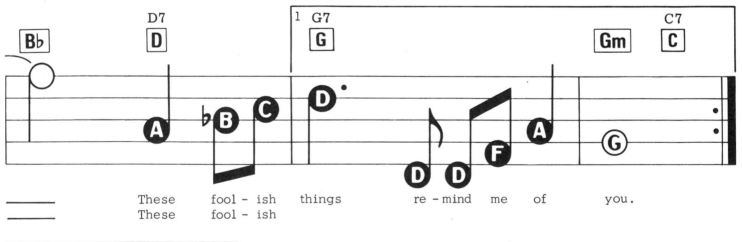

These fool-ish things re-mind me of you.
These fool-ish

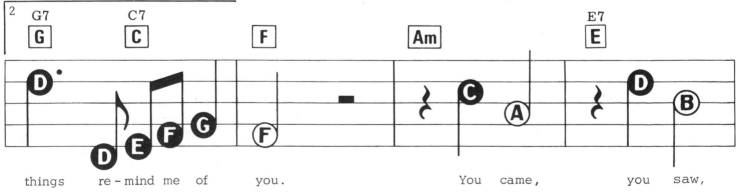

things re-mind me of you.
You came, you saw,

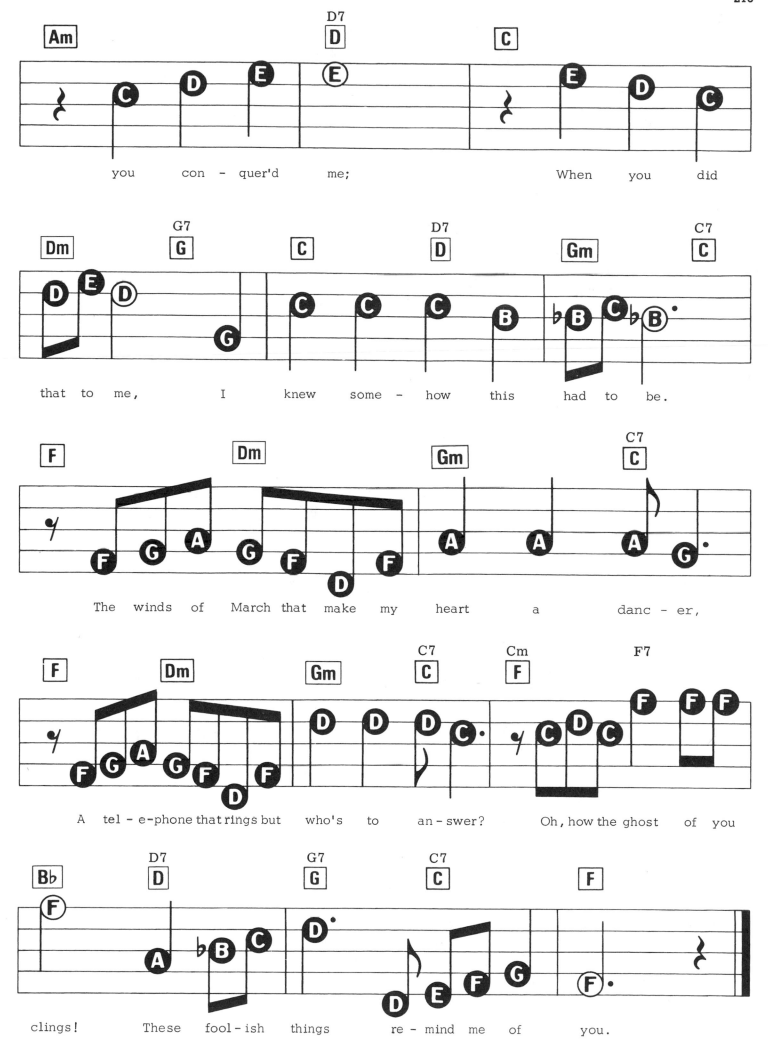

They Can't Take That Away from Me
from SHALL WE DANCE

Registration 1
Rhythm: Ballad or Fox Trot

Music and Lyrics by George Gershwin
and Ira Gershwin

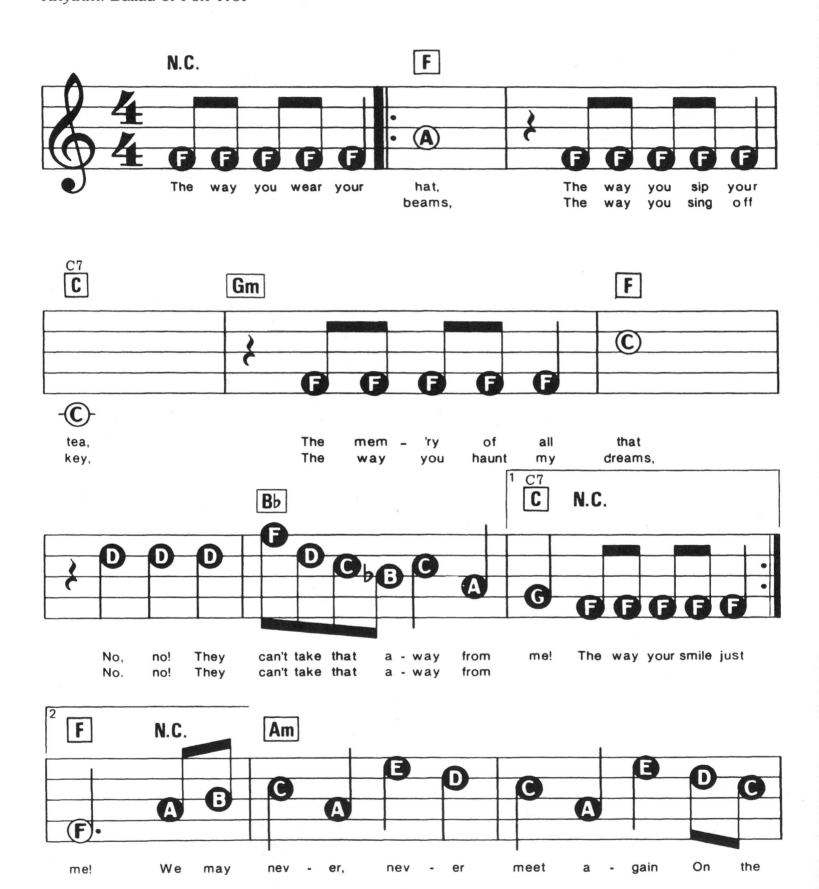

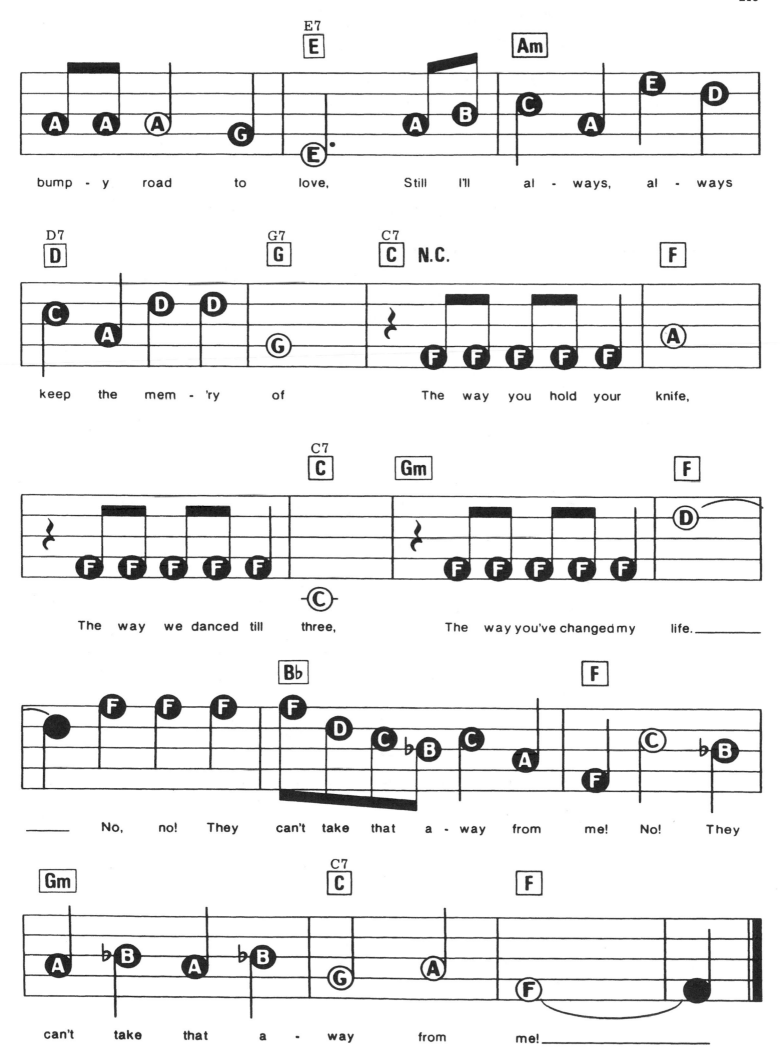

This Can't Be Love
from THE BOYS FROM SYRACUSE

Registration 1
Rhythm: Swing or Jazz

Words by Lorenz Hart
Music by Richard Rodgers

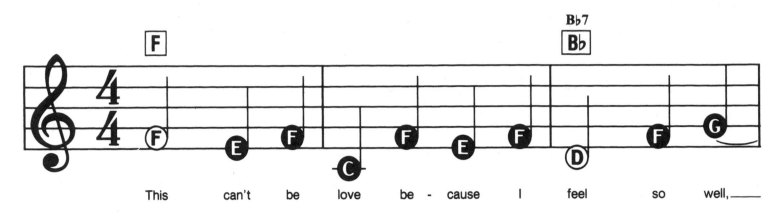

This can't be love be-cause I feel so well,___

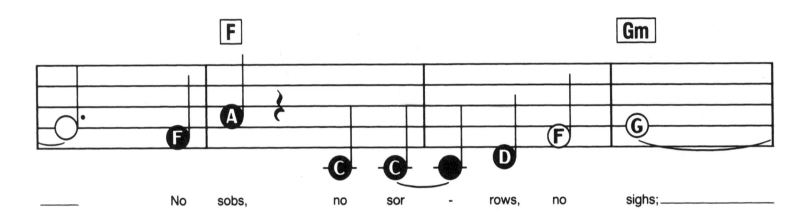

___ No sobs, no sor - rows, no sighs;___

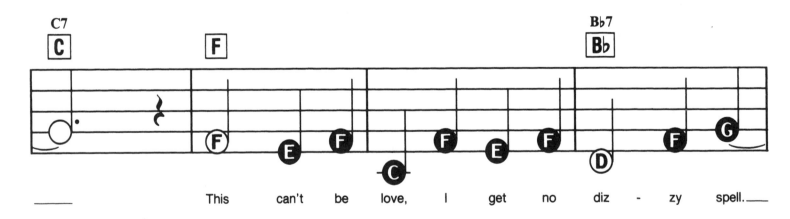

___ This can't be love, I get no diz-zy spell.___

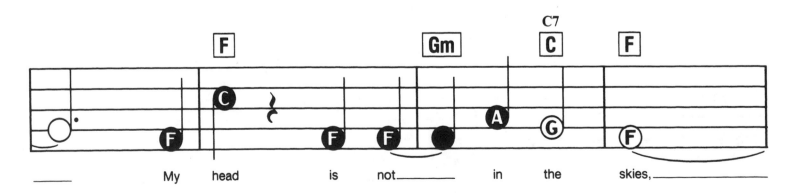

___ My head is not___ in the skies,___

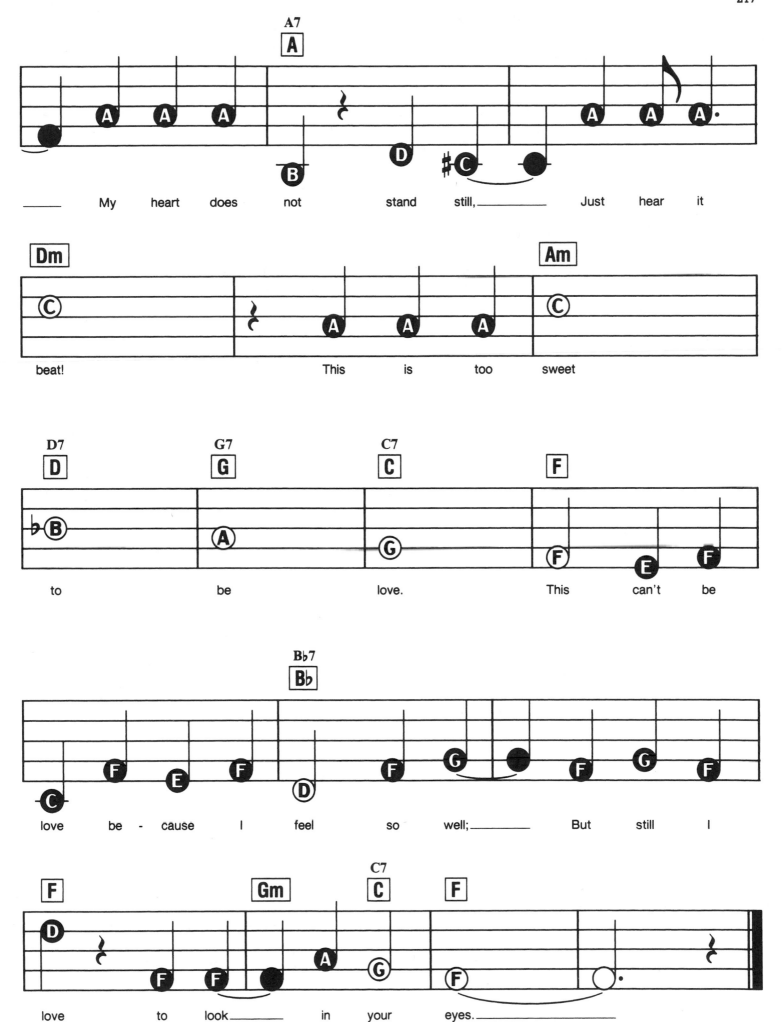

Three Little Words
from the Motion Picture CHECK AND DOUBLE CHECK

Registration 8
Rhythm: Fox Trot or Ballad

Lyric by Bert Kalmar
Music by Harry Ruby

Three lit - tle words, _____ Oh, what I'd

give for that won - der - ful phrase. _____ To

hear those three lit - tle words _____ That's all I'd

live for the rest of my days, _____ And

219

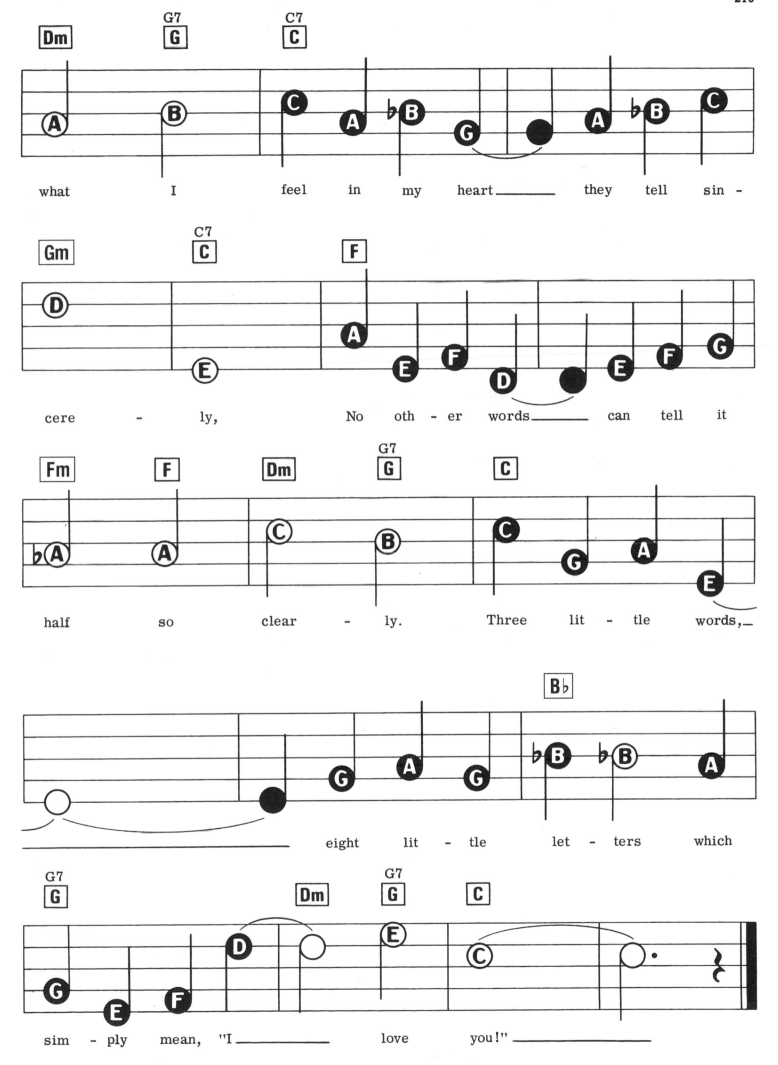

The Very Thought of You

Registration 8
Rhythm: Ballad or Fox Trot

Words and Music by
Ray Noble

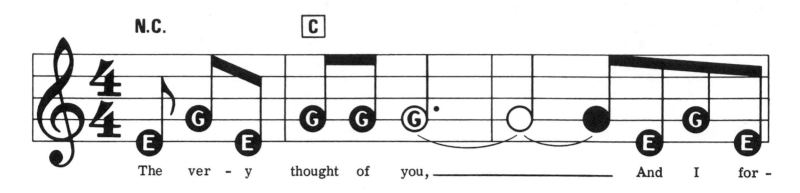

The ver-y thought of you, _____ And I for-

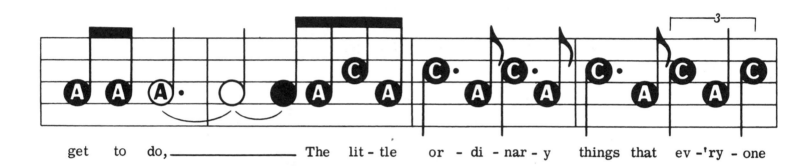

get to do, _____ The lit-tle or-di-nar-y things that ev-'ry-one

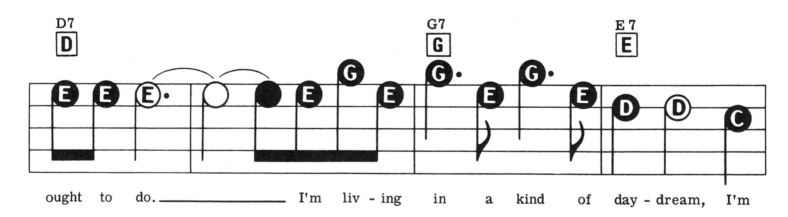

ought to do. _____ I'm liv-ing in a kind of day-dream, I'm

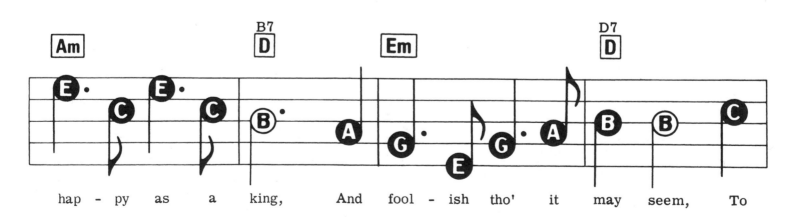

hap-py as a king, And fool-ish tho' it may seem, To

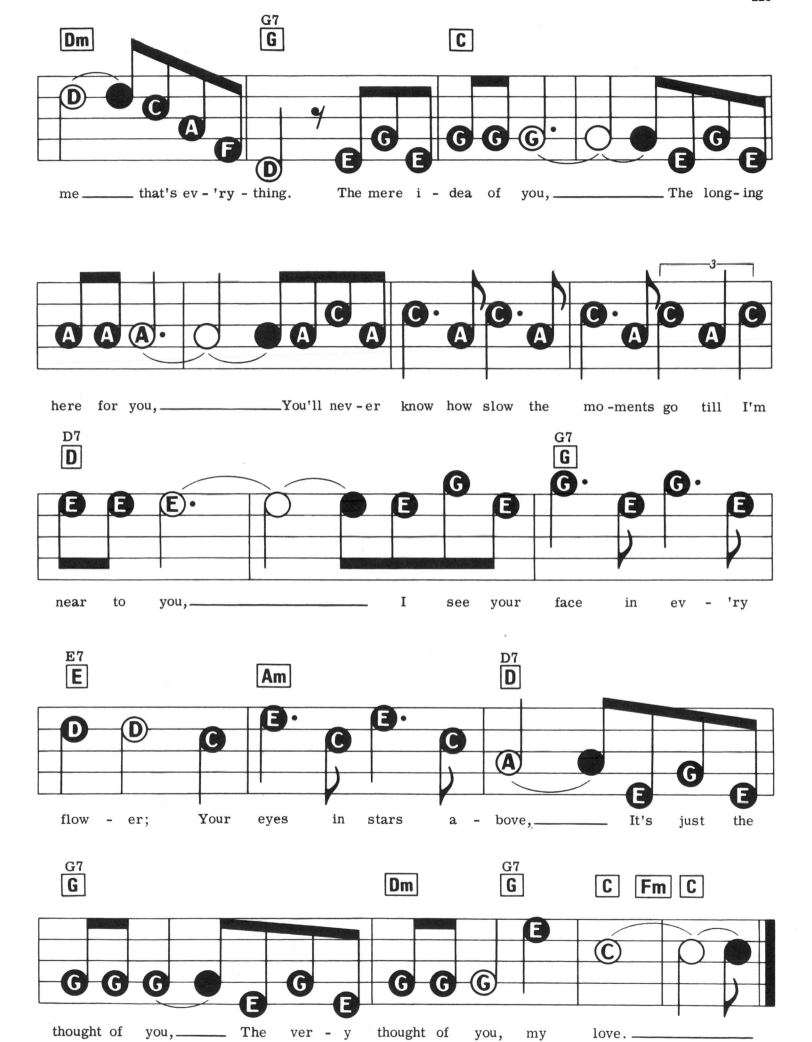

The Way You Look Tonight
from SWING TIME

Registration 1
Rhythm: Fox Trot or Ballad

Words by Dorothy Fields
Music by Jerome Kern

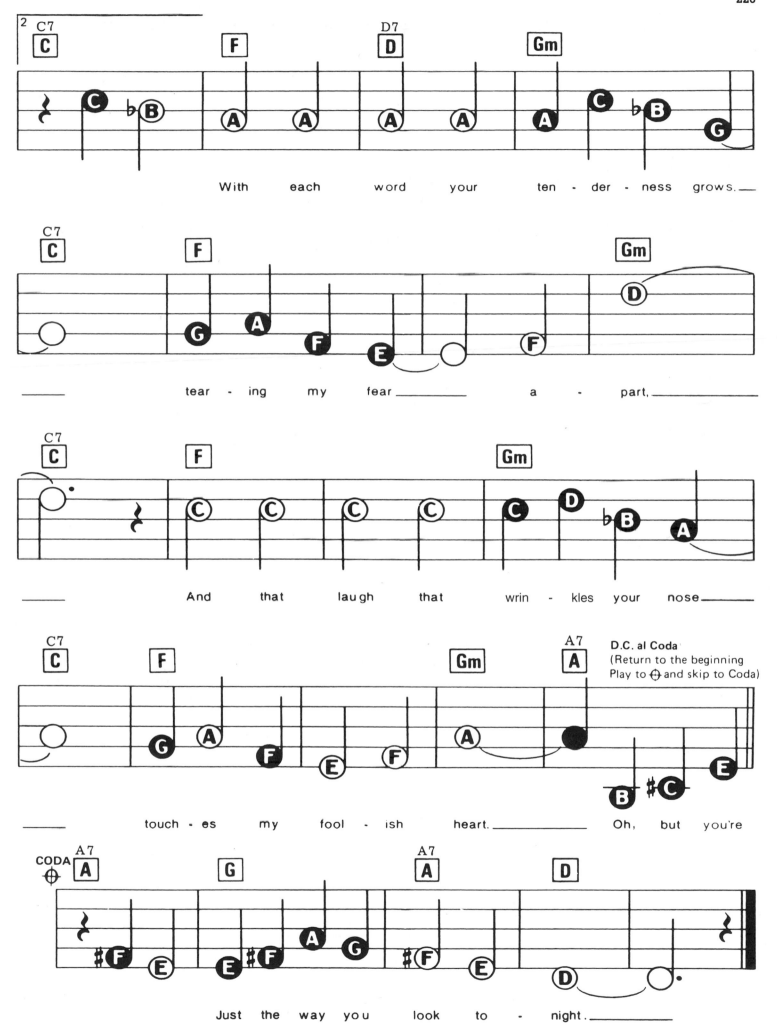

With each word your ten - der - ness grows. ___

___ tear - ing my fear ___ a - part, ___

And that laugh that wrin - kles your nose ___

touch - es my fool - ish heart. ___ Oh, but you're

D.C. al Coda
(Return to the beginning
Play to ⊕ and skip to Coda)

Just the way you look to - night. ___

What a Little Moonlight Can Do

Registration 2
Rhythm: Fox Trot or Swing

Words and Music by
Harry Woods

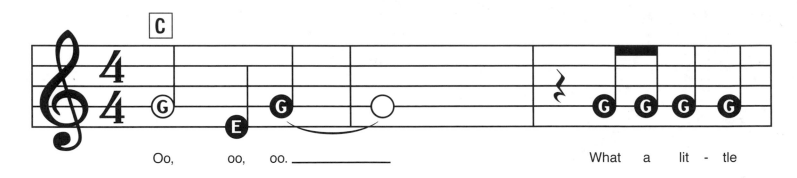

Oo, oo, oo. _____ What a lit - tle

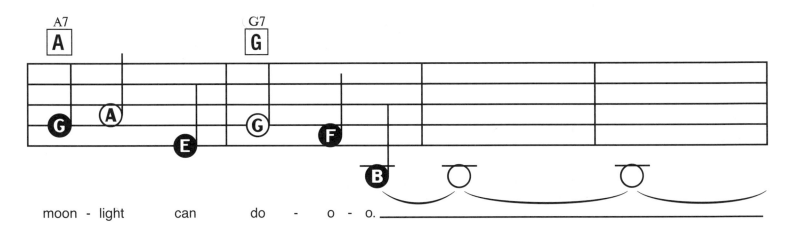

moon - light can do - o - o. _____

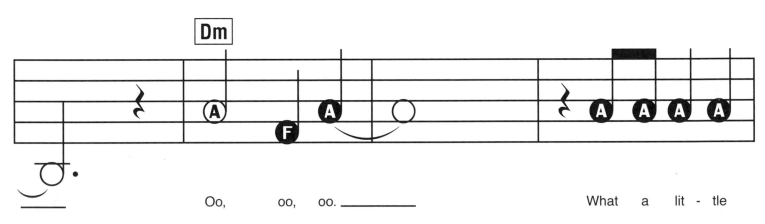

Oo, oo, oo. _____ What a lit - tle

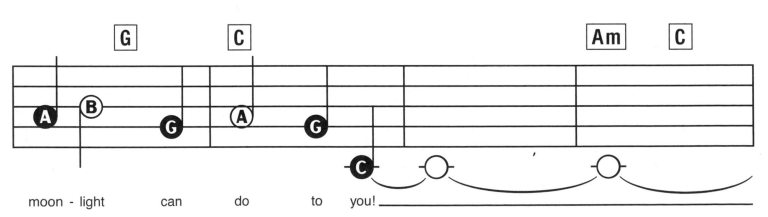

moon - light can do to you! _____

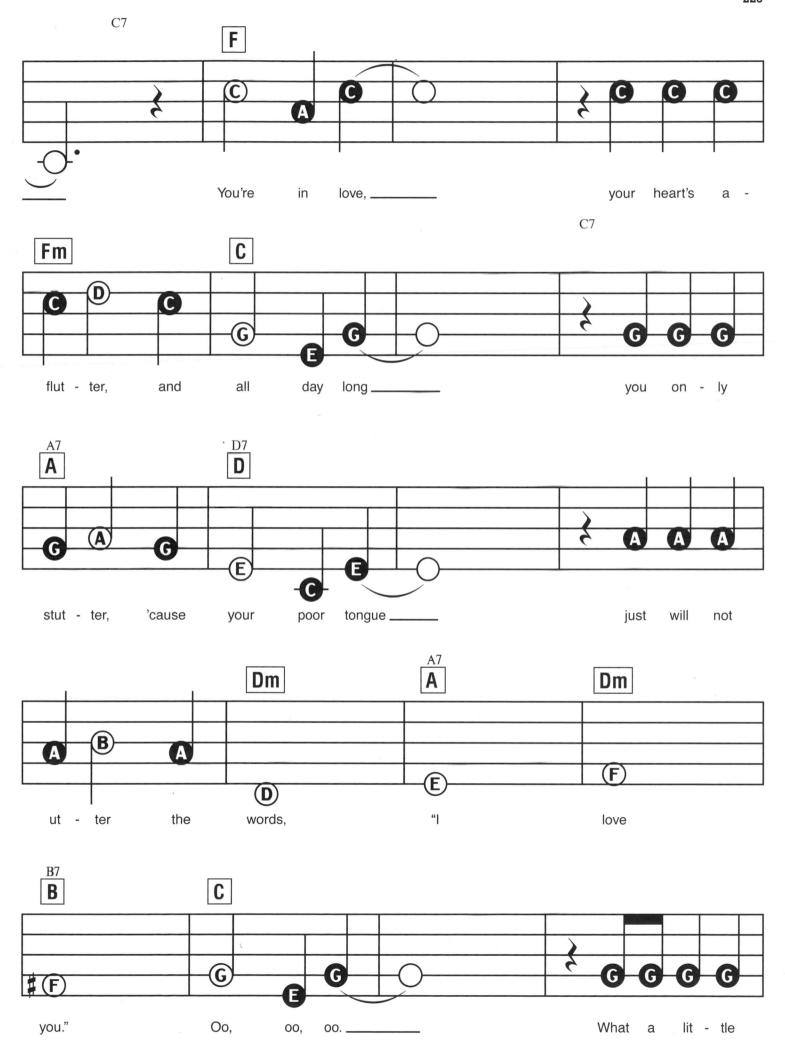

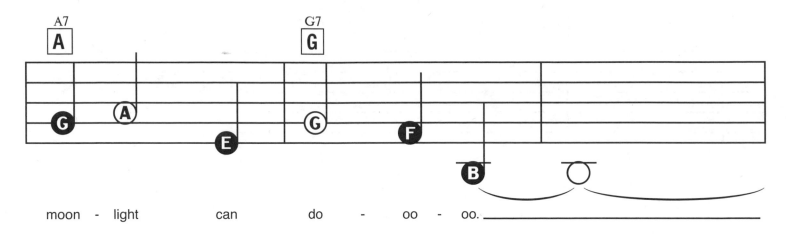

moon - light can do - oo - oo. _____

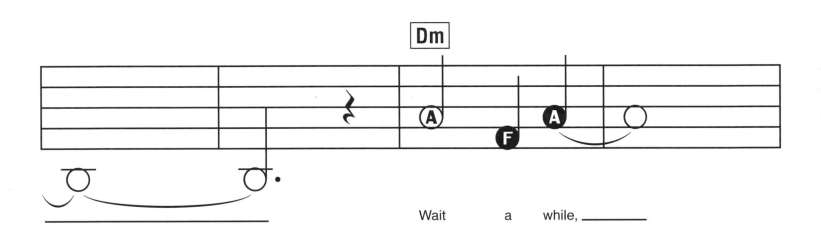

Wait a while, _____

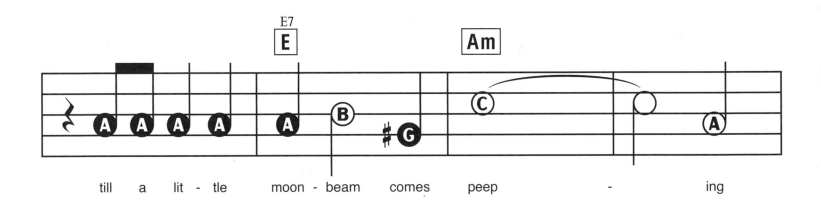

till a lit - tle moon - beam comes peep - ing

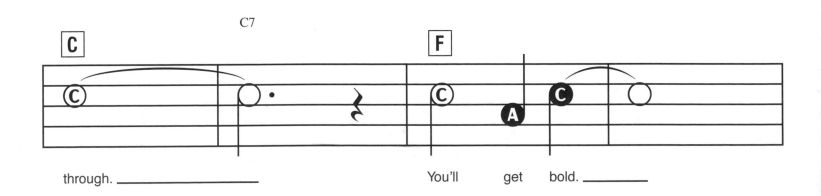

through. _____ You'll get bold. _____

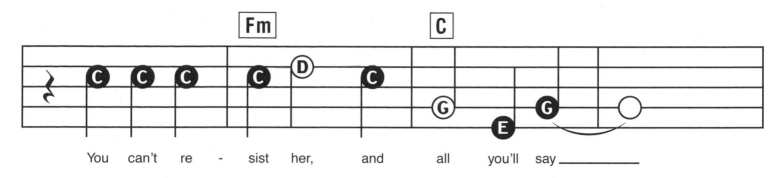

You can't re - sist her, and all you'll say _____

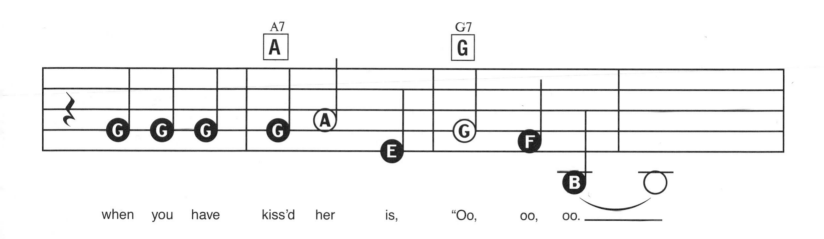

when you have kiss'd her is, "Oo, oo, oo. _____

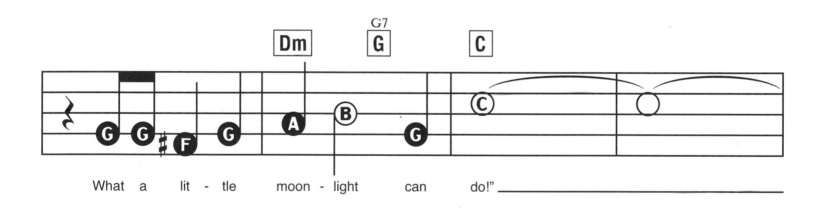

What a lit - tle moon - light can do!" _____

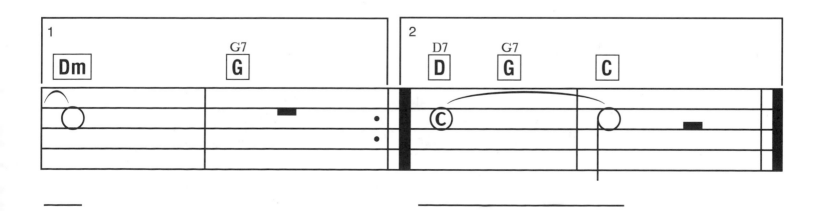

What Is This Thing Called Love?

from WAKE UP AND DREAM

Registration 7
Rhythm: Fox Trot or Swing

Words and Music by
Cole Porter

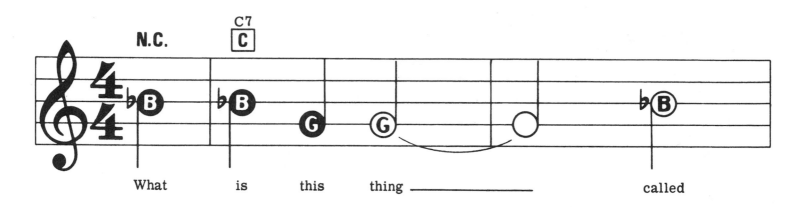

What is this thing _____ called

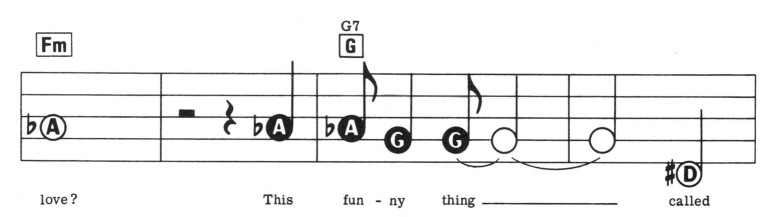

love? This fun - ny thing _____ called

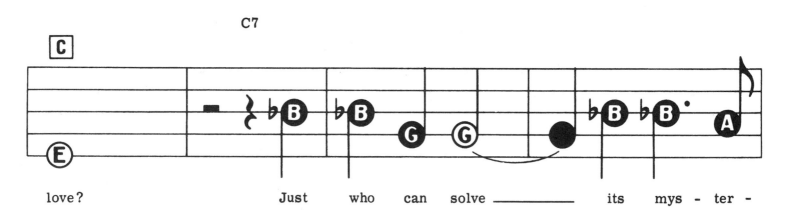

love? Just who can solve _____ its mys - ter -

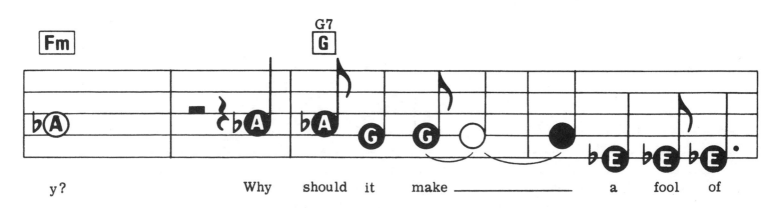

y? Why should it make _____ a fool of

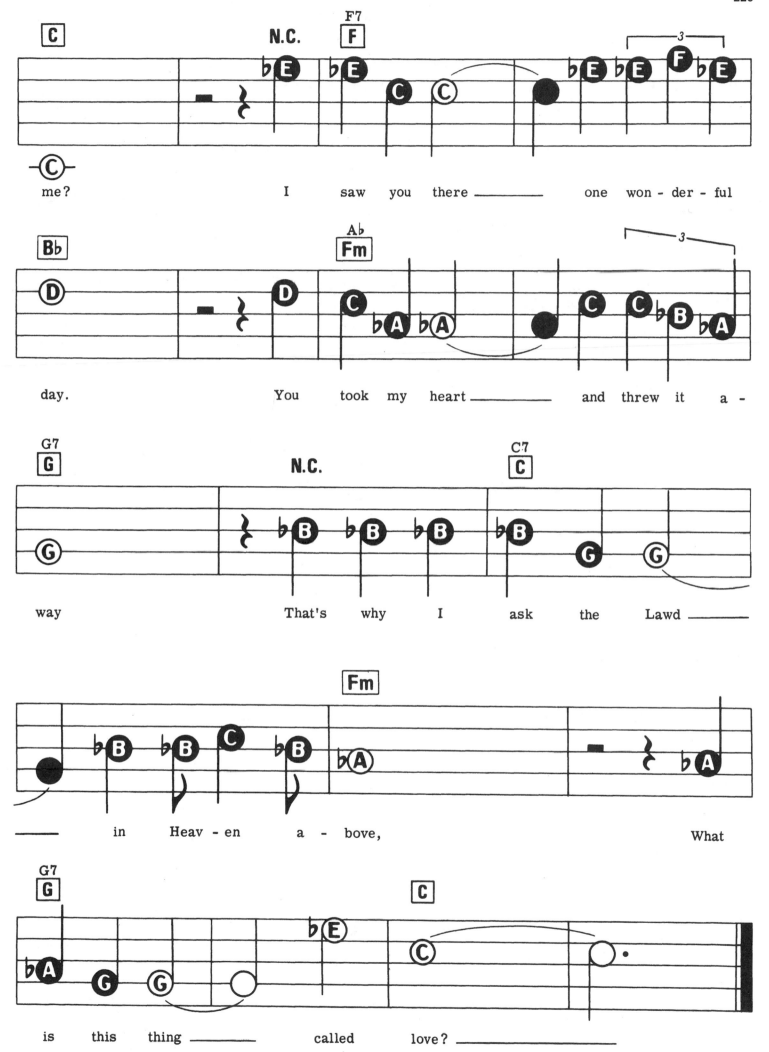

Where or When
from BABES IN ARMS

Registration 7
Rhythm: Fox Trot or Swing

Words by Lorenz Hart
Music by Richard Rodgers

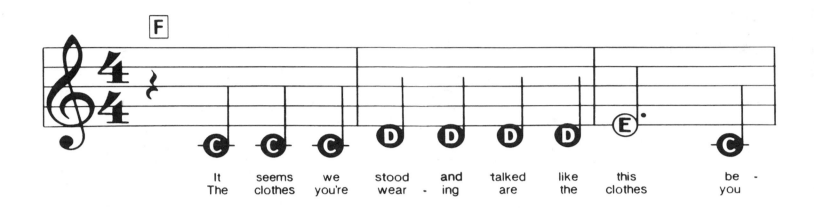

It seems we stood and talked like this be -
The clothes you're wear - ing are the clothes you

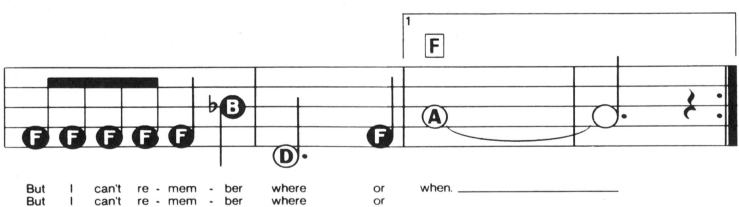

fore. We looked at each oth - er in the same way then,
wore. The smile you are smil - ing you were smil - ing then,

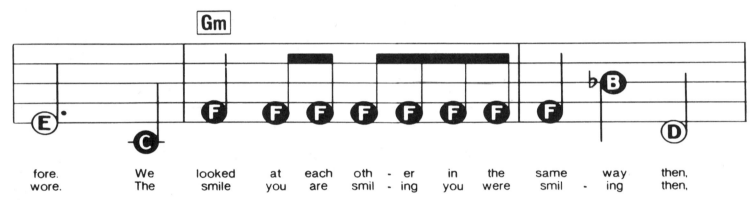

But I can't re - mem - ber where or when. _____
But I can't re - mem - ber where or

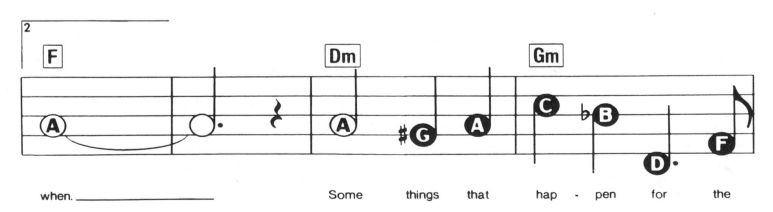

when. _____ Some things that hap - pen for the

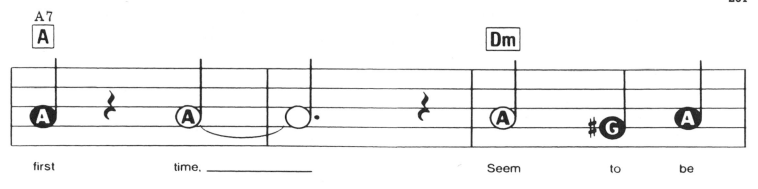

first time, _____ Seem to be

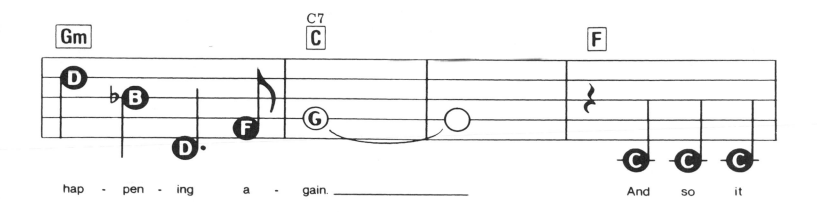

hap - pen - ing a - gain. _____ And so it

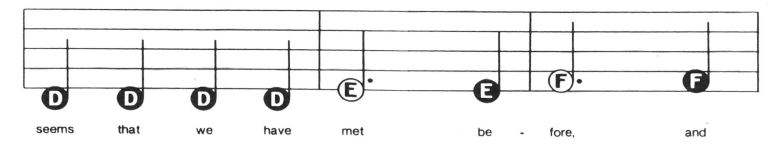

seems that we have met be - fore, and

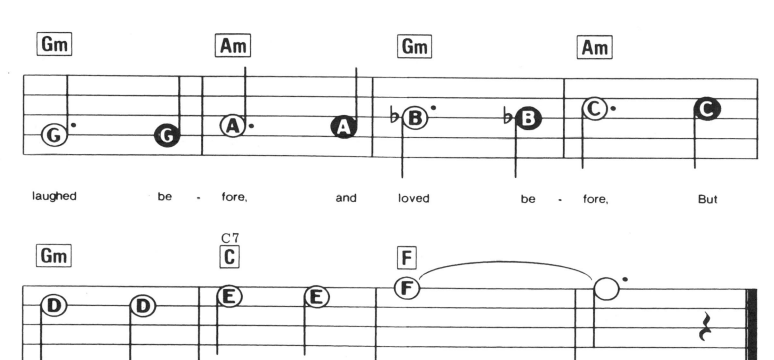

laughed be - fore, and loved be - fore, But

who knows where or when! _____

Wrap Your Troubles in Dreams
(And Dream Your Troubles Away)

Registration 4
Rhythm: Fox Trot

Lyric by Ted Koehler and Billy Moll
Music by Harry Barris

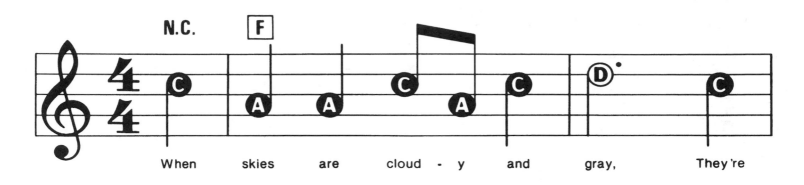

When skies are cloud - y and gray, They're

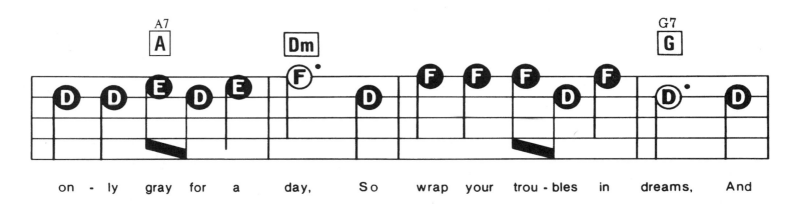

on - ly gray for a day, So wrap your trou - bles in dreams, And

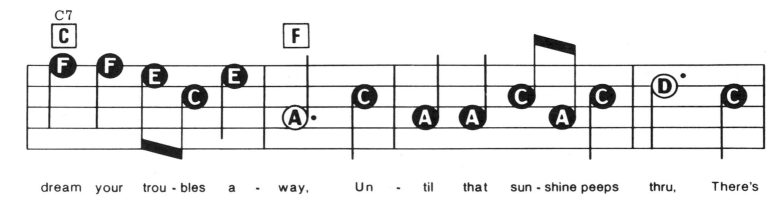

dream your trou - bles a - way, Un - til that sun - shine peeps thru, There's

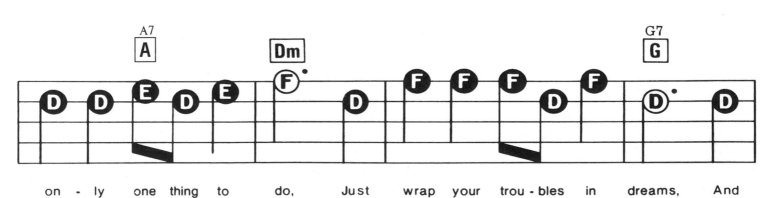

on - ly one thing to do, Just wrap your trou - bles in dreams, And

233

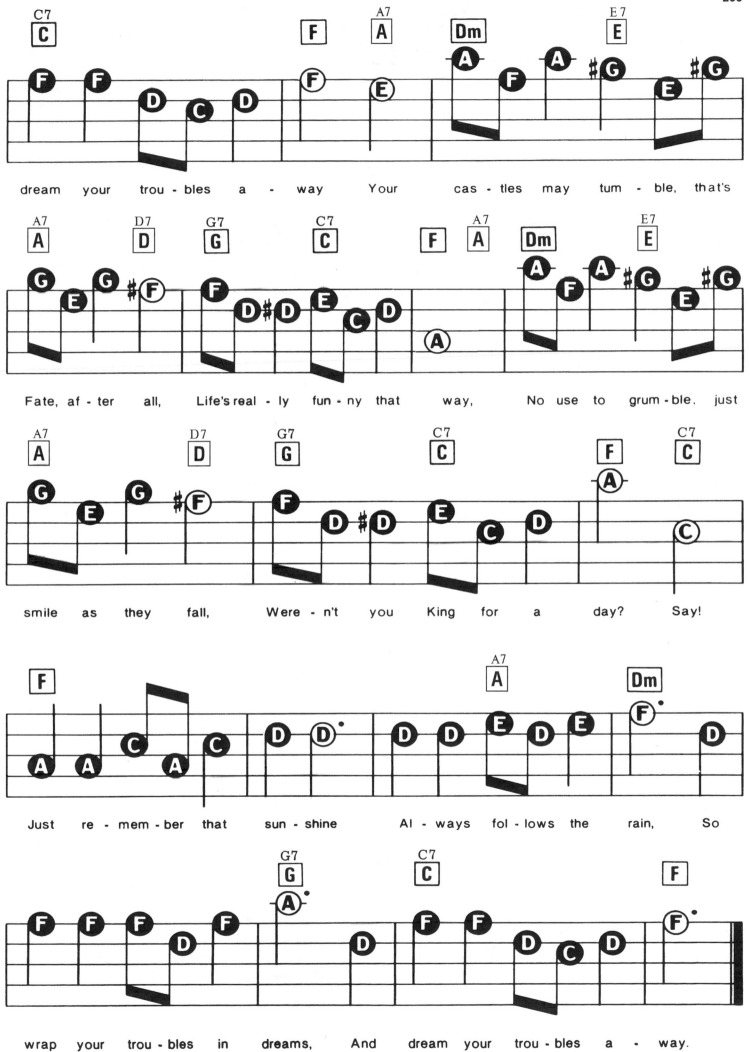

You Must Have Been a Beautiful Baby

Registration 4
Rhythm: Swing or Jazz

Words by Johnny Mercer
Music by Harry Warren

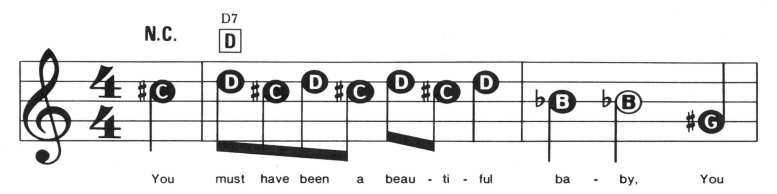

You must have been a beau - ti - ful ba - by, You

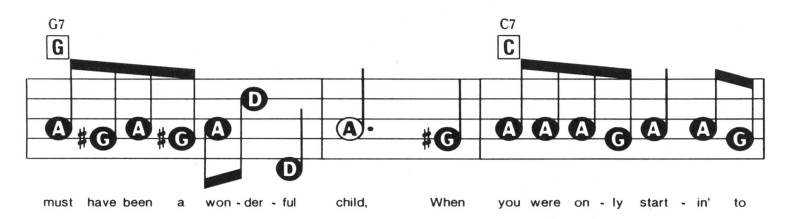

must have been a won - der - ful child, When you were on - ly start - in' to

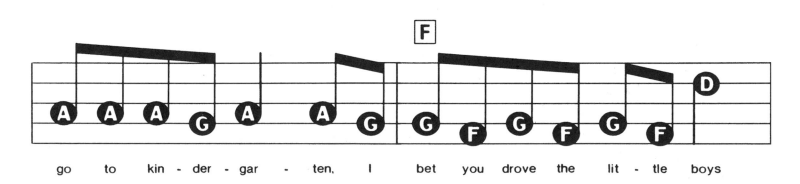

go to kin - der - gar - ten, I bet you drove the lit - tle boys

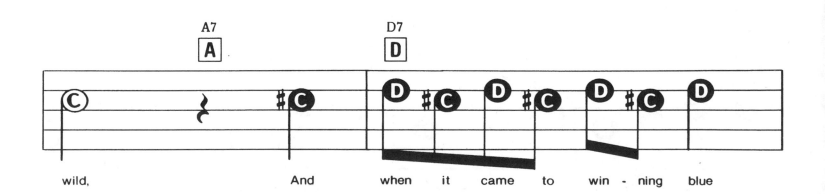

wild, And when it came to win - ning blue

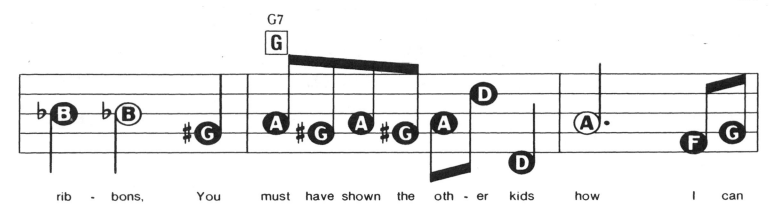

rib - bons, You must have shown the oth - er kids how I can

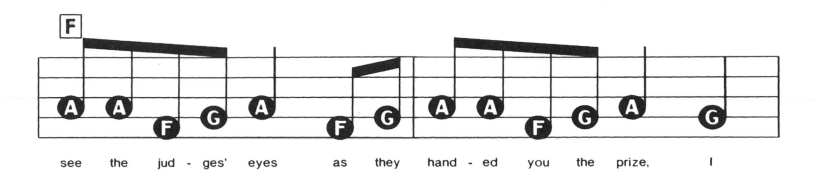

see the jud - ges' eyes as they hand - ed you the prize, I

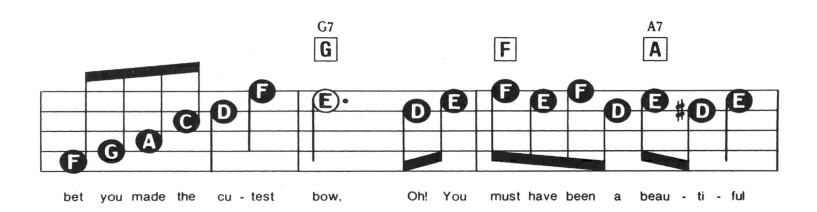

bet you made the cu - test bow, Oh! You must have been a beau - ti - ful

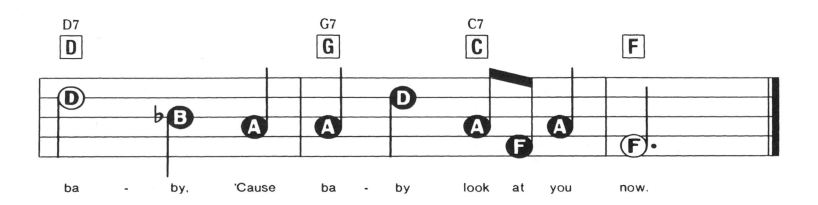

ba - by, 'Cause ba - by look at you now.

You're Getting to Be a Habit with Me

from 42nd STREET

Registration 8
Rhythm: Jazz or Swing

Lyrics by Al Dubin
Music by Harry Warren

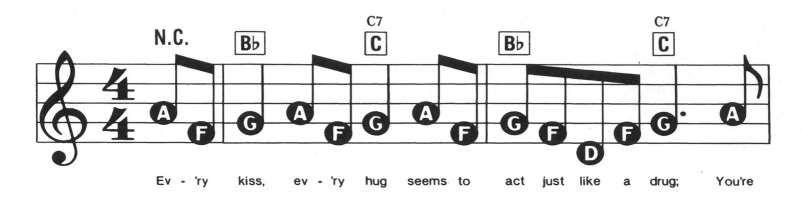

Ev - 'ry kiss, ev - 'ry hug seems to act just like a drug; You're

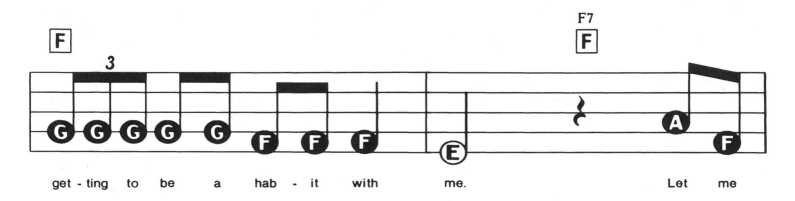

get - ting to be a hab - it with me. Let me

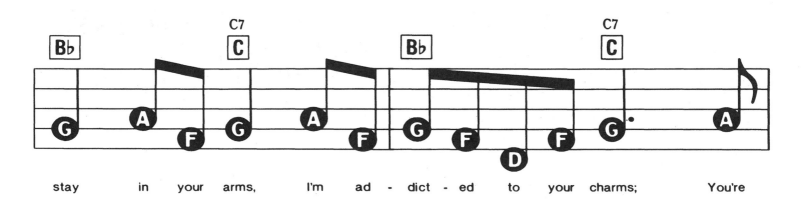

stay in your arms, I'm ad - dict - ed to your charms; You're

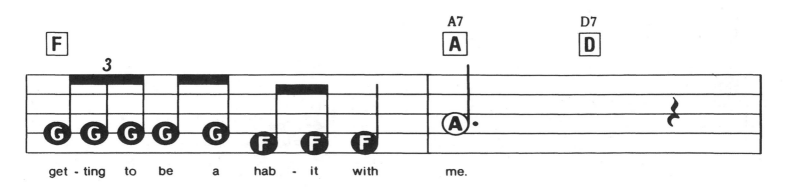

get - ting to be a hab - it with me.

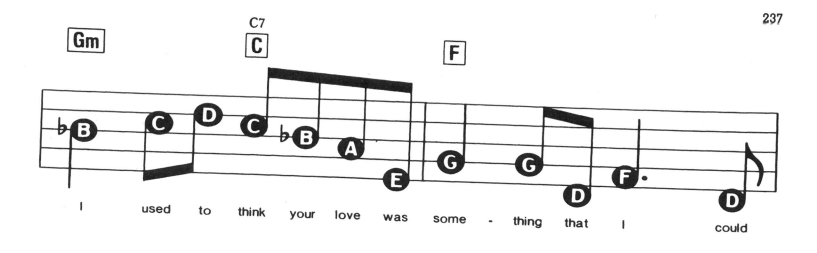

I used to think your love was some - thing that I could

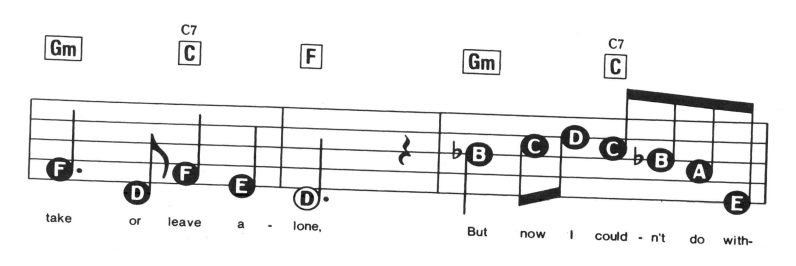

take or leave a - lone, But now I could - n't do with-

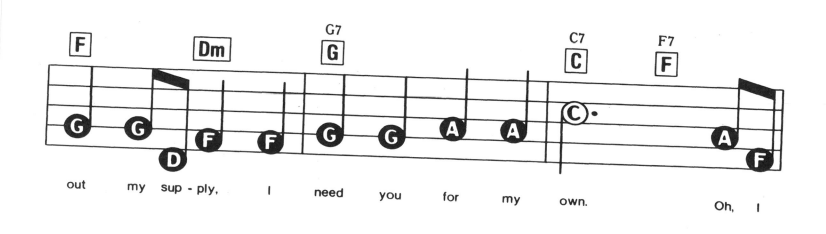

out my sup - ply, I need you for my own. Oh, I

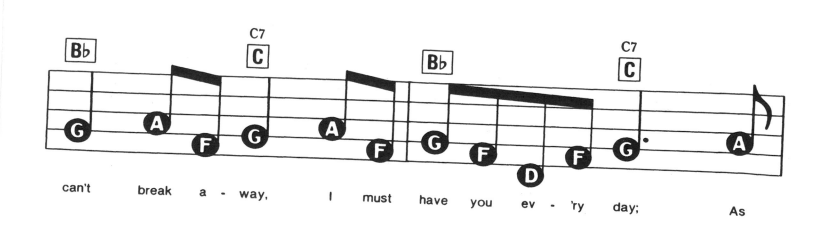

can't break a - way, I must have you ev - 'ry day; As

Registration Guide

- Match the Registration number on the song to the corresponding numbered category below. Select and activate an instrumental sound available on your instrument.

- Choose an automatic rhythm appropriate to the mood and style of the song. (Consult your Owner's Guide for proper operation of automatic rhythm features.)

- Adjust the tempo and volume controls to comfortable settings.

Registration

1	Mellow	Flutes, Clarinet, Oboe, Flugel Horn, Trombone, French Horn, Organ Flutes
2	Ensemble	Brass Section, Sax Section, Wind Ensemble, Full Organ, Theater Organ
3	Strings	Violin, Viola, Cello, Fiddle, String Ensemble, Pizzicato, Organ Strings
4	Guitars	Acoustic/Electric Guitars, Banjo, Mandolin, Dulcimer, Ukulele, Hawaiian Guitar
5	Mallets	Vibraphone, Marimba, Xylophone, Steel Drums, Bells, Celesta, Chimes
6	Liturgical	Pipe Organ, Hand Bells, Vocal Ensemble, Choir, Organ Flutes
7	Bright	Saxophones, Trumpet, Mute Trumpet, Synth Leads, Jazz/Gospel Organs
8	Piano	Piano, Electric Piano, Honky Tonk Piano, Harpsichord, Clavi
9	Novelty	Melodic Percussion, Wah Trumpet, Synth, Whistle, Kazoo, Perc. Organ
10	Bellows	Accordion, French Accordion, Mussette, Harmonica, Pump Organ, Bagpipes